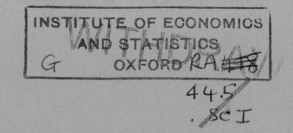

*The Scientific Basis
of Health and Safety
Regulation*

Studies in the Regulation of Economic Activity

The Scientific Basis of Health and Safety Regulation

ROBERT W. CRANDALL
LESTER B. LAVE
Editors

The Brookings Institution / Washington, D.C.

Library of Congress Cataloging in Publication Data:

Main entry under title:
The scientific basis of health and safety regulation.

(Studies in the regulation of economic activity)
Includes bibliographical references and index.
1. Public health—United States—Decision-making
—Case studies. 2. Environmental health—Government
policy—United States—Decision making—Case studies.
3. Traffic safety—Government policy—United States
—Decision making—Case studies. 4. Policy sciences
—Case studies. I. Crandall, Robert W. II. Lave,
Lester B. III. Series.
RA445.S43   363.1′0973   81-10224
ISBN 0-8157-1600-1   AACR2
ISBN 0-8157-1599-4 (pbk.)

9 8 7 6 5 4 3 2 1

THE BROOKINGS INSTITUTION is an independent organization devoted to nonpartisan research, education, and publication in economics, government, foreign policy, and the social sciences generally. Its principal purposes are to aid in the development of sound public policies and to promote public understanding of issues of national importance.

The Institution was founded on December 8, 1927, to merge the activities of the Institute for Government Research, founded in 1916, the Institute of Economics, founded in 1922, and the Robert Brookings Graduate School of Economics and Government, founded in 1924.

The Board of Trustees is responsible for the general administration of the Institution, while the immediate direction of the policies, program, and staff is vested in the President, assisted by an advisory committee of the officers and staff. The by-laws of the Institution state: "It is the function of the Trustees to make possible the conduct of scientific research, and publication, under the most favorable conditions, and to safeguard the independence of the research staff in the pursuit of their studies and in the publication of the results of such studies. It is not a part of their function to determine, control, or influence the conduct of particular investigations or the conclusions reached."

The President bears final responsibility for the decision to publish a manuscript as a Brookings book. In reaching his judgment on the competence, accuracy, and objectivity of each study, the President is advised by the director of the appropriate research program and weighs the views of a panel of expert outside readers who report to him in confidence on the quality of the work. Publication of a work signifies that it is deemed a competent treatment worthy of public consideration but does not imply endorsement of conclusions or recommendations.

The Institution maintains its position of neutrality on issues of public policy in order to safeguard the intellectual freedom of the staff. Hence interpretations or conclusions in Brookings publications should be understood to be solely those of the authors and should not be attributed to the Institution, to its trustees, officers, or other staff members, or to the organizations that support its research.

Foreword

IN CREATING regulatory agencies to protect and promote health and safety, Congress has repeatedly emphasized scientific data and analysis. For example, the Clean Air Amendments of 1970 require that air quality standards be established on the basis of scientific data, and the Occupational Safety and Health Act of 1970 stressed that regulations were to be based on the best available scientific evidence on health risks. Other statutes, such as the Toxic Substances Control Act of 1976, also require the application of scientific information. Consequently, regulatory bodies such as the Environmental Protection Agency have been given substantial budgets for research and scientific investigation.

The editors of this book, sharing a belief that scientific data and analysis in practice play a smaller role in regulatory decisions than statutes, public perceptions, or research budgets imply they should, organized a research conference at Brookings in November 1979 to explore that issue. The conference focused on five topics, each influenced by recent regulatory decisions: passive restraint devices for automobiles, occupational exposure to cotton dust, sulfur oxide air pollution standards, saccharin as a food additive, and waterborne carcinogens. For these topics, scientists were asked to summarize evidence on the nature of the risks, economists were asked to examine the benefits and costs of proposed regulations, and incumbent or former regulators were asked to comment on the adequacy of the papers prepared by the scientists and economists as the basis for regulatory judgment. The regulators, for their part, emphasized the nature of the data required, considerations other than scientific and economic that influence regulatory decisions, and the roles of scientific and economic analysis.

This volume presents the fifteen papers prepared for the conference. They are introduced and summarized by the editors and followed by comments from a businessman and a scientist reflecting discussion at the conference as well as the papers themselves. The fifty-seven conference participants, drawn from various government, business, and academic organizations, are listed on pages 301–02.

Robert W. Crandall and Lester B. Lave are senior fellows in the Brookings Economic Studies program. They are grateful to Jean Rosenblatt, who edited the manuscript; to Lisa Saunders and Valerie Harris, who typed it; to Penelope Harpold, who supervised the verification of its factual content; and to Diana Regenthal, who prepared the index.

This is the sixteenth publication in the Brookings series of Studies in the Regulation of Economic Activity. The series presents the findings of a program of research focused on public policies toward business. This study was supported by a special grant from the Andrew W. Mellon Foundation and by grants for the Brookings regulatory program from the Ford Foundation, the Alfred P. Sloan Foundation, and the Alex C. Walker Foundation.

The views expressed in this book are those of the authors and should not be ascribed to the foundations whose assistance is acknowledged above, or to the trustees, officers, or other staff members of the Brookings Institution.

BRUCE K. MAC LAURY
President

July 1981
Washington, D.C.

Contents

PART SIX: GENERAL COMMENTS

Tables

Figures

*The Scientific Basis
of Health and Safety
Regulation*

Introduction and Summary

ROBERT W. CRANDALL *and* LESTER B. LAVE

THE REGULATION of health and safety by government is not a new phenomenon in the United States. Food and drugs have been regulated at the federal level by the Food and Drug Administration for more than fifty years. A myriad of product safety, occupational safety, and environmental regulations have been enforced by state and local government authorities for more than a century. Mine safety regulation at the federal level began more than seventy years ago. The U.S. Department of Agriculture has had far-reaching regulatory powers since World War II.

Despite its long history, it is only in the last ten years that federal regulation of health and safety has become the object of major public policy concern. The Occupational Safety and Health Administration, the National Highway Traffic Safety Administration, the Environmental Protection Agency, and the Consumer Product Safety Commission were all established in the 1970s. Each agency was given responsibility for enforcing one or more new statutes, which have greatly increased the scope of federal regulation, and most have become responsible for enforcing earlier statutes. As a result of this wave of new regulation, virtually no aspect of our lives, from the air we breathe to the food we eat and the safety of our work place, is outside the scope of federal regulation.

Why has regulation increased so markedly in the past decade? Economists generally believe that health and safety regulation should be designed to cure observed "market failure"—instances when markets cannot operate efficiently to provide an effective level of health or safety. Regulation is an attempt to cope with the absence of appropriate market signals and to achieve more efficient allocation of resources by directing more of them toward, for example, the reduction of accidents, morbidity, or premature death. Undoubtedly some of the support for increased regu-

1

lation reflects a general belief that an increasingly wealthy society should trade off more private goods for improved health and safety.

Obviously there are other explanations for the growth of regulation. The political process can be used to state social goals that have nothing to do with economic efficiency or market failures. For instance, requiring motorcyclists to wear helmets is not necessary to correct a market failure. Regulation may be used to transfer wealth from producers to workers or from unorganized to organized workers through the Occupational Safety and Health Administration. Regulation can be and has been used to retard economic growth in certain areas of the country so as to prevent economic decline in other sections. The recently promulgated air-pollution standards for new coal-fired power plants were clearly an attempt to suppress competition by making western coal less attractive. Regulations that place much larger burdens on new facilities or that scrutinize new drugs or chemicals carefully while devoting less attention to existing substances have a similar anticompetitive effect.

Notwithstanding these diverse political reasons for regulation, the principal purpose of these new regulatory programs should be to enhance health, safety, and environmental quality. The extent to which they achieve this and the extent to which regulators attempt to design them for this purpose can be assessed by examining the scientific basis of individual regulations as well as how large a role such evidence has played in the design of these regulations. These issues were addressed at a conference at the Brookings Institution in November 1979, which brought scientists, economists, and regulators together to examine five recent regulatory decisions. The five are (1) the National Highway Traffic Safety Administration's requirement of passive restraint systems for automobiles; (2) the Occupational Safety and Health Administration's regulation of cotton dust; (3) the Food and Drug Administration's decision to ban saccharin; (4) the Environmental Protection Agency's drinking water standards; and (5) the Environmental Protection Agency's ambient sulfur dioxide standard.

The regulations examined in the case studies were chosen because they represent a range of issues. They cover four agencies with quite different statutory mandates, which must deal with a considerable number of health and safety problems. While these agencies' use of scientific evidence cannot be characterized definitively by only five case studies, the studies do give a sense of how regulatory bureaucracies deal with this evidence in making regulatory decisions.

Scientific Issues Underlying Regulation

Increasing the efficiency and efficacy of health, safety, and environmental regulation requires answers to four questions. First, is there a scientific foundation for government action? Regulatory actions may be motivated by a popular reaction to a recent event rather than by evidence of a problem that regulation can systematically address. Also, an agency may exacerbate concern about a trivial or nonexistent problem. Second, will setting a standard reduce risks to health and safety? Often a regulatory action is undertaken to demonstrate agency concern rather than to reduce risk. Third, is there enough scientific evidence to provide realistic estimates of the risks and costs of alternative standards? Standards are often enacted on the basis of only fragmentary evidence of a potential health or safety hazard, with no evidence about the costs of implementing the standard. Fourth, has sufficient analysis been done to identify uncertainties and to map out a prudent course, given the uncertainties and possible future events? The collection of scientific data that *suggest* a risk does not justify the imposition of a regulation. Alternative policies must be analyzed and the effects of uncertainties identified to set a reasonable course of action.

The case studies in this volume address these questions to differing degrees. For each regulatory issue, a scientist, an economist, and a regulator present their views of the scientific basis for the regulation and how the scientific evidence was used in the standard-setting process.

Coping with Scientific Uncertainty

In each of the case studies, it was obvious that regulators confronted difficult problems in dealing with uncertain evidence concerning prospective health effects and economic costs. These problems were particularly severe with the scientific evidence available on the health or safety effects. In each case, the regulator had to resolve these difficulties taking into account the political pressure being applied to him and the statute under which he was issuing the regulations. The question of how to deal with scientific uncertainty is so important that it deserves special attention in this summary.

Most economists at the conference were eager to see regulators confront the evidence on costs and benefits from a number of regulatory options and choose the option that offered the greatest positive difference between benefits and costs. Regulators generally complained that this was impossible because of the highly uncertain evidence on benefits. Extrapolations from animal studies or imperfect epidemiological studies would produce a very wide range of estimated health benefits. How were they to choose a precise estimate from this range?

The lack of precise evidence on the dose-response relationship for saccharin and the cost of acquiring additional data lead Williamson to suggest a "decision tree" approach to regulating food additives that isolates the critical policy issues and attempts to establish whether the current information is sufficient, and if not, what information is necessary. Huelke and O'Day suggest field testing air bags before they are mandated for all cars. Controversy over whether there are health effects at current levels dominates the studies of sulfur oxides and waterborne carcinogens. The latter case study provides perhaps the most thorough discussion of the role of uncertainty in decisionmaking.

In most cases, a complete review of available scientific evidence does not provide clear, definitive answers to the questions regulators must address. Uncertainty inevitably remains, inducing regulators to resort to intuitive judgment. In assessing the evidence on waterborne carcinogens, for example, Kimm, Kuzmack, and Schnare state that one approach to regulation is that of formal cost-benefit analysis. They point out that their experience with this approach has not been encouraging because of the uncertainties in estimating health benefits. They propose, however, that "another approach to regulation is to continue balancing risks and benefits intuitively." They defend the intuitive approach by saying: "We would be wary of overformalizing the approach. Ideally, each case would lead to a creative resolution of conflicting goals." Furthermore, they advocate resolving the uncertainty by assuming that a risk of cancer actually exists when the evidence is mixed. "Almost nobody understands," they write, "that although the risks may or may not exist, it is rational to treat them as real; that any reduction in cancer rates is likely to be small but still worth achieving; and that probably no one will ever know the true impact of preventive action."

These are the views of a group of regulators who have given careful attention to the scientific evidence and have attempted to quantify the risks of exposure and the uncertainty surrounding the estimates of these risks. These regulators do not dismiss the relationship between hard, scientific evidence and sensible regulation. Indeed, they show great interest in using quantitative techniques. But they refuse to deal with uncertainty in a precise, quantifiable way when it comes to setting the actual standards. To do so, they argue, would paralyze the regulatory process, since naysayers would use the evidence to delay promulgation of the standard and have a better chance of getting the courts to negate it.

The view that an intuitive approach to uncertainty should be used in the setting of a standard predominates among regulators. In the cases examined in this volume, the regulators do not address how a reduction of uncertainty would affect a decision. What would result, for example, from spending millions of dollars to narrow the range of estimates of the carcinogenic effects of chloroform in municipal water supplies from a factor of one hundred to a factor of only ten? Would the Environmental Protection Agency set a different standard? If not, why should the resources have been spent to narrow the range of uncertainty? How, indeed, does improved scientific evidence improve regulation?

Institutional Restraints on Rational Decisionmaking

There are a number of obvious constraints on regulators. These include the legal process, political forces, and limited resources. Given the complex task of promulgating and enforcing scores of standards, these constraints can be formidable. The legal process is designed to minimize the opportunity for one party to influence an outcome without equal opportunities for others to respond. All decisions must be defended subsequently on the basis of evidence provided through the legal process. Administrators must be able to acknowledge different types of information, assert that they have weighed it in their decision, and issue a decision that does not conflict with the evidence. This process accounts for the frequent pleas by regulators in this volume to allow them to rely on "judgment" rather than a formal decision analysis. To perform a formal analysis requires revealing the subjective values placed on the means and variances of important parameters, and these values could be questioned in a judicial appeal.

Given the large probability that many will be challenged, the dominance of lawyers in the regulatory field is not surprising. Good public policy is of little use if it results in endless delays or reversals in court. The lawyer's function is to draft regulations that will be held by appellate courts to comply with the statutes governing administrative procedures and the specific regulatory powers of the agency. These statutes are not generally written to induce efficient rational choices by regulators. Instead, they often provide for choosing a strategy reflecting the "best available technology" or the maximum protection "feasible" or even total proscription in the face of specified evidence. Complying with this statutory language without inviting a court reversal often requires a decision that is in conflict with rational choices based on costs and benefits.

Political forces are another serious constraint on regulatory decision-making. In their most innocuous form, these constraints require regulators to weigh all pleadings made on a given issue. Obviously, these pleadings will be dominated by a few groups that have a large stake in the outcome. In addition, most health-safety agencies are not as well insulated from the political process as the independent rate-setting agencies have been. Political pressure from small cities can be brought to bear on the Environmental Protection Agency's waterborne carcinogen standard, or the AFL-CIO can place considerable pressure on the Department of Labor over the appropriate level of cotton dust or the occupational lead standard. Coal-producing states in Appalachia can influence the Environmental Protection Agency's decision to require scrubbing of low-sulfur coal combustion gases in the West and Southwest.

Finally, the regulator faces severe problems in mustering the staff effort required to grapple with difficult health and safety issues. This volume concentrates on only five regulations. The head of the Environmental Protection Agency or the Food and Drug Administration must cope with hundreds, even thousands, of regulations in a single year. With limited staff and the natural limits of human organization, it would be naive to expect each of these decisions to reflect a careful analysis of all the scientific and economic issues raised by the regulatory problem. At best, only the "major" decisions can be given such careful scrutiny.

The Case Studies

The scientific basis of regulation, the treatment of uncertainty, and the nature of the regulatory process are not easily explored in abstract terms. The five case studies were therefore selected to elucidate these issues. In each case study a scientist presents what is known about the risks posed by each case and an economist examines the benefits and costs of a proposed regulation. Finally, a regulator comments on the adequacy of these estimates of risk, benefits, and costs for making a regulatory judgment; regulators also elaborate on the facts required and considerations other than scientific and economic ones that intrude in decision-making and discuss the roles of scientific and economic analysis.

Passive Restraints

The current three-point seat belt required on all new cars sold in the United States is potentially one of the most important and cost-effective safety features introduced in recent years. There is a consensus among experts that there would be as many as 9,000 fewer highway deaths and 40,000 fewer severe injuries each year if all vehicle occupants wore their belts. However, only about 10 percent of occupants wear their belts. Rather than require that seat belts be worn (and assuming that the law would be effective), the National Highway Traffic Safety Administration required that 1974 and early 1975 model automobiles have an interlock device preventing the operation of the automobile unless all front-seat occupants were belted. Mechanical problems and inconveniences associated with the interlock caused Congress to prohibit the agency from continuing the requirement in October 1974. Low rates of use of active belts and political opposition to mandatory belt use inevitably led to a standard for a "passive" protective system—one that would not require actions by the occupant to activate it. This system is to be phased in over model years 1983–85. This regulation requires that the occupants of the front seat be protected when a car is crashed into a rigid barrier at thirty miles per hour. Two safety devices, air bags and passive seat belts, constitute the only practical current choices for meeting this requirement.

Unlike the saccharin issue, the passive restraint issue poses no question about the cause or extent of the risk to human safety. There has, however, been controversy about the reduction of injuries that would result from passive devices. Initially, the Department of Transportation and the auto industry held very different points of view. However, scientific investigation has narrowed the range of uncertainty to the point where there is general agreement about the expected benefits from the safety equipment in various accidents.

Huelke and O'Day show that neither the current passive belt nor the air bag are as effective as the current three-point (lap-shoulder) belt.

However, the combination of air bag and lap belt is the most effective, although it seems unlikely that occupants of cars with air bags would also wear lap belts. In this case, the scientists were able to give an estimate of risk reduction that was generally accepted. Ironically, the air bag may reduce the incentive to use seat belts and could even be counterproductive.

Blomquist and Peltzman argue that the estimated reduction of injuries would not be realized in practice. Motorists would change their driving behavior in response to the safety increase obtained from air bag use, and the result would be increased injuries and fatalities, particularly for pedestrians. The authors argue that regulation cannot force drivers to consume more safety than they desire; hence, the final outcome may provide little enhancement of safety and would add substantially to the cost of the vehicle.

Nash states that the National Highway Traffic Safety Administration was instructed by Congress to enhance highway safety and has been successful in doing so, as verified by a number of analyses. He argues that the cost-effectiveness of air bags and passive belts is roughly comparable to that of previous highway safety requirements, in spite of the fact that some people are expected to dismantle their passive belts.

Cotton Dust

Merchant's paper describes the large body of scientific evidence linking cotton dust exposure to byssinosis, or brown lung disease. It is clear that workers exposed to respirable cotton dust in textile plants suffer a considerable risk of contracting byssinosis and that the severity of the disease is related to the length of time a worker has been inhaling cotton dust. While there is limited evidence that cotton dust increases mortality rates among workers, increased morbidity from byssinosis and prolonged exposures to the fine particles in cotton dust are closely related.

The etiological mechanism in the formation of byssinosis is not completely understood, but chronic exposure to cotton dust is known to reduce respiratory capacity in a way similar to the effects of chronic bronchitis and emphysema. Continued exposure to fine cotton dust particles induces respiratory disease, which progresses from simple chest tightness on Monday to an eventual reduction of respiratory capacity that can severely reduce an individual's ability to function.

Given imperfect understanding of the dose-response relationship between cotton dust and byssinosis, it is difficult to set a standard for fine

cotton dust that meets the Occupational Safety and Health Act's requirement that "no employee will suffer material impairment of health or
functional capacity."[1]

Morton Corn, the administrator of the Occupational Safety and Health
Administration when the cotton dust standard of 200 micrograms per
cubic meter was proposed, indicates that another requirement of the act
—that the standard be "feasible"—prevented the agency from proposing
a standard that would assure no "material impairment to health." As in
many other health and safety issues, it is simply not possible to achieve
zero risk if the U.S. textile industry is to survive. The proposed standard
and the final standards, which provide somewhat less stringent levels for
all sectors of the industry except yarn manufacturing, are based primarily
on an assessment of the maximum feasible control. Corn defends the final
standards as the best technically and economically achievable, arguing
that even in weaving areas (where the standard is 750 micrograms per
cubic meter) disease incidence can be reduced to below 10 percent.

Morrall analyzes the standards, using a traditional economic framework. He contends that there are major faults in the final standards although they are superior to the proposed standard of 200 micrograms per
cubic meter. In fact, Morrall shows that a standard requiring tighter controls where they are cheapest would lower the cost per case avoided.
Thus, if the final standards made sense, a tighter standard would have
been even more effective.

Morrall also criticizes the Occupational Safety and Health Administration for not allowing the option of more work practice changes or
personal protective devices for avoiding byssinosis. This is a common
criticism of so-called engineering standards, which mandate specific solutions, rather than pure performance standards, which allow employers to
choose their own solution as long as they reduce disease incidence to a
low level. Performance standards allow employers to achieve the standards at the lowest possible cost, but the Occupational Safety and Health
Administration and trade unions often object to allowing job rotation or
cumbersome personal protective devices to be used to achieve a standard,
contending that such devices do not work or are not used by the workers.

Finally, Morrall argues that the Occupational Safety and Health Administration has underestimated the cost to society of preventing byssinosis. He thinks that the cost may be $100,000 per case or more but

1. 84 Stat. 1594.

does not claim to know how much textile workers or society would be willing to pay to control the disease. Whatever this value, he argues, the Occupational Safety and Health Administration could have obtained more protection for less cost. Nowhere does he discuss feasibility. Since the conference, the Supreme Court has ruled that the Occupational Safety and Health Act does not require a comparison of costs and benefits; hence, Morrall's analysis may be useful for sensible policy, but it is not relevant to the statutory responsibilities of the Occupational Safety and Health Administration.

Saccharin

Grobstein characterizes the investigation of the toxicity of saccharin as one of the most complete ever done for a drug. A National Academy of Sciences panel, which he chaired, found that saccharin was a human carcinogen, but with little potency. That panel does not and Grobstein continues to refuse to quantify the risks to humans of ingesting saccharin at levels currently in our diets. Grobstein emphasizes that the various methods of extrapolating risks and laboratory evidence have arrived at estimates that differed by a factor of 10,000,000. The National Academy of Sciences panel concluded that the scientific evidence was not firm enough to calculate a risk estimate in which they could have confidence, but they attempted to reach some sort of agreement on weighing the health effects of saccharin. Since the National Academy of Sciences study was done, three epidemiological studies on saccharin have been published, none of which finds an increased incidence of bladder cancer at average doses (although there is an indication of an increase for individuals who smoke and who consume the equivalent of six cans of saccharin-sweetened soft drinks each day).[2] These three studies are consistent with the view that saccharin either produces no effect or is an extremely weak carcinogen.

How does one measure the benefits of saccharin? There is no conclusive evidence that saccharin lowers total calorie intake and thus lowers weight. Nevertheless members of Congress did receive a vast amount of

2. Alan S. Morrison and Julie E. Buring, "Artificial Sweeteners and Cancer of the Lower Urinary Tract," *New England Journal of Medicine,* vol. 306 (March 6, 1980), pp. 537–41; Robert Hoover and others, "Progress Report to the Food and Drug Administration from the National Cancer Institute Concerning the National Bladder Cancer Study" (Bethesda, Md.: National Cancer Institute, 1979); and Irving I. Kessler and J. Page Clarke, "Saccharin, Cyclamate, and Human Bladder Cancer: No Evidence of an Association," *Journal of the American Medical Association,* vol. 240 (July 1978), pp. 349–55.

mail when Congress was considering whether to forbid the Food and Drug Administration to ban saccharin.

Williamson does not attempt to set out the benefits and costs of using saccharin or of banning it. Rather, he prescribes an alternative framework for deciding whether saccharin or any other suspected carcinogen should be banned. The framework is designed to consider benefits of the substance as well as health effects and forces detailed quantification only if the decision cannot be made on the basis of gross effects. Furthermore, the process considers a range of options beyond simply a ban, including labeling and restricted sale.

Merrill describes the legal framework within which the Food and Drug Administration considered and banned saccharin. Under the Delaney clause,[3] the agency had no alternative to banning saccharin as a food additive after it had been found to be an animal carcinogen. However, because of a ban's effect on the quality and availability of food, there is room for discretion both in the precise classification used for each food additive and in whether the Food and Drug Administration chooses to press a particular case. Merrill argues that the present framework gives the agency adequate flexibility. He considers saccharin to be almost a unique case and thus does not think that vast changes in the law are required.

Waterborne Carcinogens

The carcinogenic risk from the organic contaminants in drinking water has been recognized only recently. These contaminants are derived from the discharge of synthetic organic compounds into lakes and streams and the interaction of natural organic compounds with the chlorine used to disinfect drinking water to protect humans from disease. The chlorine combines with a variety of organic compounds to form several chlorinated and brominated compounds. Of these, the four trihalomethanes— chloroform, bromoform, dibromochloromethane, and bromodichloromethane—have received the most attention. Of the four, chloroform appears in the greatest concentrations in drinking water.

Many of the organic compounds in drinking water have been recognized so recently that they have not been tested for carcinogenicity. According to Hoel and Crump, there are at least nineteen human or animal carcinogens and three suspected animal carcinogens in drinking water, but the degree of their carcinogenicity and their concentrations vary sub-

3. Contained in Food Additives Amendment of 1958 (72 Stat. 1786).

stantially. Although chloroform is found in the greatest concentrations, dieldrin—another chemical found in drinking water, at much lower concentrations—is 200 times as potent a carcinogen.

Extrapolating these data to establish risk to humans is perilous. Page, Harris, and Bruser argue that the surface-area extrapolation technique used by Hoel and Crump is likely to understate the rate of cancer induced by waterborne carcinogens. Hoel and Crump present other problems in extrapolating animal test data to humans: (1) lack of low-dose results; (2) differences in genetic and environmental conditions; (3) physiological and biochemical differences between experimental animals (mice) and humans; (4) potential interactions of several carcinogens acting together; and (5) controversy over the existence of a threshold level for carcinogens in the formation of cancer. Finally, Page, Harris, and Bruser argue that extrapolation of cancer risk from the available data is impossible because many, possibly carcinogenic, organic compounds in water supplies have not yet been identified.

Because of these uncertainties of extrapolating risk to humans from waterborne organic compounds, Kimm, Kuzmack, and Schnare argue that precise cost-benefit analyses cannot be done for alternative standards. They defend the use of an intuitive approach where extrapolations of the experimental health evidence vary greatly. Nevertheless, they carry out a sensitivity analysis of the cost-benefit calculations for the trihalomethane component of drinking water. As expected, the results vary with the value placed on human life, the assumed cost of treating the water, and the dose-response relationship. Conservative assumptions appear to justify the standard proposed by the Environmental Protection Agency (one hundred micrograms per liter for trihalomethanes), but an even tighter standard is apparently justified by slight variations in the important assumptions.

Sulfur Dioxide

Ferris shows that at high concentrations, particularly in combination with small particles, sulfur dioxide has an adverse effect on morbidity and mortality. A series of air pollution episodes testifies to both sets of effects. The same adverse effect appears to result from high levels of sulfates. There is almost no direct measurement of sulfate levels during episodes, but suggestive effects have been produced in laboratory experiments at high concentrations. Indeed, it is difficult to determine which sulfur oxides are the most toxic at current ambient concentrations.

Several laboratory and epidemiological studies fail to show any significant increase in health effects or even physiological changes associated with low to moderate levels of sulfur dioxide. Ferris interprets some of these studies as demonstrating that there are levels of air quality that would not cause health problems for the general population. Although there is a range of levels in which neither positive nor negative results have been detected, Ferris is willing to make a judgment about the safe level of ambient air quality. He concludes that current air quality standards are probably protective, perhaps even overprotective. He finds that there is a scientific basis for a primary air quality standard that meets the congressional requirement for protecting the health of even the most sensitive members of the population.

Lave also examines the scientific literature on the effects of sulfur oxides, concluding that sulfates, not sulfur dioxide, are the likely culprits in producing health effects and that there is no safe ambient air quality level that would protect the population completely. Rather, he concludes that the health effects appear to be proportional to air quality.

Reducing particulate and sulfate levels by 50 percent would lead to a 4.5 percent reduction in the total mortality rate; the effect on mortality (and presumably morbidity) would be proportional to ambient air quality. A table of the various costs of abatement and of possible health effects shows that stringent abatement of sulfur oxides is justified for reasonable estimates of effects and health valuations (see table 1 in the paper by Lave). Lave concludes that the current ambient air quality standards for sulfur dioxide should be changed to an acid sulfate standard and tightened.

Middleton points out that large gaps in knowledge existed at the time sulfur dioxide and particulate standards were initially set. The decision to set the standards had to be made before important questions could be answered definitively. Those decisions persist, even though the knowledge of effects has been expanded considerably. It is difficult to revise standards once they are established.

Lessons from the Case Studies

Several generalizations emerge from the five case studies. The first is that scientific evidence was not the determining factor in the regulatory action, and in only one instance—that of passive restraints—were scientists able to estimate risks with reasonable confidence. The underlying scientific basis for each regulation was far from complete in each case: anyone asserting that scientific evidence determined the regulation simply did not have the correct information.

This is not to say that the scientific evidence was totally ignored. In some cases, it clarified the issues and isolated the judgments on risk and value that were needed. The evidence did not replace the regulator's judgment, but it did provide facts and a structure in which a complicated decision could be made. The regulator needed to make judgments about risks, the effect of the regulation, induced changes in behavior, and the desirability of the regulation to the population generally and to involved interest groups. The scientific evidence at least helped in making such judgments.

Unfortunately, there is widespread perception that science determines regulations, or at least the allowable risk level of certain substances. This perception places pressure on scientists and creates a set of expectations they cannot fulfill. Good science provides only part of the required information; the rest is assumption and judgment. Having gone through the experience once, scientists question why they bothered trying so hard, given the second step.

A more realistic assessment of the role of science and scientists is that they help in the formulation of the right questions, the search for the best data and judgments, and the identification of the range of uncertainty. Putting more weight on the role of science would not only lead to the gathering of scientific information more useful to the regulatory process, but would also improve regulations by correctly reflecting the uncertainties involved.

A second conclusion that emerges from all five papers is that uncertainty confounds the attempt to use scientific information. None of the regulators provides a detailed decision analysis embodying the facts and uncertainties—both scientific and economic—involved in setting a standard. In every case, it was clear that the scientific evidence was no more than one input into a regulator's decision. In fact, Kimm, Kuzmack, and Schnare argue that the very presence of uncertainty makes quantitative approaches impossible. An administrator's judgment is required, and the decision cannot be driven by any systematic decision analysis of uncertain evidence.

In this environment, economists' modeling of costs and benefits is not taken seriously because regulators distrust point estimates of costs or health effects and are unwilling to sanction the translation of frequency distributions into cardinal or ordinal rankings. Regulators certainly do not want to set out their loss functions for public review. Moreover, the cost data are viewed as suspect or even biased, and the attempt to measure health and safety benefits is viewed as legally irrelevant or unethical. Thus, economists can usually question the cost-effectiveness of a regulation, but they are generally unable to quantify the benefits and costs of alternative standards. Uncertainty becomes the basis for informal decisionmaking.

Since scientific evidence remains uncertain, regulators need a way to deal with this uncertainty just as much as they need better scientific evidence. It is not surprising that many scientists are skeptical that more precise estimates of saccharin's or trihalomethanes' role in causing cancer would have improved the quality of regulation eventually set. No matter how much this health evidence is improved, they argue, there will still be enormous uncertainty as to dose-response relationships, interactions with other carcinogens, and differences in individual tolerances. Until regulators develop a decisionmaking framework that admits uncertainty in some systematic way, reducing the variance of the estimates of the important coefficients will not necessarily improve the quality of regulatory decisions.

Without a better approach to dealing with uncertainty, scientific evidence cannot be used to determine whether society might be better off with no regulatory intervention at all. The best example among the five case studies of the relationship between uncertainty and the decision to intervene is provided by saccharin. Williamson's decision tree provides one potential method for resolving the problem, but such methods are generally overlooked by regulators who have a statute to enforce, which rarely allows them the luxury of inaction. For instance, the National Highway Traffic Safety Administration gives little attention to Blomquist and Peltzman's argument that automobile safety standards are largely offset by drivers' adjustments of driving habits. The prospect of delaying regulations until better data are available is addressed only in the case of waterborne carcinogens by Page, Harris, and Bruser. They come the closest to actually spelling out a loss function for the Environmental Protection Agency, based on the possibility that many new carcinogens will be discovered among the organics not yet identified or tested. But most of the regulators do not spell out criteria for deciding when to regulate— largely because they appear to believe that they have no legal authority for deciding not to regulate.

Finally, the papers by regulators do not uncover a consistent set of goals for each agency. It is not clear how the Environmental Protection Agency or the Occupational Safety and Health Administration, for example, would determine how much sulfur dioxide, waterborne carcinogens, or cotton dust is "just right." In most cases, the regulatory answer to this problem is to maximize health or subject safety to a political "feasibility" constraint. In the case of the National Highway Traffic Safety Administration, seat belt interlocks were politically infeasible; thus, the agency was left with passive restraint systems or the voluntary use of seat belts. In the case of waterborne carcinogens, political opposition caused the Environmental Protection Agency to withdraw the filtration requirement. Corn is quite explicit in saying that feasibility precluded a tighter standard for cotton dust, a standard that would have been more protective of human health. And for sulfur dioxide, the Environmental Protection Agency must find a health threshold even when none may exist to make sense of the absolutist Clean Air Act.

Conclusion

The five case studies show that data and analysis are not the sole basis for setting standards; indeed, they often do not even serve as an important resource. Data and analysis can assume a more important role only if the relative importance of different aspects of the regulatory process is changed and if the goals of the process are clarified. It is ironic that the evidence for the enhanced role of scientific data and analysis is a set of case studies—soft, impressionistic material—which is being used to suggest the value of hard analysis! But we know of no better way to illuminate the role of scientific evidence in the world of regulation.

The cases concerned with exposure to toxic substances are dominated by political judgments, and the resulting regulations are inevitably challenged by those groups not favored by the regulators' judgment. Rather than ask that science play a greater part in the regulatory process, Congress seems to be looking more toward judicial and legislative review. The apparent direction of Congress seems to have come from a feeling of frustration, a feeling that regulators are not in control, are getting into areas not sanctioned by Congress, and are making unfortunate regulations. The case studies support another conclusion: regulators do not seek scientific contributions in a way that is likely to elicit the most helpful analysis and are not able to use the material they do receive. Both problems stem partly from an inability of agency heads to understand the limitations of science and to interpret inconclusive information. The problems are exacerbated by scientists' alienation from the chaotic, pressured world of the regulator, with its need for timely answers, even if such answers require making arbitrary assumptions. Regulators have learned that scientific data and analysis often cannot provide firm answers to their questions. With few scientific constraints, regulators find themselves driven by political forces, using an intuitive decisionmaking process.

The difficulty is not that science has nothing to offer; rather it is that the science is not perceived as helpful because it is inconclusive. Since regulators do not see scientific data as helpful, they assign research a lower priority and a lesser role in policy formulation. The result is self-destructive in a sense, since funding has shrunk and the research results are used to satisfy legislative requirements rather than influence decisions. For example, the Environmental Protection Agency must review its regulations on sulfur oxides, but it has supported little research that would help clarify the consequences of various alternative standards.

When a regulatory decision must be made, the scientific data will always be somewhat incomplete, and important questions will be unanswered. What decisions can and should be made in light of the prevailing uncertainties? What can be gained at various periods by additional research? How should the current uncertainties in scientific knowledge be reflected in public policy? The answers to these questions require careful policy analysis. Fortunately, such analysis can be done relatively quickly and at a relatively low cost. Unfortunately, deciding to use policy analysis requires giving more emphasis to scientific evidence and less to political horse trading. The case studies show that there is substantial room for improvement in regulatory decisionmaking through better use of scientific information, but we doubt that such improvement will be realized soon.

Part One

Part One

Passive Restraints: A Scientist's View

DONALD F. HUELKE *and* JAMES O'DAY

IN 1978 about 50,000 people in the United States died in motor vehicle accidents. About 27,000 of these people were in the front seat of an automobile at the time of the accident that caused their death.[1] Although lap and lap-shoulder belts were available to the front-seat occupants in the majority of these cars, it has been estimated that fewer than 5 percent of those fatally injured had taken the trouble to put them on.

Federal Motor Vehicle Safety Standard 208 requires that passive restraint systems be installed in all new passenger cars by the 1984 model year.[2] The term *passive restraint* implies that the car occupant will have protection against injury in a crash equivalent to that available from an active restraint system (for example, a lap-shoulder belt) but without having to take any direct action to engage the protective system. Both air bags that are mounted on the dashboard and steering wheel and belt systems that come into a protective position when a door is closed fit this definition.

There are also several combinations of simple systems that have been proposed or are actually used. The air bag alone may be supplemented by an active lap belt (that is, one that requires the occupant's action to engage it). The latter provides better protection against injury in roll-

---

1. U.S. Department of Transportation, National Center for Statistics and Analysis, *Motor Vehicle Traffic Fatalities in the United States: Trends from 1975 to 1978, and 1979 4-Month Estimates* (Government Printing Office, 1979); Department of Transportation, National Highway Traffic Safety Administration, Fatal Accident Reporting System data for 1977.

2. The Reagan administration has delayed the implementation of this regulation until 1985 and may rescind it altogether. 49 C.F.R. 571.208.

21

overs and side collisions. Automatic passive belts are usually supplemented by a redesigned lower instrument panel to provide more adequate knee protection and to limit lower torso movement.

As Federal Motor Vehicle Safety Standard 208 is now written, the use of air bags seems to be the only way to satisfy the regulation when there are more than two seated positions in the front seat. Automatic belts have been used in the front passenger seat nearest the door in some Volkswagen Rabbits for several years and in a few Chevrolet Chevettes in 1980. About 12,000 cars equipped with air bags have been produced so far, and about 9,000 of these cars are still in operation.

A significant amount of laboratory testing on passive restraints has been done, but there have not been enough real-world crashes of cars equipped with passive restraints to provide the information needed to adequately evaluate the various passive restraint designs. We agree with Haddon, Suchman, and Klein that an argument can be made "that the introduction of essentially unevaluated accident prevention measures 'can't do any harm,' but two potential dangers in this approach need to be noted. First, the introduction and enforcement of insufficiently evaluated measures may lead to an inappropriate choice of emphasis and may, as a result, dissipate funds, time, and public concern that might be applied to more effective measures. Secondly, the public and its government may conclude that everything that can be done is being done."[3]

The Effectiveness of Passive Restraint Systems

An early National Highway Traffic Safety Administration estimate by the then administrator Douglas Toms was that 24,000 persons would be saved each year by air bags.[4] An analysis conducted by General Motors engineers in 1972 of 706 fatal car crashes concluded that 18 percent of the annual front-seat fatalities would be avoided by the use of air bags alone.[5] Extrapolated data from the 1976 decision of Secretary of Trans-

3. William Haddon, Jr., Edward A. Suchman, and David Klein, *Accident Research: Methods and Approaches* (Harper and Row, 1964), p. 5.
4. John Z. DeLorean, Corp., *Automotive Occupant Protection: Safety Aircushion Expenditure Benefit Study* (Bloomfield Hills, Mich.: John Z. DeLorean, Corp., 1975), pp. 46, 49.
5. R. A. Wilson and C. M. Savage, "Restraint System Effectiveness—A Study of Fatal Accidents," in Society of Automotive Engineers, *Automotive Safety Seminar Proceedings* (Detroit: SAE, 1973). Hereafter referred to as the General Motors study.

portation William T. Coleman, Jr., predicted that 10,700 front-seat lives could be saved (39 percent of 27,200 front-seat fatalities) each year by air bags alone.[6] More recently the National Highway Traffic Safety Administration has indicated a possible saving of 9,000 lives.[7] Huelke's 1979 study judged from a review of on-the-scene investigations of fatal accidents that the use of air bags could have prevented between 23 percent and 27 percent of the deaths caused by those accidents.

The original concept of passivity was usually applied to the air bag alone, but some estimates have been made based on a combination of the air bag and lap belt—the lap belt being used to prevent partial or complete ejection and to moderate movements of the lower torso and legs. The General Motors study indicated that about 29 percent of front-seat fatalities could be prevented with the use of an air bag plus lap belt; the Coleman decision data indicated a 65 percent fatality reduction; and the Huelke 1979 study showed a 34 percent fatality reduction with the use of air bag and lap belt. In the General Motors study and in the Huelke 1979 study it was reported that about 50 percent of the fatalities would not have survived in any case because of the crash type, amount of crush, and the high speeds involved.[8]

Two reports estimated the effectiveness of passive belts for preventing deaths: the Coleman decision data indicated an effectiveness of 50 percent and the Huelke study estimated an effectiveness of 28 percent.

In addition to those people killed in motor vehicle crashes, there are a significant number who are severely injured. However, these numbers are estimates at best; the actual number of the severely injured is unknown. Similarly, there are only minimal data on precisely where in the body the severe injuries have occurred and almost no data on their causes. Without these data, estimates of passive restraint effectiveness are difficult to make and subject to wide variation.

6. "The Secretary's Decision Concerning Motor Vehicle Occupant Crash Protection" (Department of Transportation, 1976) (hereafter referred to as the Coleman decision); and Donald F. Huelke and others, *Effectiveness of Current and Future Restraint Systems in Fatal and Serious Injury Automobile Crashes,* Society of Automotive Engineers Technical Paper 790323 (Detroit: SAE, 1979) (hereafter referred to as the Huelke 1979 study).

7. Statement of Joan B. Claybrook in *Department of Transportation and Related Agencies Appropriations, Fiscal Year 1979,* pt. 3, Hearings before the Subcommittee on Transportation of the Senate Committee on Appropriations, 95 Cong. 2 sess. (GPO, 1978), p. 378; and U.S. General Accounting Office, *Passive Restraints for Automobile Occupants: A Closer Look,* Report to the Congress by the Comptroller General of the United States (GAO, 1979), pp. 13, 93.

8. Personal communication with R. A. Wilson, 1978.

The Huelke 1979 study reviewed data from the authors' own field investigations of car occupants who suffered serious nonfatal injuries. The authors estimated the effectiveness of air bags and other restraint systems and concluded that the air bag would reduce serious injuries by an average of 58 percent. Using the figure of 70,700 seriously injured occupants presented in the Coleman decision, the authors estimated that 41,000 occupants, on the average—compared to the National Highway Traffic Safety Administration's 22,840—would not have sustained serious injuries. Huelke and others also noted a higher effectiveness level of passive belts than did the administration for reducing the occurrences of serious injuries. The authors concluded that the administration significantly underestimated estimates on the effectiveness of air bags.

Potential Effectiveness of Lap-Shoulder Belts

Many studies have focused on the effectiveness of lap and lap-shoulder belts, and several have used data from a specialized accident investigation program.[9] In general, these studies have compared injury severity and fatality rates of unrestrained, lap-belted, and lap-shoulder-belted occupants. Rininger and Boak, in their study of front-seat occupants injured or killed in full-sized 1974–75 General Motors cars involved in tow-away accidents, estimated that 77 percent of the fatalities would have been prevented by the use of the lap-shoulder belts.[10] Scott, Flora, and Marsh of the Highway Safety Research Institute reviewed 1973–75 American-made passenger cars involved in tow-away accidents and showed that lap-shoulder belts are 62 percent effective in reducing the incidence of fatalities.[11]

9. A. R. Rininger and R. W. Boak, "Lap/Shoulder Belt Effectiveness," in *Proceedings of the Twentieth Conference of the American Association of Automotive Medicine* (Lake Bluff, Ill.: AAAM, 1976), pp. 262–79; Robert E. Scott, Jairus D. Flora, and Joseph C. Marsh, *An Evaluation of the 1974 and 1975 Restraint Systems* (Ann Arbor: University of Michigan, Highway Safety Research Institute, 1976); Donald W. Reinfurt, Claudio Z. Silva, and Andrew F. Seila, *A Statistical Analysis of Seat Belt Effectiveness in 1973–1975 Model Cars Involved in Towaway Crashes,* vol. 1 (Chapel Hill: University of North Carolina, Highway Safety Research Center, 1976).

10. Rininger and Boak, "Lap/Shoulder Belt Effectiveness."

11. Scott, Flora, and Marsh, *An Evaluation of the 1974 and 1975 Restraint Systems.*

Reinfurt, Silva, and Seila of the University of North Carolina's Highway Safety Research Center found that lap-shoulder belts were 55 percent effective in reducing fatal injuries.[12] European studies by Backstrom and others, Asberg, MacKay, and Tarriere have indicated that conventional three-point belts prevent serious and fatal injuries to front-seat occupants within a range of 32 percent to 55 percent.[13] A 1977 study by Huelke and others showed that there is a decrease in fatalities of 57 to 77 percent in frontal crashes and 91 percent in rollovers with the use of lap-shoulder belts.[14]

Using mass accident statistics on serious injuries, three studies concluded that lap-shoulder belts would be effective at the 42–57 percent level. Rininger and Boak and Reinfurt and others concluded that lap-shoulder belts are 57 percent effective in reducing moderate or more serious injuries as rated by the Abbreviated Injury Scale;[15] Scott, Flora, and Marsh indicated an effectiveness of 42 percent for moderate (AIS-2) or more serious injuries; and the Huelke 1977 study (see note 14) showed a 48 percent reduction in the more severe (AIS 3–5) level in frontal crashes and 51 percent in rollovers.[16]

The Huelke 1979 study reviewed the condition of seventy front-seat occupants who sustained severe, serious, or critical but nonfatal injuries

12. Reinfurt, Silva, and Seila, *A Statistical Analysis of Seat Belt Effectiveness,* vol. 1.

13. C. G. Backstrom and others, *Road Accident Research: Saab 99—Results from the First Three Years* (Malmo, Sweden: Saab-Scania, 1973); A. Asberg, "Statistical Traffic Accident Analyses Referring to Occupant Restraint Value and Crash Safety Requirements for the Experimental Safety Car," *Proceedings of the Fourth International Technical Conference on Experimental Safety Vehicles* (National Highway Traffic Safety Administration, 1973), pp. 359–92; G. M. MacKay, "Some Cost-Benefit Considerations of Car Occupant Restraint Systems," Technical Aspects of Road Safety no. 59 (September 1974), pp. 4.1–4.11; Claude Tarriere, "Efficiency of the 3-Point Belt in Real Accidents," *Proceedings of the Fourth International Conference on Experimental Safety Vehicles,* pp. 607–19.

14. Donald F. Huelke and others, "The Effectiveness of Belt Systems in Frontal and Rollover Crashes," Society of Automotive Engineers Technical Paper 770148 (Detroit: SAE, 1977).

15. The Abbreviated Injury Scale (AIS) is an index of the seriousness of injuries sustained in automobile accidents. The scale consists of the following levels of injury: AIS-0, no injury; AIS-1, minor; AIS-2, moderate; AIS-3, severe (not life-threatening); AIS-4, serious (life-threatening, but survival probable); AIS-5, critical (survival uncertain); AIS-6, maximum (currently untreatable).

16. Reinfurt, Silva, and Seila, *A Statistical Analysis of Seat Belt Effectiveness;* Scott, Flora, and Marsh, *An Evaluation of the 1974 and 1975 Restraint Systems;* and Huelke and others, "The Effectiveness of Belt Systems."

in cars involved in accidents during the same time period covered by the studies just discussed (1973–77). In this study it was concluded that all restraint systems are more effective in reducing the frequency of the more serious injuries than in reducing fatalities. According to the study, the lap belt was 39 percent effective, the air bag with lap belt was 68 percent effective, the lap-shoulder belt was 64 percent effective, and the air bag alone or the passive belt system (shoulder portion only) was 58 percent effective.

Analyses of Fatalities

Two studies have made estimates of the effectiveness of restraint systems using specific injury information, injury causation data, and type of vehicle crash. In 1972 Wilson and Savage reviewed 706 fatalities that occurred in vehicles produced between 1967 and 1972, evaluating the potential effectiveness of various restraint systems for reducing fatal injuries.[17] The researchers reviewed field accident data (including photographs, medical reports, crash data, and other information) of fatal automobile crashes and rated the probability of fatality reduction from 0 percent (essentially no chance for survival) to 100 percent (survival essentially certain). Several staff members at General Motors, all well versed in the causes of crash injuries, analyzed accidents to determine the percentage of survivability afforded by each restraint system. The results are shown in table 1.

In the Huelke 1979 study, three experienced crash investigators reviewed data concerning fatalities of front-seat car occupants that had occurred at high speeds in rural areas. The researchers investigated these deaths between January 1, 1973, and December 31, 1977. Fatalities that occurred in vans, pickup trucks, larger trucks, and the rear seats of cars were excluded from the review. Of the 101 people killed (under conditions within the range of the study), only four were wearing belts. (See table 1 for the results.)

One significant conclusion of the Huelke 1979 study was that approximately 42–51 percent of the 101 people killed had had no chance of survival, regardless of the type of restraint system used. There was a similar finding in the General Motors study. Thus, from these two studies

17. Wilson and Savage, "Restraint System Effectiveness."

Table 1. Comparison of the Potential Effectiveness of Various Restraint Systems for Reducing Fatalities

Percent

Type of restraint	General Motors	Huelke, 1979	
		Average	*Range*
Lap belt	17.0	12.8	9.2–15.9
Lap-shoulder belt	31.0	32.1	30.6–32.4
Air bag alone	18.0	25.1	23.2–27.1
Air bag and lap belt	29.0	34.2	32.6–35.3
Passive belt	Not estimated	28.0	26.8–29.6

Sources: R. A. Wilson and C. M. Savage, "Restraint System Effectiveness—A Study of Fatal Accidents," in Society of Automotive Engineers, *Automotive Safety Seminar Proceedings* (Detroit: SAE, 1973); and Donald F. Huelke and others, *Effectiveness of Current and Future Restraint Systems in Fatal and Serious Injury Automobile Crashes*, Society of Automotive Engineers Technical Paper 790323 (Detroit: SAE, 1979).

it can be concluded that known restraint systems may have no chance at all to be effective for half of the front-seat car occupants in all crash configurations.

Analyses of Fatal and Serious Injury Cases

In the Huelke 1979 study of fatal and serious injury crashes, the authors estimated the number of lives saved annually by various restraint systems and compared these numbers with the National Highway Traffic Safety Administration's figures (table 2). In addition to averaging they computed the potential fatality reduction by using the probabilities derived from the combined estimates of three experienced "estimators." Using each interval (10 percent, 20 percent, and so forth) as a probability and multiplying the number of cases in each interval by the figure of 27,200 (front-seat fatalities) yielded the effectiveness of each restraint system. These probability estimates are also shown in table 2. Estimates used in the Coleman decision of lives saved with the various restraint systems, especially the air bag and the lap-shoulder belt, are much higher than those of the Huelke study.

The problem of the variation in estimates of lives saved results from a relatively limited knowledge of the actual number of passenger car fatalities, the circumstances under which these occurred, and the location of the accidents. The National Highway Traffic Safety Administration began compiling a census of fatal highway accidents occurring in the United

Table 2. Estimated Lives Saved, by Type of Restraint[a]

Type of restraint	Huelke study		NHTSA: Coleman decision	
	Average	*Probability estimates[b]*	*Number*	*Percent*
Lap belt (100 percent use)	3,536	3,436	10,900	40
Lap-shoulder belt (100 percent use)	8,704	8,278	16,300	60
Air bag alone (100 percent activation)	6,800	6,909	10,700[c]	39
Air bag and lap belt (100 percent lap-belt use)	9,248	9,112	17,700[c]	65
Passive belt (100 percent use)	7,616	7,371	13,400[c]	50

Sources: Huelke and others, *Effectiveness of Current and Future Restraint Systems*, p. 7; and U.S. Department of Transportation, "The Secretary's Decision Concerning Motor Vehicle Occupant Crash Protection" (DOT, 1976), table A6, p. A-8.

a. Minimum to optimum number of potential lives saved of 27,200 front-seat car occupants.

b. See discussion in text.

c. Our estimate from NHTSA data.

States in the early 1970s; by 1976 this had become a rather complete set of data. It is now possible to pinpoint the number of persons killed in passenger cars each year, and although there is some uncertainty about the effectiveness of various restraints, the population that would benefit from the restraints is well known. The data are compiled in the Fatal Accident Reporting System and are available through the National Highway Traffic Safety Administration and elsewhere.

Although the total number of fatalities varies from year to year, we have chosen the fatality data from calendar year 1977 as a basis for discussion. Table 3 shows the number of front-seat occupants of passenger cars who died in 1977, their seat location, and the direction of the impact that caused the principal damage. Both the "top" and the "other and unknown" categories imply something other than a straight-on impact; both of these categories probably include rollovers.

Data on Crash Severity

The choice of the crash or impact speed at which air bags are to activate involves a trade-off between the cost of unnecessary deployment (for a low-speed crash with little anticipated injury) and the benefits of injury and fatality reduction at higher speeds. Current air bag designs call for activation with an instantaneous longitudinal change of velocity of about twelve miles per hour.

A relatively new data source is the National Crash Severity Study. This study, done under the auspices of the National Highway Traffic Safety

Table 3. Fatalities of Front-Seat Occupants of Passenger Cars, 1977

Principal collision damage	Driver	Front center occupant	Front right occupant	Other front occupant	Total
Frontal	8,813	292	2,795	8	11,908
	(961)	(38)	(337)	(1)	(1,337)
Right	1,989	108	1,508	4	3,609
	(350)	(20)	(228)	(1)	(559)
Back	457	12	170	0	639
	(82)	(4)	(52)	(0)	(138)
Left	2,764	65	488	1	3,318
	(445)	(13)	(84)	(1)	(543)
Top (rollover)	1,554	50	568	0	2,712
	(631)	(22)	(229)	(0)	(882)
Other and unknown	1,596	57	561	1	2,215
	(783)	(32)	(286)	(0)	(1,101)
Total	17,173	584	6,090	14	23,861
	(3,252)	(129)	(1,216)	(3)	(4,600)

Source: National Highway Traffic Safety Administration, Fatal Accident Reporting System data for 1977. Numbers in parentheses indicate ejected occupants.

Administration, has provided detailed crash severity and injury information for a sample of U.S. tow-away accidents involving passenger cars. When possible, an estimate has been made of the crash severity in terms of the velocity change at the instant of impact. This is usually referred to as the "Delta V" for that vehicle and is a vector sum of the longitudinal and latitudinal components.

Table 4 presents data from this study showing several categories of velocity change at impact and the injury level of the most seriously injured person in the car. In the range of one to ten miles per hour 14 percent of the frontal crashes produce more than a minor injury to an occupant of the car, although only six of ten thousand such crashes involve a fatality. Averaged over the range of eleven to twenty miles per hour, about two-thirds of the activations of air bags would occur in crashes in which only minor injuries are predicted. In this range, about four fatalities would occur in one thousand frontal crashes. The choice of twelve miles per hour as the activation level seems to be reasonable in light of these statistics, but this means that about one of four towed vehicles will need an air bag replacement after the crash.[18]

18. Leda L. Ricci, ed., *NCSS Statistics: Passenger Cars* (National Highway Traffic Safety Administration, forthcoming), pp. 84–85.

Table 4. Range of Injuries at Various Delta Vs
Number of most seriously injured persons in car

Longitudinal Delta V (miles per hour)	No or minor injury	Moderate injury	Greater than moderate injury and fatalities	Total
1–10	4,841	439	322	5,602
11–20	2,064	544	371	2,979
Over 20	335	165	341	841
Total	7,240	1,148	1,034	9,422

Source: National Highway Traffic Safety Administration, National Crash Severity Study data.

An Analogy[19]

The incidence of automobile injuries can be compared to a disease, which may be treated with special medicines (restraint systems) and through other preventive measures such as automobile and highway engineering. Each crash type may be viewed as a separate and specific disease, for which different treatment plans are needed. One medicine, or restraint system, may not be able to reduce injury or prevent death in all kinds of crashes. For maximum protection, several restraints may be needed. For example, air bags, with or without belts, which function best in head-on crashes, offer little or no protection in rear-end crashes. Because of lack of data, it is not known how effective air bags are in crashes with side or angle impacts and in rollover crashes, but their effectiveness is probably fairly low. The passive restraint concept has already been modified to include a lap belt with the air bag for additional protection. In other words, the National Highway Traffic Safety Administration now indicates that two different "medicines" may be needed for improved or optimal occupant protection.

Problems with the Data

The scientific method usually involves a combination of analytical or logical models and the acquisition of laboratory or real-world data to fit those models. Indeed, all of the estimates given earlier in the chapter

19. This section is derived from E. F. Domino and D. F. Huelke, "Belts, Bags, and Medicine: Application of a Medical Treatment and Prevention Model for Automobile Occupant Protection," Society of Automotive Engineers Technical Paper 750392 (Detroit: SAE, 1975).

were arrived at by application of this sort of procedure. The great disparity between early estimates and later ones can be attributed to a combination of inadequate data, simplistic models, and an overoptimistic view of the earlier numbers.

Scientists are ordinarily not directly involved in such decisions as the promulgation of Federal Motor Vehicle Safety Standard 208, but rather are in a position to provide information to help others form opinions and make decisions. Estimates of effectiveness (or other quantities) are typically stated in the form of a mean (or average) value along with an estimate of the variance (or the uncertainty) associated with that value. In the physical sciences some quantities are known with great precision (for example, the speed of light) and may be used to make further calculations. But determination of the average value and the standard deviation of lives saved by a particular restraint system is limited by the fact that the data available have not come from controlled experiments. One must then rely on a good deal of "engineering judgment."

The recent estimate by the National Highway Traffic Safety Administration of 9,000 lives saved by air bags is probably closer to real numbers than those previously suggested, yet it is not clear to us just how this number was generated and whether the 9,000 lives are saved by the air bag alone or by the air bag in addition to lap belts—an important differentiation. The Huelke study, for example, estimated about 9,200 lives saved with air bags and 100 percent lap belt usage; without belts (air bag alone) the estimate was approximately 6,800–6,900 lives. The two estimates represent a 35 percent difference.

Another problem can be approached through the medical treatment analogy used earlier. In the drug field the federal government must protect the public against the possibility of undesirable side effects of medication developed by manufacturers. Drugs are approved for experimental purposes, but generally with the provision that effects be monitored carefully before they are made available to the public. In the case of passive restraint systems, this situation is nearly reversed. The government has promulgated a standard that implies a blessing on widespread use of a device, but there are still questions about possible harmful effects that deserve investigation.

Additional data required for more accurately assessing the effectiveness of restraint systems are now available. For example, the Fatal Accident Reporting System file includes data on the frequency of deaths by seating position, by principal direction of impact, and by vehicle type (car, truck, and so forth). Yet even with the known frequency of driver deaths in certain types of crashes, for example, it would not be possible to assess the effectiveness of a passive restraint system. The Fatal Accident Reporting System file indicates that 8.5 percent of driver deaths occur in cars where the principal point of impact is at the passenger door area and 13.3 percent from impact at the driver's door area.[20] Because of the lack of real-world data on air bags in such side impacts, it is unknown whether the air bag would be activated in this type of crash and, if it were, whether it would give the required protection. It seems logical to assume that impacts at the driver's door are crashes in which the air bag would not be activated. But there may be drivers who would receive protection in this type of crash. Thus to totally write them off may be incorrect. An accurate estimate of the effectiveness of air bags cannot be made without further data obtained from actual crashes involving cars equipped with air bags.

The air bag has long been touted as the cure-all for the disease of automobile injuries and fatalities. However, it is not as effective as a belt system in preventing ejections, the major cause of death during rollover collisions. Also, the air bag may even contribute to the injury of an occupant who is not in a standard seating position.[21] The potential danger to young children standing close to an air bag as it activates is now being studied. Volvo has conducted tests with live animals and has shown that the present bags may cause serious or fatal injury.[22] The death or serious injury of only a few children could greatly harm the entire passive restraint program. Thus, this critical problem needs to be resolved.

One of the few actual fatalities in connection with the positioning of an air bag occurred when an infant slid from the front seat when the car was braked and hit the dashboard when the car crashed. The air bag activated above the child and was not directly responsible for the death. But the mother might have thought that placing the infant on the seat was safe.

Another problem, perhaps less well defined, is that of out-of-position

20. National Highway Traffic Safety Administration, National Center for Statistics and Analysis, *Fatal Accident Reporting System: 1977 Annual Report* (GPO, 1978), p. 27.

21. Domino and Huelke, "Belts, Bags, and Medicine."

22. Bertil Aldman, Äke Anderson, and Olov Saxmark, "Possible Effects of Airbag Inflation on a Standing Child," in *Proceedings of the Eighteenth Conference of the American Association of Automotive Medicine* (Lake Bluff, Ill.: AAAM, 1974).

adults—for example, a driver with his chest on or near the steering wheel at the time of impact. In one of the six fatal accidents in the United States involving an activated air bag there was speculation that the driver had been in this position and may have died of a fractured larynx and a cervical spinal cord injury. In the few off-axis frontal tests of air bag systems that have been performed, dummies have slid over the air bag, striking the head on the A-pillar of the car.

A similar problem has occurred in connection with the energy-absorbing steering column mandated by Federal Motor Vehicle Safety Standards 203 and 204.[23] The testing of these columns for compliance with the standard requires an axial impact with an instrumented pendulum-type device. The impact of the device on the steering wheel measures both the loading on the simulated chest and the compression of the column. A study conducted in 1972 noted that many steering columns observed in crashes did not compress as expected.[24] Some explanations were that in real crashes drivers do not always sit in a position directly behind the steering wheel and that many crashes produce a vertical or horizontal rotation of the car, which would result in an off-axis impact of the chest with the steering column. Early estimates of the effectiveness of the energy-absorbing steering column in preventing fatal injuries were shown to be optimistic. Although some progress has been achieved, the steering column remains a principal cause of fatal injury to drivers in frontal impacts.

There are many other areas of uncertainty in attempting to extrapolate laboratory results and apply them to the future. Passenger cars are being made smaller and lighter, with a different stiffness; passive restraint requirements for smaller cars are not yet known. Furthermore, predictions of effectiveness have been based on so-called standard-sized cars and not on the smaller cars becoming more and more popular.

Conclusions

There is not much question that fatalities would be reduced if occupant restraints were universally available and used. Although the numer-

23. 49 C.F.R. 571.203 and 571.204.

24. John W. Garrett and Donald L. Hendricks, "Factors Influencing the Performance of the Energy Absorbing Steering Column in Accidents," *Fifth International Technical Conference on Experimental Safety Vehicles* (National Highway Traffic Safety Administration, 1974), pp. 369–94.

ical estimates of improvements with their use have progressed from wild guesses to reasoned projections, they have yet to be confirmed (in the United States) by actual experience. All studies suggest considerable injury reduction with either the lap or lap-shoulder belt, but the National Crash Severity Study file (where a measure of crash severity is available) shows that belted people have less severe crashes. The improvement, therefore, may not be as great as would be predicted by a simple extrapolation. The estimate of 6,300 to 9,200 lives saved each year by air bags is a recent considered judgment by informed experts and includes numbers we have estimated ourselves. Although the National Highway Traffic Safety Administration has estimated the most probable number in this range as 9,000, it seems likely that economists would want to make computations using both extremes.

Past experience with other standards has indicated that initial estimates of the benefits of nearly all of them have been furnished by the promoters and found to be quite optimistic. In our experience roughly half of the fatal accidents investigated were so severe that, with present vehicle designs, no restraint system would have been adequate to prevent the fatality. In Victoria, Australia, for example, where the government made wearing seat belts compulsory in 1970, about a 15 percent actual reduction in fatalities during 1971 was attributed to the compulsory measure, with as much as 85–90 percent of the population wearing seat belts.[25] Probably—and unfortunately—even the best reasoned estimates on improvement resulting from passive restraints are optimistic.

It is likely that there will be some real dangers associated with at least the air bag approach to passive restraint. These dangers can only be identified through widespread use of air bags. The present 12,000 cars with air bags represent only about one ten-thousandth of the cars in the nation, and it is not proper to extrapolate one possible broken neck or the death of one baby to ten thousand times that number. But neither is it proper to neglect these possibilities. Such problems may well be solved by design changes that have not yet been invented, but not until the problems have been identified.

When evaluating restraint systems, there is really no substitute for actual experience. Children standing against the glove compartment, drivers slumping on the steering wheel, and babies lying loose on the seat

25. D. C. Andreassend, "Victoria and the Seat Belt Law, 1971," *Human Factors,* vol. 18 (December 1976), pp. 593–600.

have been identified as areas of concern. Modification of the activation rate of the passenger air bag may be a solution to the first; the second may not be a problem at all; and the third may be approached by states mandating or otherwise encouraging the use of children's seats and lap belts for infants and small children. The National Highway Traffic Safety Administration and the automotive industry have both monitored crashes of cars currently using air bags, and plans are being made to use the National Accident Sampling System to continue this monitoring to obtain adequate data.

Passive Restraints: An Economist's View

GLENN C. BLOMQUIST *and* SAM PELTZMAN

FOR OVER two centuries economists have explored the implications and truth of Adam Smith's assertion that the economy operates as if an invisible hand guides individual actions for the betterment of all society. By now we have defined the conditions under which Smith's principle holds and the criteria under which society is better off. If perfect competition and a set of equilibrium prices exist, if each individual acts to maximize his own well-being, and if each firm acts to maximize its own profit, then resources will be allocated efficiently. These efficiency conditions are socially desirable because under them no reallocation of goods among consumers, no reallocation of resources or productivity among firms, or no change in goods produced can make any member of society better off without making someone else worse off. The conditions under which Smith's principle generally does not hold include the presence of (1) buyers or sellers with market power and (2) externalities in production or consumption broadly defined to include public goods.[1] Put simply, the market works well as long as the signals to individuals are undistorted, but it fails to yield satisfactory results whenever individual benefits or costs do not equal social benefits or costs, that is, there is an externality. It is these divergences of private value from social value (together

The authors thank Richard Burkhauser, Peter Linneman, and Carl Nash for helpful comments; however, the views expressed here and any errors remaining are the authors' alone.

1. A more complete treatment of the relationship between social welfare and the market economy can be found in most price theory texts; for example, Walter Nicholson, *Microeconomic Theory: Basic Principles and Extensions* (Dryden Press, 1978).

with unacceptable distributions of income) that create a demand for intervention in market operations. This demand is in the public interest because policy designed to correct market failure can improve social welfare. Assuming that such a social demand for a government policy on highway safety even exists, it might be helpful to review the motivation for such policy in terms of a simple model of driver behavior.

Social Welfare and Individual Behavior

Elsewhere Blomquist[2] uses a model of lifesaving activity to analyze lap belt use. Essentially the model says that drivers have a demand for and face a supply of highway safety, and that the optimal (to the driver) amount of highway safety is determined in this implicit market. The demand emanates from the value of an increase in the probability of living and from changes in, first, the probabilities of nonfatal injury and property damage and, second, possibly a sense of security. The supply depends on costs of equipment, time, energy, and discomfort. The driver desires more highway safety as long as the additional value of safety is greater than the additional resources spent to get the safety.

However, the amount of safety chosen by the individual will be insufficient if benefits exist that he fails to take into account. Such benefits increase the social demand for driver safety and the socially optimal amount of safety. For example, a drunken driver would value driving sober and safely, but still might lose control and injure himself and others. To the extent that the drunken driver does not fully compensate others for the damage they suffer, the social benefits of a sober driver are greater than the benefits to him alone.[3] The external benefits not considered by the drunken driver cause the problem of insufficient safety. To solve the externality problem Pigou and other economists recommend placing a tax on activities with social costs greater than individual costs and instituting a subsidy for activities with social benefits greater than individual benefits.[4] One can imagine a schedule of income tax credits avail-

---

2. Glenn Blomquist, "Value of Life Saving: Implications of Consumption Activity," *Journal of Political Economy*, vol. 87 (June 1979), pp. 540–58.

3. Surprisingly little attention has been given to identifying and measuring highway safety externalities. Those dealt with by Faigin are discussed later in the text. See Barbara Moyer Faigin, *1975 Societal Costs of Motor Vehicle Accidents* (National Highway Traffic Safety Administration, 1976).

4. A. C. Pigou, *The Economics of Welfare* (London: Macmillan, 1946).

able to drivers who avoid certain types of accidents each year. Other solutions involve developing a better compensation mechanism, perhaps through clearer establishment of liability, so that benefits and costs perceived by individuals more fully reflect social values. However, it is not at all clear that a substantial externality problem now exists, and it is even less clear that tax incentives or mandatory vehicle design standards are appropriate responses.

Financial Incentives versus Standards

Two points are often forgotten in discussions of highway safety.

First, there is a private market for safety and, where costs and benefits are fully borne by the driver, there is no clear case for government intervention, whether through taxes, subsidies, *or* regulation of vehicle design.

Second, if there is a case for intervention it would rest on costs imposed by the driver on others that the driver would not bear. (Our drunken driver, for example, would bear at least some of the costs his actions imposed on others, through legal sanctions, increased insurance premiums, or other penalties.)

Current safety regulation appears to ignore the first point by assuming implicitly that design changes must be required by law to bring about significant improvements. As we argue later, this will typically lead to overestimates of the net effectiveness of the regulation. Regulatory practice ignores the second point by focusing its major effort on protecting the driver rather than his victim. That is, we are discussing, for example, an air bag that explodes inward from the steering column and dashboard when perhaps we ought to be discussing one that explodes outward from the front fender. As we also argue later, this sort of displaced concern will exacerbate rather than alleviate whatever externality problem exists. We also point out that—should it even be contemplated—an outward-exploding air bag would probably be a less efficient response to the externality problem than appropriately designed financial incentives.

If the incentive and standard were designed to yield the same level of safety, the standard would require more resources unless it imposed the cheapest solution for each driver in all circumstances. The financial incentive is more efficient because it leads drivers to produce safety as cheaply as possible. The money and time saved can then be used for important nonsafety goods and services. The incentive encourages and permits drivers to use various types of equipment and different combinations of effort (while driving) and equipment, depending on which benefits and costs apply to each driver's situation. Another advantage is that a smaller cost is imposed on low-income drivers with an incentive scheme than with regulation, and the dollar cost is even smaller, since time and effort can be substituted for equipment in producing safety.

Why, then, has highway safety policy in the United States taken the form of standards, such as that for mandatory passive restraint systems, rather than an incentive system that is flexible and more efficient? It is questionable even why there is any government effort at all, since market failures are costly to correct—that is, the government effort is not free.[5] Only some market failures call for a response by government—those failures in which the externality cost is great enough to pay for the cost of a government response. In the case of automobile safety, so much of the relevant benefits and costs are already internalized by the government through liability laws and by the market through insurance that it cannot merely be *presumed* that the remaining externality problem is large enough to merit intervention.

Of course, it is naive to think that social welfare (the economist's concept of public interest) considerations determine or even greatly influence the direction of regulation.[6] Nevertheless, until an alternative rationale for regulation is established, we have, as economists, little choice but to analyze regulation on its own presumptive terms—as a program that, in some sense, tries to yield social benefits greater than its costs.

The Effectiveness and Social Benefits of Mandatory Passive Restraints

Cost-benefit analysis is applied welfare analysis by which social benefits and social costs of a proposed policy can be evaluated to determine whether or not it increases social welfare by increasing allocative effi-

5. Weidenbaum and DeFina estimate that in 1976 the administrative costs alone of the Department of Transportation for safety regulation were $183 million. See Murray L. Weidenbaum and Robert DeFina, *The Cost of Federal Regulation of Economic Activity* (Washington, D.C.: American Enterprise Institute for Public Policy Research, 1978), p. 4.

6. Stigler and Peltzman suggest factors other than social welfare that influence regulatory decisions. See George J. Stigler, "The Theory of Economic Regulation," *Bell Journal of Economics and Management Science,* vol. 2 (Spring 1971), pp. 3–21; and Sam Peltzman, "Toward a More General Theory of Regulation," *Journal of Law and Economics,* vol. 19 (August 1976), pp. 211–48.

ciency.[7] Careful analysis can identify traffic safety externalities and indicate whether or not mandatory passive restraints are socially desirable—that is, whether they would increase social welfare more than any alternative policy such as mandatory safety belt use, accident taxes, safe driving subsidies, and so forth.

An integral part of estimating benefits is determining the reduction in fatalities, nonfatal injuries, and property damage to all highway users that will result from the safety regulation. Huelke and O'Day analyze both accident data for occupant restraints and the evidence from various studies of accident data. They estimate that occupant fatalities are reduced with the use of lap-shoulder belts by 31 to 77 percent, with passive belts by 28 percent, with air bags by 18 to 25 percent, and with air bags and lap belts by 29 to 34 percent.[8] The estimated reductions for serious injuries are also considerable. We question neither the care with which the studies were executed nor the objectivity of the investigators. However, the methodology will overestimate the effectiveness of the safety equipment in actual experience—which Huelke and O'Day suspect but fail to pursue.[9]

We can offer three reasons for this overestimation. One we have already alluded to: individuals will voluntarily purchase some safety without being required or induced to do so. This safety can take a myriad of forms, including the way a vehicle is driven as well as its particular design features. The typical approach of safety engineers ignores this private demand. Consequently their approach ignores the possibility that a car equipped with an air bag, for example, might have been built to be safer even if an air bag were not required. The second reason is closely related: since safety is the outcome of a choice, the regulation can affect the choices made. In particular, if drivers would prefer safety in another form but are forced to buy air bags, they will not buy as much of the other form of safety. This substitution of more mandated safety for less

7. Several papers on benefit-cost analysis of highway safety policy are in National Highway Traffic Safety Administration, *Proceedings of the Fourth International Congress on Automotive Safety* (Government Printing Office, 1975). Useful benefit-cost analysis would consider all relevant benefits and costs (including implicit costs) and quantify them to the extent possible. Such an analysis would focus on traffic safety externalities and thus avoid bias either for or against an active government role.

8. See the paper by Huelke and O'Day in this volume. Secretary of Transportation Coleman and National Highway Traffic Safety Administration estimates of effectiveness are higher. See "The Secretary's Decision Concerning Motor Vehicle Occupant Crash Protection" (Department of Transportation, 1976), p. A-8.

9. See the paper by Huelke and O'Day in this volume.

nonmandated safety will offset some of the benefits promised by regulation. The third reason is similar: if drivers use less care in driving as a result of mandated safety, then an increase in deaths and injuries to other roadway users will result. The increased injuries to bicyclists, motorcyclists, and pedestrians will partly offset the reduced injuries to drivers.

Voluntary Use of Safety Belts

We can illustrate the force of these points in several ways. One that is most relevant here concerns the most direct competitors of the air bag: lap-shoulder belts and the newer passive belts. To estimate the benefits of the mandatory passive restraints standard the safety obtained with the standard must be compared to the safety obtained without the standard. The difference in safety will depend on the use of lap-shoulder belts without the standard, the use of passive belts without the standard, the use of lap belts and air bags with the standard, and the effectiveness of safety equipment in crashes (as estimated by Huelke and O'Day).

Drivers do use safety belts. Marzoni found the following concerning the use of safety belts in 1970 and 1971 for cars of all model years: 17 percent of drivers "always" used lap belts for short trips, 39 percent used them for longer trips, and 44 percent used them for cross-country trips.[10] Use was confined almost totally to lap belts. For a national sample of drivers surveyed in 1972 by the University of Michigan, Blomquist reports that the use of belts by those who had them was 23 percent.[11] According to the National Highway Traffic Safety Administration, with the installation in 1973 model automobiles of the more convenient and comfortable second-generation belt systems, lap belt and lap-shoulder belt use increased to 30 percent and 6 percent, respectively, making combined belt use 36 percent.[12] Use in 1974 and 1975 model cars was greater yet—5 percent for lap belts and 40 percent for lap-shoulder belts— although this usage was not totally voluntary because of the ignition interlock device. Three recent studies show lower usage: Stowell and

10. P. Marzoni, Jr., *Motivating Factors in the Use of Restraint Systems,* prepared for the National Highway Traffic Safety Administration (New York: National Analysts, Inc., 1971), p. 14.

11. Glenn Blomquist, "Economics of Safety and Seat Belt Use," *Journal of Safety Research,* vol. 9 (December 1977), p. 182.

12. Data are for automobiles involved in tow-away accidents. See U.S. Department of Transportation, National Highway Traffic Safety Administration, *Fact Book: Statistical Information on Highway Safety* (NHTSA, 1977), p. I.5.2.1.

Bryant found that only 18.5 percent of drivers of 1964–77 cars use safety belts, Opinion Research Corporation found that 14 percent of drivers of 1964–78 cars use safety belts, and the National Highway Traffic Safety Administration found that 8 percent of occupants (not just drivers) involved in tow-away crashes use safety belts.[13] The apparent decline in safety belt use may be a result of the study design and lack of comparability to earlier studies rather than of driver behavior.

Given the importance of speed as a major contributing factor to traffic deaths, we expect that safety devices will be used more in circumstances permitting high speeds such as rural interstate travel. If a safety externality exists it is more likely to cause problems as a result of high-speed driving. But in at least one study, "the intended emphasis of the sampling plan was upon urban driving."[14] In this study Stowell and Bryant did find, even for urban driving, that safety belt use is 20 percent on freeways and 27 percent on the West Coast, where one expects higher average speeds.[15] The results of a study by Hart based on a random national survey found the following on reported safety belt use: 16 percent use safety belts almost all the time, 25 percent use belts most of the time or almost all the time, 43 percent use belts sometimes or most of the time, and 56 percent rarely or never use safety belts.[16] The usage trend is unclear because of the lack of comparability of studies on safety belt use over time.

Based on our research, in the absence of mandated safety we would expect the use of safety belts to increase. In an earlier work Blomquist analyzed lap belt use in 1972 to determine the relative importance of various factors affecting use.[17] One factor is the time cost of finding, fastening, adjusting, and unfastening the lap belts, which was reflected by the negative effect of drivers' value of time on belt use. If the second-generation belts reduced time costs by 20 percent, for example, then

---

13. See Carol Stowell and Joseph Bryant, *Safety Belt Usage: Survey of the Traffic Population,* prepared for the National Highway Traffic Safety Administration (NHTSA, 1978), p. 4, available from the National Technical Information Service, Springfield, Va.; Opinion Research Corporation, *Safety Belt Usage: Survey of Cars in the Traffic Safety Administration* (Princeton, N.J.: Opinion Research Corp., 1978), p. 1; U.S. General Accounting Office, *Passive Restraints for Automobile Occupants: A Closer Look,* Report to the Congress by the Comptroller General of the United States (GAO, 1979), p. 1.

14. Stowell and Bryant, *Safety Belt Usage,* p. 29.

15. Ibid., pp. 26, 29.

16. Peter D. Hart, *Public Attitudes toward Passive Restraint Systems,* prepared for the National Highway Traffic Safety Administration (NHTSA, 1978), p. 15.

17. Blomquist, "Economics of Safety and Seat Belt Use," pp. 179–89.

drivers would increase belt use from 23 percent to 30 percent. A second factor is growth of labor earnings, which further increases belt use. If earnings increase 5 percent, belt use will increase from 30 to 32 percent. A third factor is the degree of discomfort associated with belt use. Blomquist estimated that the annual discomfort costs associated with lap belt use are much larger than time costs ($45.38 as compared to $6.23).[18] If perceived comfort increases 5 percent, belt use would increase to 50 percent. Since the second-generation belts are more comfortable as well as more convenient, belt use—especially of lap-shoulder belts, which will eventually be used by most belt users—will increase. To predict a safety belt use rate for 1982, when passive restraints become mandatory, we must expect that voluntary use would increase with growth in earnings and the development of more convenient and comfortable belt systems. A lap-shoulder belt use rate of 40 or 50 percent is plausible, particularly during driving where risk of death or serious injury is greatest.

However, the development of third-generation safety belts—passive belt systems—indicates that even 50 percent voluntary belt use is probably an underestimation. Passive belts are and will be a good buy for drivers. The cost of passive belts is approximately $27 in 1978 dollars, according to the General Accounting Office.[19] Adjusting the annual time cost of using belts estimated by Blomquist for the difference between the average wage of the drivers sampled in 1972 to the average industrial wage in 1978, we get a time cost of $7.41. This means that, with a 10 percent discount rate, passive belts pay for themselves in potential time costs saved in less than five years for the average driver (who does not use belts) of a car with first-generation belts. Even for drivers of cars with second-generation belt systems, the passive belts pay for themselves in less than six years if time costs are reduced by 20 percent to allow for the difference between first-generation and second-generation belt systems. If the passive belts of 1982 and the future are more comfortable than second-generation belts, the passive belts will be an even better buy than the second-generation belts. A future combined safety belt use rate of 70 percent seems plausible, especially in light of the 78 percent current usage rate in Volkswagen Rabbits.[20]

The crucial point is that the increase in safety provided by the market

18. Blomquist, "Value of Life Saving," p. 552.

19. General Accounting Office, *Passive Restraints for Automobile Occupants*, p. iv.

20. As reported in Stowell and Bryant, *Safety Belt Usage*, p. 21, the safety belt use rate in Volkswagen Rabbits with passive belt systems was 77.7 percent.

reduces the marginal effect of the mandated passive restraints, specifically, the benefits. The benefits of the mandated restraints might even be
negative if the projected 70 percent use of passive belts were compared
to installation of air bags if only 5 percent of drivers used lap belts (as
drivers substituted mandatory equipment for voluntary safety activity),
since Huelke and O'Day show that passive belts are more effective in
crashes than air bags alone.[21] Estimates of benefits based on crash effectiveness of mandated equipment exaggerate the benefits that will actually
be experienced.

Driver Choice and Highway Death Rates

The impact of driver choice can be viewed from a broader perspective.
In 1972, as it was launching the latest round of mandatory design
changes, the National Highway Traffic Safety Administration announced
in its annual report the goal it then expected to achieve: a highway death
rate by 1980 of thirty-six deaths for every billion vehicle miles traveled,
or about 20 percent below the then prevailing level.[22] Peltzman analyzed driver behavior in the period before the National Highway Traffic
Safety Administration was created, when safety outcomes were the result
of choices not constrained by vehicle design regulation. Peltzman concluded that the continued working through of an unregulated choice process would in fact result in even fewer fatalities—thirty-three for every billion vehicle miles by 1980.[23] In fact, the latter figure was reached by 1977,
and the reason appears to reflect another sort of driver choice having nothing to do with vehicle design regulation. Neither the National Highway
Traffic Safety Administration nor we could then have fully compre-
hended the impact of rising oil prices, and Peltzman's estimate for 1980
assumed continued increases in average driving speeds. However, Peltzman also found that driving speeds respond to gas prices (as well as to
per capita income and the stock of imported cars). Given the rise in gas
prices that has occurred since 1972, this response (together with a rise in
imports)—a trade-off of more driving time for less gas consumption—

21. See the paper by Huelke and O'Day in this volume.
22. National Highway Traffic Safety Administration, *Traffic Safety '72: A Report
on Activities Under the National Traffic and Motor Vehicle Safety Act* (Department
of Transportation, 1973), p. 10. (This report is also included in *1972 Annual Reports
under the Highway Safety and National Traffic and Motor Vehicle Safety Acts of
1966, Message from the President*, H. Doc. 93-173, 93 Cong. 1 sess. [GPO, 1973].)
23. Sam Peltzman, "The Effects of Automobile Safety Regulation," *Journal of
Political Economy*, vol. 83 (August 1975), p. 718.

explains why it took five rather than eight years to reach a fatality rate of thirty-three deaths for every billion vehicle miles.[24] Driving speeds have in fact fallen somewhat more than can be accounted for by steadily rising gas prices.[25] The most plausible explanation for this decline is the speed limit of fifty-five miles per hour. However, the decline in death rates has not been nearly as great as we could have expected from the pre-1972 connection between driving speed and death rates; the decline in death rates has been consistent only with that portion of the decline in speed attributable to an unconstrained driver response to higher gas prices.[26]

One explanation for this is that drivers have substituted mandated safety for voluntary safety: having been forced to consume more safety than they would otherwise have chosen—in this case in the form of a fifty-five-mile speed limit—they have chosen less safety in other forms, perhaps by buying smaller cars or by driving less carefully at the slower speeds.

24. To elaborate on the basis for this conclusion, let us first convert the basic facts to percent changes per year (PPA). Peltzman's original projection (thirty-three deaths for every billion vehicle miles in 1980) meant a 3.7 PPA decline from 1972 death rates. In fact, the 1972–77 decline was 5.8 PPA, or 2.1 PPA more than projected. The 3.7 PPA projection comes from two ingredients. The first is knowledge of how death rates had responded to various causative factors in the past. This element is summarized in a regression equation in Peltzman, "The Effects of Automobile Safety Regulation," p. 692, which relates death rates to such factors as alcohol consumption, the segment of the population aged eighteen to twenty-four, and so on. Prominent among these factors was driving speed: in the period between 1947 and 1965, each PPA increase in average speed led to a 1.8 PPA increase in death rates, all else being the same. The second ingredient in the projection was an estimate of the course of these causative factors in 1972–80. Here Peltzman simply assumed that future driving speeds would increase, as they had in the past, by 1 PPA.

However, in another regression Peltzman ("The Effects of Automobile Safety Regulation," p. 703) found that before 1972 driving speed had fallen by 0.2 percent for each 1 percent rise in the price of gas (relative to the consumer price index) and by 1.3 percent for each percentage point increase in the fraction of the automobile stock made up of imports. Had the substantial increases in these variables been foreseen in 1972, Peltzman's regression would have implied a forecast of a 0.2 PPA *decline* in speed, instead of the 1 PPA increase he actually assumed. In turn, a projected 0.2 PPA decline in speed implies a 2.2 PPA greater decline in death rates than does a 1 PPA increase. This is virtually the same as the 2.1 PPA discrepancy between the actual 1972–77 decline and Peltzman's original projection.

25. Average speeds declined 2.2 PPA between 1972 and 1977 rather than the 0.2 PPA decline that is consistent with the actual rise in gas prices and imports.

26. If death rates had responded to the full 2.2 PPA decline in speed rather than just to the projected 0.2 PPA decline (see footnotes 24 and 25 above), Peltzman's regression would imply that the 1972–77 decline in death rates would have been 3.6 PPA more than the 5.8 PPA that has occurred.

This brings us to our second objection to the overselling of safety regulation, which is that drivers will probably substitute against it. This would not be perverse or stupid behavior, but a rational response to the incentives provided by regulation—that is, the forced consumption of safety in a specific form in excess of what the driver finds optimal. Indeed, in earlier work Peltzman found evidence that there was considerable substitution against the earlier generation of traffic safety standards.[27] Huelke and O'Day also allude to their disappointment with the results of Australia's mandatory belt-wearing law.[28] They neglect to mention that Australian researchers found that, although driver deaths fell much more than the 15 percent overall figure they cite, pedestrian deaths and injuries rose dramatically (about 20 to 30 percent).[29] This is consistent with a rational choice process: if the driver is forced to be safer than he would otherwise choose to be when an accident occurs—and this is precisely the message of a belt law—his incentive to avoid accidents, including those that involve pedestrians, is correspondingly reduced. Air bags and the gamut of mandated vehicle design changes will create the same sort of incentives; Peltzman found evidence that these changes led to the same sort of substitution found in Australia—the substitution of pedestrian for occupant deaths.[30] This sort of substitution creates conditions under which a smaller cost is absorbed by the driver and a larger cost is imposed on other parties.

The conclusion of this analysis of equipment effectiveness is that compelling theoretical explanations and ample empirical evidence show that the National Highway Traffic Safety Administration is substantially overestimating the benefits of mandatory passive restraint systems by the methodology it is currently using.

The Value of Safety Gained and the Costs of Safety Policy

So far we have discussed the effectiveness of safety policy in purely physical terms, that is, reduced accident injury. In doing this we have

27. Peltzman, "The Effects of Automobile Safety Regulation."
28. See the paper by Huelke and O'Day in this volume.
29. A. P. Vulcan, R. Ungers, and P. W. Milne, "Australian Approach to Motor Vehicle Safety Standards," in *Proceedings of the Fourth International Congress on Automotive Safety,* pp. 849–50.
30. Peltzman, "The Effects of Automobile Safety Regulation."

emphasized the importance of driver response in the measurement of expected gain. To further analyze benefits and costs of safety policy it is necessary to place a value on any gain in safety and to estimate the costs of the policy.

Value of Lifesaving

Determining the benefits of saving lives is essential if efficient allocation of scarce resources to public programs affecting human health is to be achieved. Along with the increasing concern for systematic evaluation of highway safety regulations, interest in the value of lifesaving—what is called the value of life—is growing. It has become apparent that treating the benefits of lifesaving as if they were infinitely great leads to the untenable position that all government expenditures should be devoted to health and safety programs and that the government should prohibit all individual behavior that reduces health and safety. To say that it is necessary to value safety and that the value is not infinite does not mean, of course, that it is easy to determine practical values of life for the purposes of cost-benefit analysis. Although measuring the value of life is usually viewed as being much more difficult than estimating the effectiveness of policy designed to improve highway safety, we have shown in the previous section that estimating overall effectiveness for all highway users is more complex than most people think. Despite the difficulties, meaningful progress in measuring the benefits of lifesaving is being made, theoretically and empirically.

The value of life, in the context of cost-benefit analysis of highway safety policy, is the value of a small change in the probability of survival, not the value of avoiding certain death. Such a value of life is determined by the marginal rate of substitution between consumption or wealth and probability of survival. The value of this marginal change is usually extrapolated to a unit (0 to 1) change. It is called "value of life" or "value of lifesaving" only because such terminology permits easy comparison among situations with small but different changes and because of the lack of another accepted unit of measure.

A value of life based on the individual's value or willingness to pay is superior to the more easily measured and less theoretical value of expected future labor earnings (future earnings). Linnerooth's review of the recent theoretical literature on value of life concludes that there is no theoretical basis for an empirical relationship between value of life based on willingness to pay (for safety) and future earnings.[31] Her review also shows that theoretically value of life typically exceeds future earnings. This is plausible since accounting of market earnings or market consumption ignores important nonmarket (household) counterparts.

There is a growing body of empirical evidence on the premiums that individuals are willing to pay to reduce the risk of death by a small amount. In a recent review of the estimates of what people are willing to pay for safety, Blomquist concludes that there is a strong indication that the value of life exceeds future earnings.[32] The estimates were derived from two types of studies. The estimates based on observable behavior consider the value implied by production or consumption activity. The other type is based on replies to questionnaires that pose situations risky to individuals. The estimates based on observable behavior range from $310,000 to $2.5 million, and those based on replies to questionnaires range from $50,000 to $8.9 million (in 1979 dollars). While theory suggests that the value of life will vary with individual circumstances, the wide range suggests that a sensitivity analysis of results that are in terms of benefits and costs is warranted. It should also be recognized that these values of life are individual values; to the extent that there are others who value the individual's well-being and to the extent that their values are not already taken into account by the individual through love, friendship, insurance, or legal sanction, the social value of life would be greater than the individual value. Bailey has estimated that the increase in social value of life over private value is due to factors such as income tax.[33] (Faigin includes costs of vehicle repair, court proceedings, and insurance processing, but most of these costs would already be considered in the individual's value of life.[34]) The increase is small in relation to the range of individual values of life.

We conclude that although measuring the benefits of lifesaving is still an imprecise process, cost-benefit analysis of safety policy can be improved by using recent theoretical and empirical advances.

31. Joanne Linnerooth, "The Value of Human Life: A Review of the Models," *Economic Inquiry,* vol. 17 (January 1979), pp. 52–74.

32. Glenn Blomquist, "The Value of Human Life: An Empirical Perspective," *Economic Inquiry,* vol. 19 (January 1981), pp. 157–64.

33. Martin J. Bailey, *Reducing Risks to Life: Measurement of the Benefits* (American Enterprise Institute for Public Policy Research, 1980).

34. Faigin, *1975 Societal Costs of Motor Vehicle Accidents.*

Implicit Costs

Systematic analysis of highway safety policy can be improved further by recognizing that not all costs are the result of explicit market transactions or congressional appropriations. It is ironic that after years of following a sound practice of measuring part of the benefits of expressway and interstate highways by travel time saved, additional time expenditures by drivers are now ignored. Errors resulting from the failure to recognize implicit costs bias the analysis of safety programs toward those with high implicit costs paid by drivers. The *National Highway Safety Needs Reports,* which considers mandatory safety belt use and the nationwide fifty-five-mile speed limit—two of the best safety policy options—makes this evident.[35] We have already shown that these options will not be and are not as effective in improving safety as claimed. They also cost more than is claimed.

According to the Department of Transportation, the discounted present cost of ten years of mandatory safety belt use is $45 million, with no user costs.[36] But Blomquist finds that user (time and disutility) costs associated with safety belt use are important in explaining voluntary belt use. If 50 percent of all drivers are already using safety belts, the time cost of mandatory use imposed on drivers will be $436 million per year.[37] Disutility costs raise driver costs even further, making mandatory belt use even less attractive. If more drivers use safety belts voluntarily, the costs of mandatory use fall, but the benefits decrease also.

The costs of the nationwide speed limit of fifty-five miles an hour are also misleading. The social costs are estimated to be $676 million (the present value of ten years of costs), with no driver costs.[38] However, the Department of Transportation acknowledges that added time costs might be at least $1 billion per year.[39] If this estimate is correct, then the social costs are approximately ten times what the Department of Transportation reported them to be in evaluating the fifty-five-mile limit in relation to other highway safety measures. Since many drivers began driving slowly

35. Department of Transportation, *The National Highway Safety Needs Report* (DOT, 1976), p. II-2.

36. Ibid., p. VI-2.

37. Blomquist, "Value of Life Saving."

38. Department of Transportation, *The National Highway Safety Needs Report,* p. VI-2.

39. Ibid., p. VI-7.

because of rising fuel costs, the costs of the fifty-five-mile speed limit were probably overestimated; however, the benefits are also overestimated. Even with effectiveness measured correctly and the lifesaving value measured appropriately, the assumption of no implicit costs to drivers biases policies toward those with high costs in driver time and prevents citizens from getting the socially optimal amount of highway safety at the least social cost.

Toward Improved Highway Safety Policy

Successful highway safety policy must be formulated with a keen awareness of the nonregulatory demand for and supply of safety. Policy designed with no recognition of likely driver response or of what driver behavior will be without the policy risks a government failure that could be greater than any market failure safety policy is trying to correct. A successful policy must also consider traffic safety externalities and whether the costs of the problems caused by these externalities are greater than the costs of correcting them. If intervention is warranted, successful policy should choose the most efficient way, including incentives, to correct the externality problem. An estimate of the effectiveness of a particular policy should consider only the additional increase in safety over what drivers would experience anyway. A systematic evaluation of the resulting benefits and costs should place a value on reductions in fatalities using estimates based on willingness to pay for safety and should include implicit social costs.

Current regulation fails on at least two counts: it is excessively costly in that it fails to let the driver make the best use of safety resources already available to him, and it specifies precisely the wrong mix of resources, which includes more external costs than would otherwise occur.

In light of these considerations, we ought to greet skeptically the claims now being made for mandatory passive restraints. These claims are exaggerated partly because other devices and driver responses would have done part of the job mandated equipment promises to do, and (although this is partly another way of saying the same thing) because some of these other driver responses will not occur when the use of air bags is imposed. Unfortunately, the dynamics of this interaction between regulations and drivers cannot always offset regulatory costs, which happens when drivers respond to regulation by taking greater risks. The most obvious sort of response that air bags will elicit is a reduction in safety belt use. We can easily imagine this leading to pressure for mandatory seat belt laws and other rules designed to induce belt-wearing. We believe, however, that this would reduce the marginal impact of air bags to virtually zero and, in retrospect, the entire effort devoted to mandatory passive restraints would have been wasted. Future efforts should be devoted to formulating a highway safety policy that increases overall social welfare—not safety equipment or even highway safety—as much as possible.

Passive Restraints:
A Regulator's View

CARL E. NASH

ONE OF the unfortunate by-products of the extensive political debate on air bags has been a lot of misinformation about the government's policy toward automatic crash protection. Therefore, this chapter begins by describing the legal and scientific basis for the National Highway Traffic Safety Administration's automatic occupant crash protection standard.

The Legal Basis for the Standard

The legislation under which Federal Motor Vehicle Safety Standard 208 was promulgated is the National Traffic and Motor Vehicle Safety Act of 1966.[1] This act was amended in 1974 to give Congress an opportunity to review the promulgation of standards for occupant restraints other than safety belts.[2]

The act requires that the secretary of transportation issue motor vehicle safety standards that (1) meet the need for motor vehicle safety; (2) are written in performance terms; (3) provide objective criteria; and (4) are practicable.[3] There is no explicit requirement in the act that standards be cost-effective or justified on any other economic basis.

In reviewing this and other standards, the courts have refused to im-

1. 80 Stat. 718.
2. The Motor Vehicle Schoolbus Safety Amendments of 1974 (88 Stat. 1470) allowed Congress sixty days to pass resolutions of disapproval in both houses of any occupant restraint requirements for other than manual safety belts.
3. 80 Stat. 719.

pose economic conditions on safety rulemaking but have indicated that safety standards should consider economic factors. The National Highway Traffic Safety Administration agrees and has conducted economic analyses that date back to the early 1970s.[4]

An automatic crash protection standard was first promulgated in 1977.[5] Like the original standard, the present standard specifies that front-seat occupants must be protected in frontal collisions into rigid barriers (that is, head-on crashes and crashes up to thirty degrees off center—collisions that make up about half of those in which people are seriously injured or killed) at speeds of up to thirty miles per hour. This protection must be provided automatically. The standard, like all other motor vehicle safety standards, is a minimum standard and does not cover all aspects of safety for all motor vehicle occupants.

Manufacturers can use any system or vehicle design that will allow them to comply with the standard's performance requirements, including even the suggestion that passive protection be provided by making the interior of a vehicle and its structural crash pulse resilient enough so that no additional restraint systems are needed to protect unbelted occupants.[6]

The Scientific Basis for the Standard

The automatic crash protection standard is based on one of the most fundamental scientific principles of public health: that passive measures designed to protect public health are more successful than active ones.[7]

4. Barbara M. Faigin, *Societal Costs of Motor Vehicle Accidents* (National Highway Traffic Safety Administration, 1972); National Highway Traffic Safety Administration, "Benefit and Cost Analysis of Methodology" (NHTSA, 1972).

5. U.S. Department of Transportation, National Highway Traffic Safety Administration, "Part 571: Federal Motor Vehicle Safety Standard; Occupant Restraint Systems," and "Part 572: Anthropomorphic Test Dummy: Occupant Crash Protection," *Federal Register,* vol. 42 (July 5, 1977), pp. 34289–305. These rules were amendments to the occupant crash protection standard, Federal Motor Vehicle Safety Standard 208.

6. John D. States, M.D., "Static Passive Occupant Restraint Systems Without Airbags and Without Belts—Is It Possible?" in *Proceedings: Fifth International Congress on Automotive Safety* (National Highway Traffic Safety Administration, 1978), p. 419.

7. See, for example, William Haddon, M.D., "Strategy in Preventive Medicine: Passive vs. Active Approaches to Reducing Human Wastage," *Journal of Trauma,* vol. 4 (April 1974), p. 353.

This principle underlies the purification of water systems to prevent water-borne disease, the addition of fluorides to drinking water to improve dental resistance to cavities, and the use of electrical system fusing to prevent electric shock.

The current low rate of manual safety belt use shows the importance of this principle to automobile safety. In our research we have found that about 11 percent of all drivers use belts and that less than 9 percent of all occupants of cars involved in tow-away crashes use them.[8] When air bags are built into cars, they can provide protection in virtually all of the frontal crashes in which they would be needed. The use of automatic, or passive, belts will probably be well over 50 percent. Use of the Volkswagen Rabbit automatic belts was reported to be over 70 percent.[9]

Most motor vehicle safety standards are based on the concept of passive public health protection. These standards include the windshield retention and energy absorption requirements, the energy-absorbing steering column requirement, instrument panel padding requirements, and the tire and braking standards. The safety belt standard is an anomaly that resulted from the fact that there was no feasible and effective way to provide occupant restraint passively when the standard was written. As soon as passive occupant-restraint technologies became available, the Department of Transportation acted to ensure that they would be incorporated into new cars.[10]

A second important scientific principle underlying the standard—first articulated by Dr. William Haddon, Jr., and popularized by Ralph Nader in 1965[11]—is that crash injuries are caused by the so-called second collision. When an automobile strikes something, it is only about one-

8. Opinion Research Corporation, "Safety Belt Usage—Survey of Cars in the Traffic Population (November 1977–June 1978)" (Princeton, N.J.: Opinion Research Corp., 1978), p. 7; James Hedlund, "Preliminary Findings from the National Crash Severity Study" (National Highway Traffic Safety Administration, 1979), p. 6.

9. Opinion Research Corporation, "Safety Belt Usage," p. 21; Albert Westefeld and Benjamin M. Phillips, "Passive vs. Active Safety Belt Systems in Volkswagen Rabbits: A Comparison of Owner Use Habits and Attitudes" (Opinion Research Corp., 1976).

10. U.S. Department of Transportation, Federal Highway Administration, "Inflatable Occupant Restraint Systems: Advanced Notice of Proposed Rule Making," *Federal Register,* vol. 34 (July 2, 1969), p. 11148.

11. William Haddon, Jr., Edward A. Suchman, and D. Klein, *Accident Research Methods and Approaches* (Harper and Row, 1964); and Ralph Nader, *Unsafe at Any Speed* (Grossman, 1965), chap. 3.

twentieth of a second later that an unrestrained occupant begins to collide with the hostile interior of the car and becomes injured. More than sixty years ago, Hugh deHaven first articulated the principle that aircraft crash injuries could be reduced or eliminated if the aircraft interior remained relatively intact and occupants were restrained from the second collision.[12] In an automobile, some of the most hostile parts of the interior are in front of the driver and front-seat passengers: the steering wheel, the instrument panel, the windshield, and its frame. Safety belts are intended to prevent people from smashing into these surfaces and to slow down the speed of the second collision so that serious injury is avoided in crashes in which the barrier is hit at the equivalent of up to thirty to forty miles an hour.

A third important principle underlying the automatic crash protection standard is that performance standards, which regulate the results of a product rather than its design, materials, or construction, are most likely to achieve the desired results cost-effectively with the greatest amount of product innovation. Protection of vehicle occupants from injuries resulting from collisions with a car's interior is the performance sought by the automatic crash protection standard. The critical performance measurements are taken from an anthropomorphic test dummy in a simulated frontal crash.[13]

The National Highway Traffic Safety Administration believes that the automatic crash protection standard is a major innovation in safety regulation because it measures vehicle crashworthiness in realistic, repeatable tests and does not rely on secondary safety measures. By contrast, the safety belt standard that now applies to new vehicles has only secondary performance requirements: static testing of the strength of the belts and their mounting hardware, durability testing, and general specifications for location points of belt mountings. The matching of belt performance with the crush characteristics of the vehicle is not required.

Belt systems have been improved since 1968, primarily in comfort and convenience, in response to more stringent federal requirements. However, manufacturers are not required to crash test cars to test belt safety performance.

12. Martin W. Kraegel, "Sensible Sensor," United Technologies *Beehive* (Spring 1979), reprinted in Insurance Institute for Highway Safety, *Highway Loss Reduction Status Report,* vol. 14 (August 21, 1979), pp.14–17.
13. See "Anthropomorphic Test Dummies," 49 C.F.R. 572.

Reviews of the Standard

The first court test of the automatic crash protection rule was *Chrysler Corporation* v. *Department of Transportation,* which challenged the standard on a range of issues. The lawsuit was decided in the government's favor in 1972, on all points but one.[14]

The court found that the crash test instrument—the dummy—was insufficiently defined and therefore that the standard did not meet the test of "objectivity." The court specifically held, however, that the secretary of transportation had the authority to promulgate standards that require advancing safety technology, that the standard was practicable, and that the standard addressed the need for motor vehicle safety.

In 1977 the Pacific Legal Foundation also filed suit against the newly reissued standard on several counts. The decision in this lawsuit, which was appealed all the way to the Supreme Court, upheld the standard in every respect.[15]

At the same time, Ralph Nader and Public Citizen sued, claiming that the secretary of transportation had overstepped his authority in deciding to phase in the automatic crash protection requirements over several years by defining automobile types according to wheelbase length. Nader also claimed that the Department of Transportation had distorted its rulemaking on the standard to avoid a two-house legislative veto, provided for in the 1974 Amendments to the Safety Act, in violation of the 1946 Administrative Procedure Act. Again, the court upheld the secretary in all respects, and the decision was not appealed.[16]

It is important to note that the National Highway Traffic Safety Administration has no legislative authority to order fleet testing of new technologies that might be used to meet federal motor vehicle safety standards. Nor can it base decisions on such standards strictly on economic factors. In fact, the requirement that standards be written in performance terms

14. *Chrysler Corporation* v. *Department of Transportation,* 472 F.2d (6th Cir. 1972).

15. *Pacific Legal Foundation et al.* v. *Department of Transportation,* and *Ralph Nader and Public Citizen* v. *Department of Transportation,* 593 F.2d 1338 (D.C. C. 1979), *cert. denied,* 444 U.S. 830 (October 1, 1979).

16. Ibid.

would make either suggestion impractical, since manufacturers choose the technology used to comply with a performance standard.

The Coleman decision, under which a few manufacturers agreed to provide the production *capacity* for a few hundred thousand cars equipped with air bags, was essentially unenforceable.[17] Furthermore, in promulgating the present standard, the secretary of transportation provided sufficient lead time for the production of cars under the Coleman plan to proceed without interfering with the implementation of the standard.[18] (The Coleman plan called for production of cars with automatic restraints in the 1980 and 1981 model years, and the standard takes effect in the 1982 model year.)

It appears that the automobile manufacturers are being very cautious about commercializing air bags. The industry will introduce only a small number of them before the standard takes effect, and initial production will be at a relatively low volume (roughly comparable to the volume called for by the Coleman plan).[19] At least in the early years after the standard takes effect, the industry will rely mostly on automatic belts.

The National Highway Traffic Safety Administration will have an extensive and detailed evaluation program for Federal Motor Vehicle Safety Standard 208, the plan for which was published for public comment in 1979.[20] By 1983 or 1984 remaining doubts about the value of and market demand for air bags and automatic belts should be resolved, even for those who confuse the scientific method with excessive caution.

There have also been legislative reviews of the standard. Under the 1974 revisions of the National Traffic and Motor Vehicle Safety Act, resolutions of disapproval of standard 208 were introduced in both houses of Congress. The House and Senate commerce committees each held extensive hearings and debates on the standard, and both prepared detailed reports on their findings, in addition to hearing records, that strongly sup-

17. William T. Coleman, Jr., "The Secretary's Decision Concerning Motor Vehicle Occupant Crash Protection" (Department of Transportation, 1976).

18. National Highway Traffic Safety Administration, "Part 571: Federal Motor Vehicle Safety Standard," p. 34295.

19. National Highway Traffic Safety Administration, *Occupant Protection Program Progress Report No. 2* (NHTSA, 1979), p. 45.

20. National Highway Traffic Safety Administration, *Evaluation Plan for Federal Motor Vehicle Safety Standard 208, Occupant Crash Protection* (NHTSA, 1979).

ported the standard.[21] Both committees recommended that the resolutions of disapproval not be approved. The House committee voted to table the measure and the Senate committee sent the resolution to the floor with a negative recommendation. The full Senate voted, sixty-five to thirty-one, to table the resolution.[22]

Because of doubts expressed by several members of the House of Representatives, the House twice, in 1978 and 1979, voted for a restriction on the traffic safety administration's appropriations bill. The House vote did not affect the standard or the administration's activities but was a symbolic expression of House views of the standard.[23] In neither case, however, was the House vote based on any systematic review of the standard.

The General Accounting Office carried out a major review of four aspects of the standard: the effectiveness of automatic crash protection systems; the safety of sodium azide (used as a gas-generating material for air bags); the cost of air bags; and insurance savings that might be expected from implementing automatic crash protection standards.[24] Although the report was cautionary and somewhat critical of the National Highway Traffic Safety Administration's estimates in support of the standard, the General Accounting Office did not recommend modification or repeal of the standard.

The General Accounting Office found that the safety administration had been overly precise and, in some cases, overly optimistic in its estimates of the effectiveness of automatic crash protection systems, the cost

21. *Automobile Crash Protection*, S. Rept. 95-481, 95 Cong. 1 sess. (Government Printing Office, 1977); and *The Department of Transportation Automobile Passive Restraint Rule*, Report of the Subcommittee on Consumer Protection and Finance of the House Committee on Interstate and Foreign Commerce, Committee Print 95-23, 95 Cong. 1 sess. (GPO, 1977).

22. S. Cong. Res. 31 (October 12, 1977).

23. The 1979 amendment states: "Sec. 317. None of the funds provided in this Act may be used to implement or enforce any standard or regulation which requires any motor vehicle to be equipped with an occupant restraint system (other than a belt system). Nothing in this section shall be construed to prohibit the use of funds provided by this Act for any research and development activity relating to occupant restraint systems." Department of Transportation and Related Agencies Appropriation Act, 1980 (93 Stat. 1039).

24. U.S. General Accounting Office, *Passive Restraints for Automobile Occupants: A Closer Look*, Report to the Congress by the Comptroller General of the United States (GAO, 1979).

of air bags, and the insurance savings that would result from such automatic protection. The office recommended additional research and testing of automatic restraints with out-of-position occupants and on the safety of disposal procedures for cars equipped with air bags.

The traffic safety administration responded to the General Accounting Office by declaring that its estimates were the best available at the time they were made.[25] Indeed, the General Accounting Office did not provide any estimates of its own or cite other, more accurate estimates. The traffic safety administration also stated that the research that has been and continues to be conducted by automobile manufacturers and the government is responding to the need for safe disposal of cars equipped with air bags. Finally, the traffic safety administration stated that it believes that the safety of out-of-position occupants can best be addressed in developmental testing by the manufacturers of automobiles equipped with automatic restraint systems that will actually be sold to the public. The administration's views were strongly supported by General Motors Corporation's announcement that it had resolved the difficulties it was having in meeting its corporate criteria for protecting out-of-position children in cars with air bags, and that General Motors would start producing cars with air bags in the 1982 model year. Nevertheless, the government is addressing this question further in its research program and expects to report its findings in 1981.[26]

The National Transportation Safety Board is reviewing the rulemaking procedures used by the National Highway Traffic Safety Administration and is using standard 208 and other rules as examples for this study. The board released a history of the standard in September 1979 and issued its analysis of the safety administration's rulemaking in April 1980.[27]

Federal Motor Vehicle Safety Standard 208 is one of the most extensively reviewed standards ever promulgated by the federal government. And yet the standard has held up well under scrutiny. When it goes into effect, it is most likely to achieve a substantial reduction in crash fatalities at a reasonable cost to the public.

25. Ibid., p. 74.

26. "Statement by Joan B. Claybrook," National Highway Traffic Safety Administration, October 1, 1979.

27. National Transportation Safety Board, *Safety Effectiveness Evaluation of the National Highway Traffic Safety Administration's Rulemaking Process*, vol. 2: *Case History of Federal Motor Vehicle Standard 208: Occupant Crash Protection* (NTSB, 1979); and vol. 4, *Analysis, Conclusions, and Recommendations* (NTSB, 1980); available from National Technical Information Service, Springfield, Va.

Evaluation of Automatic Crash Protection

There is an ongoing debate in the United States about what constitutes due care in implementing a public policy or in commercializing a new product or service. In the case of the automatic crash protection standard, there exists both a policy (that cars sold in the United States shall have a minimum level of automatic crash protection built into them) and a product (cars equipped with air bags or automatic belts). Although the policy has not yet gone into effect, the products have already been commercialized.

There are three major questions that one generally asks in evaluating a new policy or product affecting public health and safety. Is the policy or product effective in improving public health and/or safety? Does the policy or product have significant side effects that may offset its benefits? Does the policy or product produce benefits at a reasonable cost and with the fewest and least serious side effects? Answers to these questions can be found through development and laboratory testing, analysis, and field testing and evaluation.

These methods are not necessarily useful in answering all three of the questions posed. For example, it would be virtually impossible to field test something like an intercontinental ballistic missile or a strategic defense policy. And no one has suggested that it was necessary to field test automatic belts before they were commercialized, because of their similarity to manual belts and the substantial proving ground test data developed by Volkswagen.[28]

Air bags have already been commercialized and field tested to some extent. After an initial field test involving two fleets of about 1,000 cars each, General Motors sold about 10,000 cars equipped with air bags to the public. General Motors and the National Highway Traffic Safety Administration extensively evaluated air bag field performance and investigated virtually every case in which the air bag was activated.[29]

28. See, for example, H. Schimkat and R. Weissner, "Passive Vehicle Safety as Cars Grow Smaller," Technical Paper 780282 (Detroit: Society of Automotive Engineers, 1978); and S. R. Miller, U. W. Seiffert, and J. D. States, "Volkswagen's Passive Seat Belt/Knee Bolster Restraint, VWRA: A Preliminary Field Performance Evaluation, Progress Report," Technical Paper 780436 (SAE, 1978).

29. Using special investigation teams, the National Highway Traffic Safety Administration investigates known tow-away crashes of cars equipped with air bags. Owners of these cars are given instructions on whom to contact if their car is in-

General Motors' decision not to manufacture large numbers of air bag systems during the gasoline shortage and economic downturn in 1974 and 1975 has prevented researchers from determining with any degree of statistical certainty that air bags have a specific effectiveness level in reducing crash injuries and fatalities. However, experience with cars equipped with air bags is consistent with estimates of effectiveness based on proving ground testing and analysis.[30]

On the basis of the available evidence, most experts agree that air bags will be effective in reducing fatalities and serious injuries in automobile collisions.[31] Disagreements focus on the number of lives that would be saved or the severity and number of injuries that would be reduced or eliminated. Estimates of potential lives that would be saved each year if all cars had air bags range from about 3,000 lives to about 12,000.

The field experience with cars equipped with air bags does not indicate any serious side effects. The only allegations that have been made—but not proven—on the basis of actual crash injuries that occurred in cars equipped with air bags have been that they have not provided as much protection as some believe they should have. There have been no claims that air bags have exacerbated injury or caused injuries that would not have occurred in their absence.

To answer the question about the cost-effectiveness of air bags, one need only look at use rates. Even if, for purposes of argument, the effectiveness of air bags is somewhat lower than that of safety belts and the cost is several times as high, air bags' cost-effectiveness is comparable with that of manual safety belts because air bags can provide protection in so many more crashes. We know that safety belts are used by fewer than 10 percent of the people involved in crashes, which means that if the belts reduce serious crash injuries and fatalities by 50 percent, they have a net effectiveness of about 5 percent. On the other hand, since air bags are available

---

volved in a crash. Local police departments have been informed of the need to report crashes of these cars to the Department of Transportation. Also, if a dealer orders parts to replace a deployed air bag, the order triggers an inquiry to the dealer and an investigation of the crash.

30. National Highway Traffic Safety Administration, *Occupant Protection Program Progress Report No. 2*, pp. 6–17.

31. See, for example, Donald F. Huelke and others, "Effectiveness of Current and Future Restraint Systems in Fatal and Serious Injury Automobile Crashes," Technical Paper 790323 (SAE, 1979); and Insurance Institute for Highway Safety, "Air Bags and Lap/Shoulder Belts—An Updated Comparison of Their Effectiveness in Real World, Frontal and Front Corner Crashes" (Washington, D.C.: IIHS, 1977).

virtually 100 percent of the time and have an effectiveness of at least 40 percent, even if lap belts are not worn, they have a net effectiveness of about 40 percent.[32] Air bags would have to cost much more than safety belts for the bags to be less cost-effective than safety belts.[33]

Air bag is a generic term. There are as many varieties of air bags as there are of cars. Inflators, for example, can use stored gas, a combination of stored gas and a pyrotechnic, or pyrotechnics alone to generate the gas needed to inflate the bags. Bag styles, shapes, folds, and materials also vary, and they can be mounted in a variety of places. Because of the wide variation in their designs, a government-sponsored field test of one or two air bag systems probably will not reveal all of the potential performance advantages and shortcomings of each system. Manufacturers, of course, can field test their own systems.

Finally, it is important to note that it is the automobile manufacturers who are ultimately responsible for the safety performance of their products. The manufacturers decide how much field testing should be done for their products. They have indicated to the government that they will be cautious in their initial introduction of air bag systems to the public.[34] The total production of cars equipped with air bags through 1983 will be well under a million.

The National Highway Traffic Safety Administration's evaluation program will assess the performance of these cars and should, with the manufacturers' evaluations, detect significant problems early enough so that they can be resolved. By 1983 air bag performance in the field should be well known.[35]

32. The National Highway Traffic Safety Administration estimates the effectiveness of air bags without lap belts to be 40 percent in preventing serious and fatal injuries in all crashes. With lap belts, the effectiveness is estimated to be 66 percent. Field experience with cars equipped with air bags has indicated an effectiveness of 41 to 54 percent in preventing fatalities and of 40 to 53 percent in preventing moderate to serious injuries, with lap belt use in these cars estimated to be around 15 percent.

33. Front-seat safety belts currently installed in passenger cars are estimated to cost the consumer between $40 and $100. With comparable production volumes, the cost of air bags has been estimated to be $200 to $250.

34. See, for example, National Highway Traffic Safety Administration, *Occupant Protection Program Progress Report No. 2*, p. 45; or General Accounting Office, *Passive Restraints for Automobile Occupants: A Closer Look*, p. 54.

35. National Highway Traffic Safety Administration, *Evaluation Plan for Federal Motor Vehicle Safety Standard 208, Occupant Crash Protection*, p. 76.

The Economics of Automatic Crash Protection

The economics of automatic crash protection are dominated by several factors, listed below.

1. The price charged for automatic restraint systems is established by automobile manufacturers, not by the government. The price is determined by factors such as the design features of the system, contract arrangements with suppliers, amortization policies, the volume of production, and marketing strategies.

2. In evaluating the cost of automatic restraints, it is important not to confuse the cost of initial, low-volume production with the cost of regular, high-volume production and not to confuse either of those with the prices paid by consumers.[36]

3. Although manual safety belts may be cheaper to produce than automatic systems, the latter are more effective because of their higher use rates.

4. Automatic restraints, like other power-assisted and automatic equipment on a car, have secondary benefits that, at least to some degree, justify their higher cost.

5. Because the automobile industry in the United States is a virtual monopoly and because occupant restraints cannot be sold separately from an automobile, traditional analyses of supply and demand cannot evaluate the economics of occupant protection systems accurately, particularly by assessing the degree to which the market response reflects demand.

6. Traditional economic analysis also fails to adequately assess the supply and demand for automobile safety because consumers do not have enough information on which to base rational decisions about the safety of one car over another.[37]

36. In 1979 General Motors and Ford submitted estimates of the cost of air bags in initial, low-volume production at $500 to more than $800. Earlier estimates of the cost of air bags in higher production volumes were $193 and $235 for General Motors and Ford, respectively. The National Highway Traffic Safety Administration is currently assessing the cost of the Ford system to be introduced in 1981; it seems likely that the systems of both companies will have a manufacturing cost consistent with the earlier estimates.

37. The Motor Vehicle Information and Cost Savings Act of 1972 (86 Stat. 947) was passed because of the finding that consumers lacked adequate knowledge of the crashworthiness and damageability of new cars. Title II of that act authorizes

7. Automobile insurance and other compensation do not adequately cover losses resulting from motor vehicle accidents. Compensation decreases as the seriousness of the injury increases. This means that insurance rates will not accurately reflect safety improvements resulting from automatic restraints because the improvements will mainly include the reduction of serious and fatal injuries rather than minor and moderate ones.[38] Furthermore, as the seriousness of injuries increases, it becomes more and more difficult to assess the cost of the injury in strictly economic terms; thus, proper compensation becomes even more difficult to determine. It is important to note, in this context, that the pain and suffering associated with crash injuries and deaths is compensated for only by third party insurance coverage. Thus, insurance savings derived from the reduced pain and suffering made possible by automatic restraints will occur only after a substantial number of cars with automatic restraints have been on the road, and will be divided among all insured drivers.

Finally, I address the absurd notion that people treat safety as a commodity and are satisfied with something less than virtually complete safety. Some researchers claim that there is evidence to support this view in that people, if forced to consume more safety than they want (through automatic protection), will compensate by not behaving safely in other respects.

Evidence contradicts this proposition. Since 1975, Volkswagen has marketed both passive (automatic) and active restraint systems in its Rabbit automobiles. Except for their restraints, these cars are basically identical. About 35 percent of the drivers of the standard Rabbits use seat belts—a percentage higher than the average for all cars. For the automatic belt cars, the rate of use is above 70 percent. The National Highway Traffic Safety Administration's Fatal Accident Reporting System has recorded a commensurate reduction in fatalities as a result of the increased belt use in the Rabbits equipped with automatic belts.

The Highway Loss Data Institute, which compiles extensive statistics on insurance claims for cars, has also followed the claims submitted by drivers of the two types of Rabbits. If the people in the Rabbits with automatic

---

the Department of Transportation to establish regulations for developing and disseminating such information, and the department is currently working toward automotive ratings.

38. John A. Volpe, *Motor Vehicle Crash Losses and Their Compensation in the U.S.: A Report to Congress and the President* (Department of Transportation, 1971), p. 41.

belts were actually being forced to consume more safety than they might otherwise want, there should be more claims for physical damage to the Rabbits that have automatic belts because their drivers would be more reckless. In fact, the institute's data show that physical damage claims for the two types of Rabbits have been virtually identical, demonstrating that the drivers who have the additional automatic protection perform no differently from drivers who have manual belts.[39]

Conclusions

The automatic occupant crash protection standard is based on sound scientific and economic principles and fulfills the requirements of safety legislation. Congressional and court reviews of the standard support this view.

The National Highway Traffic Safety Administration believes that the field testing of automatic restraint systems adequately justifies widespread commercialization. However, the automobile industry, which is ultimately responsible for the safety performance of its products, has apparently decided to introduce a limited quantity of air bags in the early years after the standard takes effect to allow for more field experience before committing itself to large-scale production. This pattern is typical of the industry's introduction into the marketplace of almost any new technology.[40]

39. Highway Loss Data Institute, "Comparison of Claim Frequencies of Volkswagen Rabbits with Automatic and Manual Seat Belts: 1975, 1976, and 1977 Models," Research Report HLDI A-10 (Washington, D.C.: HLDI, 1979), p. 10.

40. Since this was written, several automobile companies and the federal government have changed their policies on automatic crash protection. General Motors and Ford have discontinued their air bag programs and canceled production plans. Mercedes-Benz has postponed its air bag production plans. The government has postponed the requirement for automatic crash protection in large cars for one year, to the 1983 model year.

Secretary of Transportation Drew Lewis has also proposed that the implementation schedule be further changed or that the standard be dropped. The primary justification for changing the standard is that the original schedule would have put U.S. manufacturers at a competitive disadvantage because large American cars would have been required to have automatic crash protection one to two years before most small foreign cars. This situation is considered particularly acute because of the current financial difficulties of the American industry.

Furthermore, since automatic safety belts will be used in virtually all cars, at issue is the degree to which motorists will disconnect automatic belts. Although the use of automatic belts in Volkswagen Rabbits is over 80 percent, there is good rea-

Although it is important to use economic analysis as a tool in making decisions on public policies, the National Highway Traffic Safety Administration does not believe that public policy should become a slave to cost-benefit considerations. The view that all policy decisions should be based on a strict accounting of the costs and benefits associated with that decision is a philosophical position, not a scientific one. It ignores several realities: that economic analysis is an imprecise science, that many aspects of a policy are not susceptible to economic quantification, and that many human values transcend the materialistic approach implied by a strict economic analysis.

---

son to believe that use of the more easily detached belts that will be installed in most other cars will be substantially lower. If installing automatic belts does not increase the use of belts, the automatic crash protection standard will have little effect on motor vehicle safety.

Part Two

Cotton Dust:
A Scientist's View

JAMES A. MERCHANT

BYSSINOSIS is the generic name for acute and chronic respiratory disease among those who process cotton, flax, and hemp fibers. Observations of respiratory disease attributable to these vegetable dusts date to the early eighteenth century when Ramazzini noted the "offensive and highly injurious odor . . . perceptible from a considerable distance" and arising from the "maceration of hemp and flax. One may see these men always covered with dust from the hemp, pasty-faced, coughing, asthmatic, and blear-eyed."[1]

Today only the processing of cotton remains as a major industry, although flax and hemp are still processed in certain regions. Production and consumption of cotton products are commercially vital to developed and undeveloped countries alike. Thus, several million workers worldwide are exposed to cotton dust. In the United States more than 300,000 workers are directly exposed to cotton dust, primarily in the textile industry, but also in cotton ginning, cotton warehousing and compressing, classing offices, cotton seed oil and delinting mills, bedding and batting manufacturing, and cotton waste utilization plants.

Also associated with the textile industry are at least two syndromes characterized by fever, cough, and other constitutional symptoms such as headache and malaise, which occur most frequently with exposure to low-grade, spotted cotton. Mattress-makers' fever and weavers' cough may be considered together because of their characteristically high attack rate and probable common etiology. Mill fever, which results in less fre-

1. B. Ramazzini, *A Treatise on the Diseases of Tradesmen* (London: Bell, 1705).

quent and severe symptoms, is a common complaint of those first exposed
to the dust of cotton, flax, and hemp.

Epidemiology

Epidemiological studies of the textile industry began in the nineteenth
century.[2] The periodicity of "Monday chest tightness" was first described
in 1845 by Mareska and Heyman and by Greenhow in 1861.[3] In 1877,
Proust first described this respiratory disease as *byssinosis*.[4] The disease
had previously been referred to as *stripper's and grinder's asthma*. Collis,
who examined a large number of workers as His Majesty's Inspector of
Factories in 1908, provided the following lucid clinical description of
byssinosis:

> As soon as the individual begins to suffer, he finds his breathing affected on
> Monday morning, or after any interval away from the dust; on resuming work
> he has difficulty in getting his breath. This difficulty is worse the day he comes
> back. Once Monday is over, he is all right for the week. I cannot explain this
> fact, but it is very generally reported. The man gradually gets "tight" or "fast"
> in the chest, and he finds difficulty in filling his lungs; to use his own expres-
> sion, "the chest gets puffled up." At the same time the man loses flesh and any
> fresh colour he may have had. Consequently he becomes thin in face and body.
> As the chest trouble develops into a typical form of asthma, the action of the
> diaphragm becomes less and less effective, until the only action of this great
> respiratory muscle is to fix the lower ribs; at the same time the superior inter-
> costal muscles are being brought more and more into use, and the extraordi-
> nary muscles of respiration are more and more called into play to carry on the
> ordinary act of breathing. The sternum becomes more prominent, and the
> chest becomes barrel-shaped. Meanwhile the extra tax thrown on the lungs
> leads to some degree of emphysema. There is little or no sputum produced, and
> what little there is is expectorated with difficulty.[5]

Mortality studies began with the data (on people exposed to cotton
dust) found in the decennial supplements to the *Annual Report of the*

2. J. P. Kay, "Trades Producing Phthisis," *North of England Medical and Sur-
gical Journal*, vol. 1 (1831), pp. 358–63; and C. T. Thackrash, *The Effects of Arts,
Trades, and Professions and of Civic States and Habits of Living on Health and
Longevity* (London: Longmans, 1831).

3. E. H. Greenhow, *Report of the Medical Officer of the Privy Council, with
Appendix, 1860*, 3d Report (London: Her Majesty's Stationery Office, 1861), app.
6, pp. 172–76.

4. A. A. Proust, *Traite d'Hygiene Publique et Privée* (Paris: G. Masson, 1877).

5. E. L. Collis, *Annual Report of the Chief Inspector of Factories, 1908* (London: His Majesty's Stationery Office, 1908), pp. 203–05.

Registrar General of Births, Deaths, and Marriages in England and Wales between 1880 and 1932. Caminita reviewed these data and found a "marked excess" of deaths in higher age groups, particularly from bronchitis and pneumonia.[6] Later reports emphasized that excess mortality from respiratory disease occurred chiefly among cardroom and blowing room operators and strippers and grinders rather than among other cotton workers. These observations were reconfirmed by Schilling, who showed that a substantial proportion of cardiovascular deaths should have been classified as respiratory deaths (cardiovascular disease was traditionally given priority in multiple certifications of death before 1939).[7]

Barbero studied one hundred consecutive deaths among hemp workers and compared the results with one hundred consecutive deaths among farm workers from the same region in Spain between 1938 and 1943. The mean age of death for hemp workers was 39.6 years; that for farm workers was 67.8 years. Cardiorespiratory disease was listed as the cause of death twice as frequently among hemp workers.[8]

More contemporary studies of cotton textile workers' mortality have not revealed consistent excesses in overall mortality. It has been difficult to assess respiratory mortality because of a lack of adequate work history data in one study[9] and relatively small cohorts in two other studies.[10] Enterline studied 6,281 white male textile workers employed in Georgia mills.[11] He found that their overall mortality experience was similar to

6. B. H. Caminita and others, *A Review of the Literature Relating to Affection of the Respiratory Tract in Individuals Exposed to Cotton Dust,* Public Health Service Bulletin 297 (Government Printing Office, 1949).

7. R. S. F. Schilling and N. Goodman, "Cardiovascular Disease in Cotton Workers, Part I," *British Journal of Industrial Medicine,* vol. 8 (1951), pp. 77–90; and R. S. F. Schilling, N. Goodman, and J. G. O'Sullivan, "Cardiovascular Disease in Cotton Workers, Part II: A Clinical Study with Special Reference to Hypertension," *British Journal of Industrial Medicine,* vol. 9 (1952), pp. 146–53.

8. A. Barbero and R. Flores, "Dust Disease in Hemp Workers," *Archives of Environmental Health,* vol. 14 (April 1967), pp. 529–32.

9. David V. Bates, Peter T. Macklem, and Ronald V. Christie, *Respiratory Function in Disease: An Introduction to the Integrated Study of the Lung,* 2d ed. (Philadelphia: Saunders, 1971).

10. S. Daum, *Proceedings of the American Conference of Governmental Industrial Hygienists on Cotton Dust,* Atlanta (1975); and James A. Merchant and C. E. Ortmeyer, "Mortality of Employees of Two Cotton Textile Mills in North Carolina," *Chest,* vol. 79 (1981), pp. 65–115.

11. Philip E. Enterline and Mildred A. Kendrick, "Asbestos-Dust Exposures at Various Levels and Mortality," *Archives of Environmental Health,* vol. 15 (August 1967), pp. 181–86.

that of asbestos building product workers and asbestos friction material workers, while that for asbestos textile workers was clearly increased. There was, however, no evidence of excess respiratory disease deaths among all cotton workers when cause-specific rates were compared to U.S. white male mortality rates. Daum investigated a cohort consisting of a South Carolina local union membership employed between 1943 and 1949. Initially, these South Carolina mills processed cotton, but later they processed cotton synthetic blend. In this small cohort, moderate increases in respiratory deaths were found among male carders with ten to twenty years of exposure and among female spinning room workers with more than twenty years of exposure. Evidence of self-selection out of mill work by those with poorer health was also noted.[12] Similarly, a recent mortality study of two mills in North Carolina found moderate but significant excesses in cardiovascular deaths among men and women in cotton processing areas. The mortality rate for respiratory deaths was more than twice as high for men with over thirty years of exposure as for men with less than twenty years of exposure.[13]

Early morbidity studies of cotton and flax workers identified an unusually high prevalence of respiratory disease, particularly among those working in preparation areas.[14] In Great Britain, byssinosis was made a compensable disease in 1942 and, based on the number of cases compensated, was thought to be a disappearing disease. Schilling rediscovered byssinosis when he went into the Lancashire mills to investigate an apparent increase in cardiovascular deaths.[15] In a series of studies extending over ten years, Schilling contributed significantly to our understanding of the epidemiology of respiratory diseases of cotton textile workers.

12. Daum, *Proceedings of the American Conference of Governmental Industrial Hygienists on Cotton Dust.*

13. Merchant and Ortmeyer, "Mortality of Employees of Two Cotton Textile Mills."

14. Collis, *Annual Report of the Chief Inspector of Factories, 1908;* and A. B. Hill, *Sickness Amongst Operatives in Lancashire Cotton Spinning Mills, with Special Reference to the Cardroom,* Rep. Industrial Health Res. Board Report 59 (London: Her Majesty's Stationery Office, 1980); and A. G. Malcolm, "The Influence of Factory Life on the Health of the Operative as Funded upon the Medical Statistics of the Class in Belfast," *Journal of the Royal Statistical Society,* vol. 19 (1856), p. 170.

15. Schilling and Goodman, "Cardiovascular Disease, Part I"; and Schilling, Goodman, and O'Sullivan, "Cardiovascular Disease, Part II."

He developed, along with Roach—and tested for reliability and validity—a questionnaire from which the following grading scheme for byssinosis was developed:[16]

Grade 0—No symptoms of chest tightness or breathlessness on Mondays.

Grade ½—Occasional chest tightness on Mondays, or mild symptoms such as irritation of the respiratory tract on Mondays.

Grade 1—Chest tightness and/or breathlessness on Mondays only.

Grade 2—Chest tightness and/or breathlessness on Mondays and other workdays.

Schilling's questionnaire and grading scheme have been used worldwide in studies of exposure to cotton, flax, and hemp. Schilling also showed that cotton workers with increasing grades of byssinosis have increasing airways obstruction. Together with Roach he reported a strong dose-response relationship between total and respirable cotton dust and the prevalence of byssinosis, a relationship that largely explained differences in the prevalence of byssinosis in various mill work areas. He also first reported that smoking was an important risk factor affecting byssinosis prevalence.[17]

Since Schilling's reports, similar findings have been reported from many regions of the world where cotton is processed. In addition to being found in primary textile mills, byssinosis has been found among cotton ginners; workers in cotton seed oil and delinting operations;[18] workers in cotton waste operations;[19] garneting (bedding and batting) workers;[20]

16. S. A. Roach and R. S. F. Schilling, "A Clinical and Environmental Study of Byssinosis in the Lancashire Cotton Industry," *British Journal of Industrial Medicine,* vol. 17 (1960), pp. 1–9.

17. Ibid.

18. Mostafa A. El Batawi, "Byssinosis in the Cotton Industry of Egypt," *British Journal of Industrial Medicine,* vol. 19 (April 1962), pp. 126–30; and Madbuli H. Noweir, Yassin El-Sadek, and Abdel Aziz El-Dakhakhny, "Exposure to Dust in the Cottonseed Oil Extraction Industry," *Archives of Environmental Health,* vol. 19 (July 1969), pp. 99–102.

19. I. Dingwall-Fordyce and J. G. O'Sullivan, "Byssinosis in the Waste Cotton Industry," *British Journal of Industrial Medicine,* vol. 23 (January 1966), pp. 53–57.

20. U.S. Department of Health, Education, and Welfare, Public Health Service, National Institute for Occupational Safety and Health, *Health Hazard Evaluation,* Report 76-73-523 (GPO, 1978).

and those who process soft hemp[21] and flax.[22] Byssinosis has not been found among those processing jute.[23] Several investigations have confirmed Schilling's early dose-response findings with remarkable uniformity considering the differences in measurement techniques, study populations, and areas from which the raw product was obtained.[24] More recent studies have shown that total dust measurements may provide a misleading indication of risk and that measures of fine dust (up to fifteen milligrams) should be used instead.[25] Most of these studies have concentrated on preparation and yarn production workers and paid little atten-

21. Arend Bouhuys and others, "Byssinosis in the Hemp Workers," *Archives of Environmental Health,* vol. 14 (April 1967), pp. 533–44; and Arend Bouhuys and others, "Chronic Respiratory Disease in Hemp Workers," *American Journal of Medicine,* vol. 46 (April 1969), pp. 526–37.

22. G. C. R. Carey and others, *Byssinosis in Flax Workers in Northern Ireland,* prepared for the Minister of Labour and National Insurance, Government of Northern Ireland (Belfast: Her Majesty's Stationery Office, 1965); P. C. Elwood, "Respiratory Symptoms in Men Who Had Previously Worked in a Flax Mill in Northern Ireland," *British Journal of Industrial Medicine,* vol. 22 (January 1965), pp. 39–42; P. C. Elwood and others, "Byssinosis and Other Respiratory Symptoms in Flax Workers in Northern Ireland," *British Journal of Industrial Medicine,* vol. 22 (January 1965), pp. 27–37; and P. C. Elwood and others, "Prevalence of Byssinosis and Dust Levels in Flax Preparers in Northern Ireland," *British Journal of Industrial Medicine,* vol. 23 (July 1966), pp. 188–93.

23. A. Mair and others, "Dust Diseases in Dundee Textile Workers: An Investigation into Chronic Respiratory Disease in Jute and Flax Industries," *British Journal of Industrial Medicine,* vol. 17 (October 1960), pp. 272–78; and C. B. McKerrow and others, "Respiratory Function and Symptoms in Rope Makers," *British Journal of Industrial Medicine,* vol. 22 (July 1965), pp. 204–09.

24. Mostafa A. El Batawi and others, "Byssinosis in the Egyptian Cotton Industry: Changes in Ventilatory Capacity During the Day," *British Journal of Industrial Medicine,* vol. 21 (January 1964), pp. 13–19; Elwood and others, "Prevalence of Byssinosis and Dust Levels in Flax Preparers in Northern Ireland"; A. J. Fox and others, "A Survey of Respiratory Disease in Cotton Operatives, Part II: Symptoms, Dust Estimations, and the Effect of Smoking Habit," *British Journal of Industrial Medicine,* vol. 30 (January 1973), pp. 48–53; James A. Merchant and others, "Dose Response Studies in Cotton Textile Workers," *Journal of Occupational Medicine,* vol. 15 (March 1973), pp. 222–30; and M. B. K. Molyneaux and G. Berry, "The Correlation of Cotton Dust Exposure with the Prevalence of Respiratory Symptoms," *Proceedings of the International Conference on Respiratory Disease in Textile Workers,* Alicante, Spain (1968), pp. 177–83.

25. James A. Merchant and others, "Byssinosis and Chronic Bronchitis Among Cotton Textile Workers," *Annals of Internal Medicine,* vol. 76 (March 1972), pp. 423–33.

tion to weavers and others exposed to cotton dust. One study examined both preparation and yarn workers, who had responded similarly to similar doses of cotton dust, as well as weavers, who experienced different dose-response relationships. Based in part on this data, the U.S. Department of Labor promulgated a standard of maximum exposure to raw cotton dust: for preparation and yarn production workers a time-weighted concentration of 200 micrograms per cubic meter and for weavers 750 micrograms per cubic meter.[26] There is some evidence that the composition of cotton dust is different in cotton processes outside the primary textile industry.[27] Similarly, some conflicting evidence suggests that the toxicity of cotton, soft hemp, and flax may differ.[28]

Assessment of chronic cough and phlegm as derived from the British Medical Research Council questionnaire has been an integral part of most studies of cotton hemp and flax textile workers.[29] Most surveys have reported increased rates of chronic cough and phlegm among those exposed to large amounts of cotton dust, especially among those with symptoms of byssinosis.[30] Similarly, indices of dyspnea (difficulty in breathing) as assessed by the British Medical Research Council questionnaire—although studied less thoroughly than chronic cough and phlegm—have been shown to be strongly associated with dustier exposures and to have increased especially among those with more severe grades of

26. 29 C.F.R. pt. 1910.1043.

27. P. R. Morey and others, "Variation in Trash Composition in Raw Cottons," *American Industrial Hygiene Association Journal,* vol. 37 (July 1976), pp. 407–12.

28. J. C. Gilson and others, "Byssinosis: The Acute Effect on Ventilatory Capacity of Dusts in Cotton Ginneries, Cotton, Sisal, and Jute Mills," *British Journal of Industrial Medicine,* vol. 19 (January 1962), pp. 9–18; and F. Valić and E. Zuškin, "Effects of Different Vegetable Dust Exposures," *British Journal of Industrial Medicine,* vol. 29 (July 1972), pp. 293–97.

29. "Standardized Questionnaires on Respiratory Symptoms," prepared for the Medical Research Council, Committee on Aetiology of Chronic Bronchitis, *British Medical Journal,* vol. 2 (1960), p. 1665.

30. Harold R. Imbus and Moon W. Suh, "Byssinosis: A Study of 10,133 Textile Workers," *Archives of Environmental Health,* vol. 26 (April 1973), pp. 183–91; B. Lammers, R. S. Schilling, and J. Wolford, "A Study of Byssinosis, Chronic Respiratory Symptoms, and Ventilatory Capacity in English and Dutch Cotton Workers, with Special Reference to Atmospheric Pollution," *British Journal of Industrial Medicine,* vol. 21 (April 1964), pp. 124–34; and James A. Merchant and others, "An Industrial Study of the Biological Effects of Cotton Dust and Cigarette Smoke Exposure," *Journal of Occupational Medicine,* vol. 15 (March 1973), pp. 212–21.

byssinosis.[31] Smoking has also consistently been found to be an important risk factor for those with chronic cough and phlegm and dyspnea.[32]

Two major effects of vegetable dusts on ventilation have been reported. The first is a chronic obstruction of airways. The second effect is an acute increase in airways obstruction over a period (working shift) of exposure to cotton dust, particularly after an absence from such exposure of two or more days. Spirometric evaluations (measurements of the air entering and leaving the lungs), typically conducted before the Monday shift in western counties, have confirmed Schilling's observation that byssinotics, as a group, generally have lower airflow rates than comparable controls. Furthermore, those with chronic cough and phlegm, in addition to symptoms of chest tightness, have been found to have a further decrease in lung function.[33] In large cross-sectional studies, smoking significantly decreases preshift lung function and as a risk factor is equally as important as or less important than cotton dust, depending on the study.[34] These variations probably result from different levels of exposure to different amounts of cotton dust experienced by the study populations.

McKerrow and others first observed the acute reduction in expiratory flow (most marked after an absence from exposure) among workers in areas with higher dust levels.[35] Based on these observations the research-

---

31. Bouhuys and others, "Byssinosis in Hemp Workers"; Bouhuys and others, "Chronic Respiratory Disease in Hemp Workers"; Elwood, "Respiratory Symptoms in Men Who Had Previously Worked in a Flax Mill in Northern Ireland"; and Valic and Zuskin, "Effects of Different Vegetable Dust Exposures."

32. James A. Merchant, "Epidemiological Studies of Respiratory Disease Among Cotton Textile Workers, 1970–1973" (Ph.D. dissertation, University of North Carolina, 1973); and James A. Merchant and others, "Intervention Studies of Cotton Steaming to Reduce Biological Effects of Cotton Dust," *British Journal of Industrial Medicine,* vol. 31 (October 1974), pp. 261–74.

33. Imbus and Suh, "Byssinosis: A Study"; Lammers, Schilling, and Wolford, "A Study of Byssinosis, Chronic Respiratory Symptoms, and Ventilatory Capacity"; Merchant and others, "Intervention Studies of Cotton Steaming"; and F. Valic and others, "Byssinosis, Chronic Bronchitis, and Ventilatory Capacities in Workers Exposed to Soft Hemp Dust," *British Journal of Industrial Medicine,* vol. 25 (July 1968), pp. 176–86.

34. Arend Bouhuys and others, "Epidemiology of Chronic Lung Disease in a Cotton Mill Community," *Lung,* vol. 154 (September 1977), pp. 167–86; Merchant and others, "Byssinosis and Chronic Bronchitis Among Cotton Textile Workers"; and James A. Merchant and others, "Preprocessing Cotton to Prevent Byssinosis," *British Journal of Industrial Medicine,* vol. 30 (July 1973), pp. 237–47.

35. C. B. McKerrow and others, "Respiratory Function During the Day in Cotton Workers: A Study in Byssinosis," *British Journal of Industrial Medicine,* vol. 15 (January 1958), pp. 75–83.

ers suggested that symptoms of Monday chest tightness and dyspnea might be explained by the rate of reduction in airflow, a hypothesis that has been questioned because many byssinotics do not exhibit shift decrements and because the degree of airflow reduction, although significant, is often not marked.[36] Others have confirmed that those with higher grades of byssinosis have greater reductions in flow rates after each day of the working week.

It has also been observed that workers with bronchitis *and* byssinosis tend to have greater work shift decrements in expiratory flow than those with byssinosis or bronchitis alone.[37] Based on the association between grades of byssinosis and mean decreases in expiratory flow, Bouhuys proposed a functional grading scheme that was later modified.[38] Subsequent reports have shown that the relationship between a Monday fall in forced expiratory volume in one second (of 200 milliliters or greater) and byssinosis is not uniform. An appreciable proportion of nonbyssinotics have a clear Monday decline in airflow whereas many byssinotics do not even show a moderate decline.[39]

Because expiratory flow can be easily measured in untrained subjects and provides an objective indicator of biological effect, spirometry has been used widely in epidemiological studies. People exposed to the dust of cotton, soft hemp, and flax usually have greater decrements in expiratory flow than those exposed to similar dust levels from hard fibers.[40] Those exposed to higher dust levels have been found to show more marked decrements, and the dose-response relationship between respirable dust and decrements in flow rates approximates those for byssinosis symptoms.[41] Although smoking clearly affects baseline spirometry levels,

36. Bates, Macklem, and Christie, *Respiratory Function in Disease.*

37. Imbus and Suh, "Byssinosis: A Study"; and Valić and others, "Byssinosis, Chronic Bronchitis, and Ventilatory Capacities in Workers Exposed to Soft Hemp Dust."

38. Arend Bouhuys, John C. Gilson, and Richard S. Schilling, "Byssinosis in the Textile Industry," *Archives of Environmental Health,* vol. 21 (October 1970), pp. 475–78.

39. Imbus and Suh, "Byssinosis: A Study"; and M. K. B. Molyneaux and J. B. L. Tombleson, "An Epidemiological Study of Respiratory Symptoms in Lancashire Mills, 1963–66," *British Journal of Industrial Medicine,* vol. 27 (July 1970), pp. 225–34.

40. Gilson and others, "Byssinosis: The Acute Effect on Ventilatory Capacity"; and Valić and Zuškin, "Effects of Different Vegetable Dust Exposures."

41. Batawi and others, "Byssinosis in the Egyptian Cotton Industry"; Merchant and others, "Preprocessing Cotton to Prevent Byssinosis"; and Merchant and others, "Dose Response Studies in Cotton Textile Workers."

there is conflicting evidence on the influence of smoking on acute changes in lung function.[42]

Three prospective studies have reported a reduction in forced expiratory volume per second over time. In each of these studies, conclusions were necessarily based upon a survivor population, which complicates interpretation of data. A study of twenty-eight workers exposed to fine cotton in Yugoslavian mills over a nine-year period revealed no greater decline in forced expiratory volume than would be expected as a result of aging alone.[43] Berry and others reported that cotton workers experienced roughly twice as much decline annually as synthetic workers.[44] The decline attributable to cotton dust was slightly greater but similar to that attributable to smoking, and it was somewhat greater among those in dustier areas and among those exposed to the dust for up to four years, as opposed to longer periods of exposure. Merchant and others found that those exposed to high levels of cotton dust, many of whom were new employees with acute reactions, had declines as high as 280 milliliters over a ten-month period, which was much greater than that experienced by those exposed to lower dust concentrations over a longer period of employment.[45] Data collected by Bouhuys and others also suggest that workers exposed to cotton dust who show acute changes in breathing rates are more likely to rapidly develop ventilatory impairment.[46] Other studies have not been able to confirm this suggestion, possibly because of the migration of those with acute symptoms to jobs with lower dust exposures or out of the industry.[47]

In a study of a cotton mill community, Bouhuys found that 18 percent

42. Imbus and Suh, "Byssinosis: A Study"; and Merchant and others, "An Industrial Study of the Biological Effects of Cotton Dust and Cigarette Smoke Exposure."

43. Fedor Valić and Eugenija Zuškin, "Byssinosis: A Follow-Up Study of Workers Exposed to Fine Grade Cotton Dust," *Thorax,* vol. 27 (July 1972), pp. 459–62.

44. G. Berry and others, "A Study of the Acute and Chronic Changes in Ventilatory Capacity of Workers in Lancashire Cotton Mills," *British Journal of Industrial Medicine,* vol. 30 (January 1973), pp. 25–36.

45. Merchant and others, "Intervention Studies of Cotton Steaming."

46. Bouhuys and others, "Chronic Respiratory Disease in Hemp Workers"; and Arend Bouhuys and K. P. van de Woestijne, "Respiratory Mechanics and Dust Exposure in Byssinosis," *British Journal of Industrial Medicine,* vol. 49 (January 1970), pp. 106–18.

47. Berry and others, "A Study of the Acute and Chronic Changes in Ventilatory Capacity of Workers"; and Merchant and others, "Intervention Studies of Cotton Steaming."

of workers retiring before the age of sixty-five gave chest symptoms as the primary reason. Significantly more textile workers than nontextile workers were severely impaired. Based on these data, Bouhuys estimated that there are at least 35,000 men and women in the United States suffering from severe lung impairment associated with their work in textile mills.[48]

Clinical Signs and Symptoms

The hallmark of byssinosis is the characteristic symptom of chest tightness, which typically occurs following a weekend away from work. Although the time of the onset of chest tightness after dust exposure varies, chest tightness is most often observed two to three hours after exposure. This time interval is one important feature that distinguishes byssinosis from asthma, which has an immediate onset with exposure.[49] Affected individuals often compare the feeling of chest tightness to that of a chest cold. Frequently chest tightness is accompanied by a cough that often is more prominent on Monday. Among older workers who have been exposed to cotton dust for many years, a history of exertional dyspnea (dyspnea provoked by physical exertion) is common. Among those severely affected, chest tightness and dyspnea occur on all work days, with relief only on weekends and holidays, if then.

All of these symptoms become more severe if the time away from cotton dust exposure is prolonged; that is, the affected individual appears to lose exposure tolerance. (Conversely, Monday symptoms do not occur if exposure occurs seven days per week). Symptoms are often more severe and more frequent among smokers. Occasionally workers with typical byssinosis have reported that their symptoms of Monday chest tightness disappeared when they stopped smoking, even though their exposure to cotton dust did not change.

There are no typical or characteristic signs found in physical examinations of byssinotic subjects who are not severely affected. Although subjects often exhibit a productive cough, their lungs are usually relatively quiet, except for occasional rhonchi (rattling or snoring sounds). Wheez-

48. Bouhuys and others, "Epidemiology of Chronic Lung Disease."
49. J. D. Hamilton and others, "Byssinosis in a Nontextile Worker," *American Review of Respiratory Disease*, vol. 107 (March 1973), pp. 464–66.

ing is not commonly found early in the course of byssinosis. All of the physical signs of advanced chronic bronchitis or emphysema are evident among those severely affected.

People with or without byssinosis who have been exposed to cotton dust have several nonspecific symptoms. Cotton dust is an irritating material that dries and inflames mucous membranes, resulting in mild conjunctival irritation, sneezing, and hoarseness. Chronic cough and phlegm and exertional dyspnea are also evident among cotton workers who have not smoked and can recall no typical history of byssinosis. Whether these individuals merely forgot they once had symptoms on Monday or whether they developed nonspecific symptoms without the typical periodicity is not well understood. Available data suggest the latter.

New workers and those who first go into dusty cotton processing areas for a few hours may experience mill fever, which has been also called weavers' fever, cardroom fever, dust chills, dust fever, cotton cold, cotton fever, and, among flax workers, heckling fever.[50] Symptoms, which occur within twelve hours of exposure, consist of chills, headache, thirst, malaise, sweating, and nausea and vomiting, accompanied by a transient fever. Without further exposure these symptoms subside spontaneously within a day or two. With repeated exposure, such as that experienced by a new worker, these symptoms may occur for several days until the worker is "seasoned" or develops tolerance. Another common complaint of new workers or mill visitors is tobacco intolerance following exposure to concentrations of cotton dust higher than they are used to. These symptoms are not often observed at lower dust exposures and are therefore becoming less common as dust control improves within the cotton processing industry.

A second group of febrile syndromes associated with cotton processing includes mattress-makers' fever and weavers' cough. These conditions occur among experienced workers and are characterized by a high attack rate, a clear-cut febrile episode, severe cough, and dyspnea. Most of these epidemics have been attributed to mildewed yarn. An endotoxin containing a gram-negative bacillus, *Aerobacter cloacae,* has been isolated and was thought to be the likely etiological agent in one of the epidemics.[51]

50. J. T. Arlidge, *The Hygiene Diseases and Mortality of Occupations* (London: Percival, 1892); and Caminita and others, *A Review of the Literature.*

51. Paul A. Neal, Roy Schneiter, and Barbara H. Caminita, "Report on Acute Illness Among Rural Mattress-Makers Using Low Grade, Stained Cotton," *Journal of the American Medical Association,* vol. 119 (August 1942), pp. 1074–82.

Pathology

Schilling reviewed pathological observations made by several investigators of lungs of workers with long cotton dust exposure and concluded that the pulmonary pathology observed was that of nonspecific chronic bronchitis and emphysema.[52] The report of Dunn and Sheehan (as cited by Schilling) is notable in that they had obtained good occupational (although no smoking) histories and in that the lungs they examined were fixed in inflation.[53] Of the autopsies performed on ten workers, evidence of pulmonary disease was found in nine, all of whom had worked in dusty areas of cotton mills for over twenty years. All nine showed evidence of chronic bronchitis and/or emphysema, which was most marked among the five with histories of stripping and grinding carding machines. These five and two others also had evidence of right ventricular hypertrophy; four of these seven were judged to have died from heart disease due to pulmonary hypertension secondary to disease of the lung's blood vessels. Schilling also described pathological observations made by Gough and Woodcock of lungs of workers with histories of byssinosis.[54] Both described emphysema as a prominent lesion. Gough described inflammation of the bronchi with replacement of cells normally lining the airways by cells similar to those found in the skin and emphysema that was generalized but somewhat more pronounced in relation to dust deposits. The lungs were also described as having some increase in dust content, which appeared to be mainly rich in carbon and only slightly conducive to the development of fibers. Gough also described "byssinosis bodies," which consisted of a core of black dust surrounded by a yellowish material that had a high iron content. These bodies were characteristically round or oval and varied in size up to ten micrograms.

The most extensive pathological study of byssinosis was published by Edwards and others.[55] Lungs from forty-three patients who had long

52. R. S. F. Schilling, "Byssinosis in Cotton and Other Textile Workers," *Lancet,* vol. 2 (1956), pp. 261–65, 319–24.

53. J. S. Dunn and H. L. Sheehan, in Home Office, *Report of the Departmental Committee on Dust in Card-rooms in the Cotton Industry* (London: Her Majesty's Stationery Office, 1932), app. 3.

54. Personal communication from J. Gough and R. C. Woodcock to Schilling, "Byssinosis in Cotton and Other Textile Workers," p. 320.

55. C. Edwards and others, "The Pathology of the Lung in Byssinosis," *Thorax,* vol. 30 (December 1975), pp. 612–23.

exposure to cotton dust and who had been receiving industrial benefits for byssinosis were distended with formalin in postmortem examinations. In all cases the principal pathological finding was bronchitis. Lungs from twenty-seven (63 percent) of the patients showed no significant emphysema, ten (23 percent) showed varying degrees of centrilobular emphysema, and six (14 percent) showed varying degrees of panacinar emphysema. Although seventeen of the forty-three were known to be cigarette smokers and all subjects were from the Lancashire area, this study did not assess the possible influence of smoking or air pollution.

Pathogenesis

To explain byssinosis fully, an etiological mechanism must account for the following phenomena: chest tightness upon return to dust exposure after an absence from it, constricted airways among many with acute chest tightness, and chronic airway obstruction after prolonged exposure to cotton dust. Because byssinosis has been defined through acute symptoms often associated with airway narrowing and because the chronic phase of byssinosis is nonspecific and difficult to model, research has focused on acute events and given little attention to the chronic stage of the disease. As with most diseases of obscure etiology, many hypotheses about the cause of byssinosis have been proposed. They fall into three broad categories: a pharmacological mechanism, an immunological mechanism, and a microorganism etiology.

Pharmacological Mechanism

The similarities between asthma and byssinosis suggested to early investigators that byssinosis may be secondary to histamine and/or histamine-like substances, which were subsequently found in small quantities in vegetable dusts.[56] Researchers suggested that dust might release histamine from the lung following accumulation of histamine stores over the weekend, when the afflicted person was not exposed to dust. With the release of histamine, Monday chest tightness would occur but dis-

56. H. B. Maitland, H. Heap, and A. D. MacDonald, "The Presence of Histamine in Cotton Dust," in *Report of the Departmental Committee on Dust in Cardrooms in the Cotton Industry*, app. 6; and C. Prausnitz, *Investigation on Respiratory Dust Disease in Operatives in the Cotton Industry*, Privy Council, Medical Research Council Special Report Series 212 (London: Her Majesty's Stationery Office, 1936).

appear after the stored histamine had been consumed by normal body metabolism.[57]

To examine this hypothesis, several investigations have assessed histamine release from animal and human chopped lungs *in vitro;* isolated smooth muscle preparations; and change in airflow rates among affected textile workers or volunteers exposed to various aqueous dust extracts. With these techniques used as assays, dust extracts have been found to contain contractor substances that are water soluble, dialyzable, resistant to boiling, steam volatile, unstable in strong acids and alkali, not destroyed by proteolytic enzymes, and having some fever-inducing activity.[58] In addition to small amounts of histamine, serotonin and a kinin-like substance have been identified in cotton dust extracts.[59] Paper chromatography of extracts has led some to conclude that polypeptides are the causal agents for histamine release.[60] Methyl piperonylate has been identified as one component of cotton bract capable of releasing histamine.[61] Although there is now a great deal of evidence that a nonimmunologic pharmacological mechanism is involved with bronchoconstriction resulting from vegetable dust exposure, it does not necessarily explain the chest tightness that often occurs independently of measured changes in airflow rates, nor does it adequately explain the chronic stage of byssinosis. Therefore, pharmacological events are probably only part of the mechanism of byssinosis.

Immunological Mechanism

The known relationship between skin reactivity and asthma led several early investigators to suggest that an allergy to some component of

57. Arend Bouhuys, S. E. Lindell, and G. Lundin, "Experimental Studies on Byssinosis," *British Medical Journal* (January 30, 1960), pt. 1, pp. 324–26; and Arend Bouhuys, "Experimental Studies in Byssinosis," *Archives of Environmental Health,* vol. 6 (June 1963), pp. 742–47.

58. John D. Hamilton and others, "Differential Aerosol Challenge Studies in Byssinosis," *Archives of Environmental Health,* vol. 26 (March 1973), pp. 120–24; and Margaret Hitchcock, "*In Vitro* Histamine Release from Human Lung as a Model for the Acute Response to Cotton Dust," *Annals of the New York Academy of Sciences,* vol. 221 (February 28, 1974), pp. 124–31.

59. H. Antweiler, "The Histamine Releasing Capacity of Cotton Dust Extracts Inhaled by Guinea Pigs," *Annals of the New York Academy of Sciences,* vol. 221 (February 28, 1974), pp. 136–40.

60. Hubert Antweiler, "Observations about a Histamine Liberating Substance in Cotton Dust," *Annals of Occupational Hygiene,* vol. 2 (July 1960), pp. 152–56.

61. Hitchcock, "*In Vitro* Histamine Release from Human Lung."

cotton dust might be involved in the etiology of byssinosis. Skin testing, often with crude extracts, has yielded highly variable results that have not contributed to our understanding of byssinosis.[62] Massoud and Taylor proposed a classical immunological mechanism unrelated to skin reactivity as a possible cause of byssinosis.[63] Finding precipitating antibodies to a condensed polyphenol in the serum of textile workers, especially carders and byssinotics, led Massoud and Taylor to suggest that byssinosis might represent an atypical pulmonary disease similar to farmers' lung. Although the researchers knew that granuloma formation typical of farmers' lung was not a feature of byssinosis, they suggested that its absence might be attributable to altered "handling" of inhaled dust.[64] Examination of condensed polyphenols by Edwards later showed that the precipitin observed by Taylor and others was probably nonspecific precipitation of IgG mediated by the polyphenolic polymer.[65] Similarly, Antweiler found little liberation of histamine with the polyphenolic materials.[66]

Although the serum precipitins of Taylor's condensed polyphenol may well be nonspecific, double blind trials with byssinotic and nonbyssinotic cardroom workers and unexposed controls remain to be explained. In these clinical trials, Taylor and his colleagues found that aerosol exposure to condensed tannin produced typical Monday chest tightness in those with byssinosis but not in textile workers without byssinotic symptoms or in unexposed controls. Although concomitant changes in spirometry were not observed, it is of particular interest that these experimental ex-

62. H. R. Cayton, G. Furness, and H. B. Maitland, "Studies on Cotton Dust in Relation to Byssinosis," *British Journal of Industrial Medicine,* vol. 9 (1952), pp. 186–96; V. Popa and others, "An Investigation of Allergy in Byssinosis: Sensitization to Cotton, Hemp, Flax, and Jute Antigens," *British Journal of Industrial Medicine,* vol. 26 (April 1969), pp. 101–08; and Prausnitz, *Investigation on Respiratory Dust Disease.*

63. Aly Massoud and Geoffrey Taylor, "Byssinosis: Antibody to Cotton Antigens in Normal Subjects and in Cotton Card-room Workers," *Lancet,* vol. 2 (1974), pp. 607–10.

64. Geoffrey Taylor, A. A. E. Massoud, and F. Lucas, "Studies on the Aetiology of Byssinosis," *British Journal of Industrial Medicine,* vol. 28 (April 1971), pp. 143–51.

65. J. H. Edwards and B. M. Jones, "Immunology of Byssinosis: A Study of the Reactions Between the Isolated Byssinosis 'Antigen' and Human Immunoglobulins," *Annals of the New York Academy of Sciences,* vol. 221 (February 28, 1974), pp. 59–63.

66. H. Antweiler and S. Pallade, "Polyphenolic Actions on Guinea Pig Smooth Muscle and Mast Cells in the Rat," *Annals of the New York Academy of Sciences,* vol. 221 (February 28, 1974), pp. 132–35.

posures blocked or markedly diminished byssinotic symptoms when workers with byssinosis returned to mill work the following day.[67]

Microorganism Etiology

Both bacterial and fungal microorganisms have been extensively studied as possible etiological agents of byssinosis. They are found in substantial quantities in textile mill air.[68] The occurrence of mill fever and the description of mattress-makers' fever, both thought to be caused by endotoxins, suggested to early investigators that microorganisms and/or their products may play an important role in byssinosis pathogenesis. Early studies of bacterial and fungal species, however, showed that textile workers are rarely infected. Attention then turned to endotoxin produced by gram-negative bacteria in mill dust as a possible etiological candidate. Among the biological features common to endotoxin and byssinosis are: tachyphylaxis; fever-inducing properties; leukocytosis; anaphylaxis in laboratory animals; the liberation of histamine; a decrease of circulating platelets; fever and tachypnea in rabbits sensitized with both cotton dust extract and endotoxin; and cross-reactivity between cotton dust and endotoxin.[69] Peris concluded that byssinosis may result from the protracted inhalation of small amounts of endotoxin, which he interpreted as a condition of "immunological hypersensitivity."[70] Antweiler, however, pointed out that the small amount of endotoxin found in vegetable dust was incapable of releasing histamine; that the smooth muscle constricting substances were stable with boiling; that the endotoxin hypothesis could not explain quantitative differences with different (cotton) plant parts; and finally, that the clinical picture of byssinosis was not consistent with hypersensitivity or endotoxin effect, fever being conspicuously absent.[71]

67. Taylor, Massoud, and Lucas, "Studies on the Aetiology of Byssinosis."

68. Cayton, Furness, and Maitland, "Studies on Cotton Dust in Relation to Byssinosis"; and Neal, Schneiter, and Caminita, "Report on Acute Illness Among Rural Mattress-Makers."

69. B. Peris and others, "The Role of Bacterial Endotoxins in Occupational Diseases Caused by Inhaling Vegetable Dust," *British Journal of Industrial Medicine,* vol. 18 (April 1961), pp. 120–29; and Prausnitz, *Investigation on Respiratory Dust Disease.*

70. Peris and others, "The Role of Bacterial Endotoxins in Occupational Diseases," p. 128.

71. H. Antweiler, "Histamine Liberation by Cotton Dust Extracts: Evidence Against Its Causation by Bacterial Endotoxins," *British Journal of Industrial Medicine,* vol. 18 (April 1961), pp. 130–32.

Nevertheless, recent attention has again focused on endotoxin or enzymes contained in gram-negative organisms as possible etiological agents. Braun, Rylander, Cinkotai, and their colleagues have recently shown that the prevalance of byssinosis is roughly correlated with the number of airborne gram-negative bacteria or their products in mill air.[72] This correlation has not been as strong, however, as that between the prevalence of byssinosis and nonspecific respirable dust. Because of the stronger association between fine cotton dust and byssinosis prevalence, the dose-response relationship observed between gram-negative organisms and byssinosis prevalence is probably a secondary one, the organisms being closely associated with the vegetable dust from which they arise. Therefore, although often consistent both epidemiologically and experimentally with certain characteristics of respiratory disease resulting from cotton dust exposure, endotoxin causality has not been established.

Recently, the observations of Kilburn have stimulated studies with experimental animals focusing on acute airway changes. Kilburn found polymorphonuclear cell recruitment to airway surfaces with exposure to raw cotton dust or cotton dust extracts consisting of Taylor's polyphenolic material and quercetin.[73] Control exposures to large amounts of carbon dust, barium sulfate dust, and silica flour produced no such cell recruitment. Rylander, using similar techniques, has observed that an increase in polymorphonuclear cells was found within five hours of exposure, peaked after twenty hours of exposure, and when the cotton dust extract was diluted, resulted in a distinct dose-response relationship.[74] Studies of chemotaxis (the orientation of an organism in relation to chemical agents) in Boyden chambers suggest that complement is not necessary for the

72. Daniel C. Braun and others, "Physiological Response to Enzymes in Cotton Dust," *Journal of Occupational Medicine,* vol. 15 (March 1973), pp. 241–44; Ragnar Rylander, Annie Nordstrand, and Marie-Claire Snella, "Bacterial Contamination of Organic Dusts: Effects on Pulmonary Cell Reactions," *Archives of Environmental Health,* vol. 30 (March 1975), pp. 137–40; and F. F. Cinkotai, M. G. Lockwood, and R. Rylander, "Airborne Micro-Organisms and Prevalence of Byssinosis Symptoms in Cotton Mills," *American Industrial Hygiene Association Journal,* vol. 8 (October 1977), pp. 554–59.
73. Kaye H. Kilburn and others, "Leukocyte Recruitment through Airway Walls by Condensed Vegetable Tannins and Quercetin," *Laboratory Investigation,* vol. 28 (January 1973), pp. 55–59.
74. Ragnar Rylander and Marie-Claire Snella, "Acute Inhalation Toxicity of Cotton Plant Dusts," *British Journal of Industrial Medicine,* vol. 33 (August 1976), pp. 175–80.

leukocyte response to occur.[75] Anecdotal studies of affected workers during dust exposure have shown no change in complement levels.

Recent studies of complement activation *in vitro* are particularly interesting in relation to polymorphonuclear cell recruitment and other pharmacological events. Kutz and others found that human complement is consumed by both cardroom dust and to a lesser degree by treated (washed and extracted) cardroom dust.[76] They also showed that nanogram quantities of endotoxin found in cardroom dust could not explain the complement consumption, which would have required microgram quantities of endotoxin. They therefore concluded that other unidentified hemolytically active substances are involved and speculated that antibody-independent complement activation could explain the accumulation of polymorphonuclear cells in the airways. Such complement activation, secondary to complement cascade-releasing chemotactic factors, may induce airway changes by releasing histamine and other pharmacologically active mediators. Similarly, Kilburn noted that polymorphonuclear cells are rich in lyzosomal enzymes, among which are collagenases and elastases, which may contribute to airway narrowing and the chronic airway changes found among severely affected workers.[77] Clearly, further research is needed on possible etiological agents and their cellular and pharmacological interactions.

Treatment

As with research on the pathogenesis of byssinosis, research on therapy for byssinosis has been confined to acute events. Clinical trials have relied almost exclusively on changes in airflow rates among active workers as the indicator of effect. While propranolol has been shown to increase bronchoconstriction with hemp dust exposure, antihistamines and ascorbic acid have been found to protect against this effect.[78] Similarly, it has

75. Letter to the author from Kaye H. Kilburn.
76. S. A. Kutz and others, "Antibody-Independent Complement Activation by Cardroom Cotton Dust," *Environmental Research* (forthcoming).
77. Kilburn and others, "Leukocyte Recruitment through Airway Walls."
78. E. Zuškin, F. Valić, and A. Bouhuys, "Byssinosis and Airway Responses to Exposure to Textile Dust," *Lung,* vol. 154 (December 1976), pp. 17–24; and Zuškin and Bouhuys, "Protective Effect of Disodium Chromoglycate Against Airway Constriction Induced by Hemp Dust Extraction," *Journal of Allergy and Clinical Immunology,* vol. 57 (May 1976), pp. 473–79.

been found that inhaled bronchodilators (salbutamol, isoprenaline, and orciprenaline) will prevent or reverse airflow rate changes.[79] Finally, it has been found that pre-exposure treatment with disodium chromoglycate tends to block bronchoconstriction.[80] Inhaled beclamethazone also seems to decrease airflow rate response.[81]

These beneficial effects are all functional and are undocumented in regard to symptomatology. Although the bronchoconstriction caused by hemp and cotton dust is usually not severe and may be blocked or reversed, there is no evidence that use of the drugs named above will necessarily suppress byssinosis symptoms or retard the progress of obstructive airway disease induced by cotton dust. Therefore, these drugs cannot be considered preventive measures. For severely affected people, therapy does not differ greatly from that for chronic bronchitis and emphysema.

Prevention

Given our current knowledge about the etiology of byssinosis and lack of a biological assay, risk assessment depends on assessment of dust concentrations. Similarly, prevention depends largely on dust control in the work place. Significant improvements in exhaust ventilation dust control technology and application have recently resulted in reduced risk in most areas in the United States where textile mills are found. A second control technology, which appears promising experimentally, is washing cotton.[82] Although this procedure has been found to reduce symptoms and functional changes, largely through the removal of fine dust, it is not yet clear whether cotton washing is technically feasible on a large scale.

79. I. W. Fawcett and others, "The Effect of Sodium Chromoglycate, Beclamethasone Diproprionate and Salbutamol on the Ventilatory Response to Cotton Dust in Mill Workers," *British Journal of Diseases of the Chest,* vol. 72 (January 1978), pp. 29–38; G. R. Kamat and others, "Pressurised Bronchodilator Aerosols in Byssinosis," *Indian Journal of Medical Science,* vol. 29 (August–September 1975), pp. 208–12; and F. Valić and Eugenija Zuškin, "Pharmacological Prevention of Acute Ventilatory Capacity Reduction in Flax Dust Exposure," *British Journal of Industrial Medicine,* vol. 30 (October 1973), pp. 381–84.

80. Fawcett and others, "The Effect of Sodium Chromoglycate, Beclamethasone Diproprionate and Salbutamol on the Ventilatory Response"; Zuškin, Valić, and Bouhuys, "Byssinosis and Airway Responses"; and Zuškin and Bouhuys, "Protective Effect of Disodium Chromoglycate Against Airway Constriction."

81. Fawcett and others, "The Effect of Sodium Chromoglycate, Beclamethasone Diproprionate and Salbutamol on the Ventilatory Response."

82. Merchant and others, "Preprocessing Cotton to Prevent Byssinosis."

Although dust control is the foundation of respiratory disease prevention in the cotton processing industry, medical surveillance and employee education also play important roles. Smoking and the interaction between smoking and cotton dust exposure are clearly important risk factors in byssinosis. Therefore, it is essential that workers exposed to cotton dust be provided with information about the adverse effects of smoking, particularly in combination with cotton dust exposure. It is also essential that work practices affecting individual dust exposure be stressed. Periodic medical examinations designed to detect those affected acutely by cotton dust exposure and those with chronic lung disease are important and can be effective. Through the use of a standard questionnaire, it is possible to obtain a sound occupational and smoking history as well as to screen for byssinosis, bronchitis, dyspnea, and other medical complaints. Simple spirometry applied routinely will identify many of those affected acutely and nearly all with significant impairment.

All of these prevention provisions—allowable dust concentrations, work practices, and medical surveillance—are detailed in the Department of Labor cotton dust standard promulgated in 1978.[83] Compliance with the provisions of that standard would largely eliminate byssinosis and prevent significant occupationally related pulmonary impairment among U.S. cotton textile workers.

83. 29 C.F.R. pt. 1910.1043.

Cotton Dust:
An Economist's View

JOHN F. MORRALL III

THIS PAPER summarizes the medical information on byssinosis, or brown lung disease, that is relevant to an economic evaluation of the cotton dust standards issued by the Occupational Safety and Health Administration on June 23, 1978,[1] and analyzes the standards' rationale, cost-effectiveness, and costs and benefits.

Ideally the economic evaluation of health and safety regulations involves (1) quantifying to the extent possible social costs and social benefits; (2) examining cost-effective alternatives in light of the benefits the alternatives provide; (3) making explicit to policymakers the nonquantifiable costs and benefits of various alternatives; and (4) determining and communicating clearly the implications of the transfer of income that will be required among the various identifiable groups involved in the alternatives.[2]

1. See U.S. Department of Labor, Occupational Safety and Health Administration, "Occupational Safety and Health Standards: Occupational Exposure to Cotton Dust," *Federal Register,* vol. 43 (June 23, 1978), pp. 27350–463. These regulations did not go into effect immediately since the U.S. Court of Appeals of the District of Columbia granted a stay pending a decision. On October 24, 1979, the court upheld the standard although it asked the Occupational Safety and Health Administration to reexamine it as it applied to the cottonseed oil industry. The industry appealed the decision to the Supreme Court, which will probably decide the case during the spring 1981 term.

2. For an example of an attempt at such an analysis for another Occupational Safety and Health Administration standard, see John F. Morrall III, "Exposure to Occupational Noise," in James C. Miller III and Bruce Yandle, eds., *Benefit-Cost Analysis of Social Regulation* (Washington, D.C.: American Enterprise Institute for Public Policy Research, 1979), pp. 33–58.

Although most economists believe that this approach is quite reasonable, some believe that the gains such analysis might lead to are not worth the moral cost to society of placing a collective value on health benefits.[3]

Byssinosis

As James Merchant points out, byssinosis is the generic name applied to acute and chronic airways disease among those who process cotton. Among the more important features of the disease from the regulatory point of view are that byssinosis is progressive—proceeding from a reversible, relatively mild stage to a chronic, irreversible, and disabling stage—and that it is strongly correlated with respirable cotton dust.

Merchant (quoting Schilling) lists the progression of byssinosis in terms of grades—grade ½ being occasional chest tightness on Mondays or mild symptoms such as irritation of the respiratory tract on Mondays; grade 1 being chest tightness and/or breathlessness on Mondays only; and grade 2 being chest tightness and/or breathlessness on Mondays and other workdays.[4] The Occupational Safety and Health Administration has also listed a grade 3, consisting of "grade 2 symptoms accompanied by evidence of permanent incapacity from diminished effort tolerance and/or reduced ventilatory capacity."[5] According to Merchant, the progression of the disease from its reversible acute stage to its irreversible chronic stage suggests that periodic medical examinations can help identify many of those affected acutely and almost everyone with significant impairment. It appears, then, that for new workers exposed to cotton dust, a medical surveillance program that identified workers with grades ½ or 1 and removed them from exposure would prevent the disease from progressing to its irreversible stages and thus prevent, for the majority, significant impairment. Ideally, of course, it would be desirable to eradicate the acute grades of the disease as well.

3. See Steven E. Rhoads, "How Much Should We Spend To Save a Life?" *The Public Interest,* no. 51 (Spring 1978), pp. 74–92.

4. James A. Merchant and others, "An Industrial Study of the Biological Effects of Cotton Dust and Cigarette Smoke Exposure," *Journal of Occupational Medicine,* vol. 15 (March 1973), pp. 212–21 (quoting R. S. F. Schilling and others, "A Report on a Conference on Byssinosis," in *International Congress Series* 62 [Amsterdam: Excerpta Medica Foundation, 1963], pp. 137–45).

5. Occupational Safety and Health Administration, "Occupational Exposure to Cotton Dust: Proposed Standards and Notice of Hearing," *Federal Register,* vol. 41 (December 28, 1976), p. 56500.

The second salient feature of byssinosis from the regulatory point of view is the strong association between the prevalence of byssinosis and respirable cotton dust. The Occupational Safety and Health Administration has relied heavily on results found by James Merchant—who has probably published the most comprehensive work in the area—to predict the reduction in byssinosis cases that might be expected from lowering exposure levels.[6] However, questions remain about the actual dose-response relationship, the cotton processing industry predictably arguing that the Occupational Safety and Health Administration has overstated byssinosis prevalence. There is some basis for this concern since the Merchant study predicts higher rates than do several other studies.[7]

An important piece of information that is missing is the actual byssinosis incidence rate and the average progression of the disease over time. The estimates we have are point in time estimates only. Byssinosis results from the worker's past history of exposure, individual susceptibility, and smoking habits.[8] Thus if cotton dust levels were higher in the past than they were in 1970–71, when the dust samples for the Merchant study were taken, incidence rates based on past estimates would be overstated. This is likely to be the case, since cotton dust was not recognized in the United States as a problem until 1964, when the American Conference of Governmental Industrial Hygienists placed cotton dust on its tentative list of threshold limit values, and was not regulated by the United States until 1968 (under the Walsh-Healey Public Contracts Act of 1936).

It is also not clear what reducing cotton dust levels would do for workers who have already been exposed to higher levels of cotton dust and who have or do not have some stage of byssinosis. The technical report prepared by the Research Triangle Institute for the Occupational Safety and Health Administration and the preamble to the final standard both estimate annual incremental benefits only by the reduction of byssinosis incidence among new workers.[9]

6. See James Merchant and others, "Dose Response Studies in Cotton Textile Workers," *Journal of Occupational Medicine,* vol. 15 (March 1973), pp. 222–30.
7. See the discussion in Occupational Safety and Health Administration, "Occupational Safety and Health Standards: Cotton Dust," pp. 27355–58.
8. See Merchant and others, "Dose Response Studies."
9. See Research Triangle Institute, "Inflationary Impact Statement: Cotton Dust" (Research Triangle Park, N.C., July 26, 1976), pp. III-11–III-14; and Occupational Safety and Health Administration, "Occupational Safety and Health Standards: Cotton Dust," p. 27379. The regulations corrected the Research Triangle Institute calculations only by increasing the estimated total number of workers exposed and by increasing the estimate of the new hire accession rate.

A final piece of missing medical information that is important is the etiology of byssinosis. Although there is a strong correlation between the respirable dust in cotton processing areas and byssinosis, it is not known which agent or agents cause the disease. In fact, there is strong evidence that the toxicity of the dust varies considerably with the grade of cotton processed, the way it is harvested, the stage of processing, whether it is steamed or chemically treated, and the amount of respirable dust in the outside air.

The Cotton Dust Standard

The final regulations issued by the Occupational Safety and Health Administration in June 1978 were different from previous health standards the agency had promulgated because for the first time different permissible exposure levels to a toxic substance were set for different manufacturing stages within a given industry. Instead of the standard the Occupational Safety and Health Administration had originally proposed mandating a maximum exposure over an eight-hour day of 200 micrograms of respirable dust per cubic meter, the agency mandated the following exposure levels: 200 micrograms per cubic meter for yarn manufacturing, 750 micrograms per cubic meter for fabric manufacturing, and 500 micrograms per cubic meter for cottonseed oil mills, waste processing, and warehousing. A separate set of regulations with no exposure limit was issued at the same time for cotton ginning. Since not all employees would be protected by these levels (the Merchant study predicts a byssinosis prevalance of 13 percent for workers in yarn manufacturing exposed to 200 micrograms of respirable cotton dust per cubic meter), medical surveillance, employee training, safe work practices, and respirator requirements were also included in the final standards. The agency stated in the preamble of the standards:

The record indicates that while medical surveillance is not fool-proof in detecting cotton dust induced health effects, a properly managed program should identify affected workers well before the onset of chronic obstructive pulmonary disease.[10]

The final standards are also different from ones set in the past in that the agency relaxed health requirements for several sectors that had been

10. Occupational Safety and Health Administration, "Occupational Safety and Health Standards: Cotton Dust," p. 27359.

affected by the standards promulgated under the Walsh-Healey Public Contracts Act of 1936 and adopted by the agency in 1971 under section 6(a) of the Occupational Safety and Health Act.[11] There are four possible reasons why the agency chose the variable standard rather than the uniform one: technical feasibility, economic feasibility, equalization of risk, and cost-effectiveness. Evidence for each of these rationales is in the standards' preamble (which is not surprising since preambles are usually written in anticipation of litigation).

The Occupational Safety and Health Act instructs the agency to

set the standard which most adequately assures, to the extent feasible, on the basis of the best available evidence, that no employee will suffer material impairment of health or functional capacity even if such employee has regular exposure to the hazard dealt with by such standard for the period of his working life.[12]

Since the agency has determined that no level of exposure to cotton dust is safe, the lowest feasible level of exposure determines the permissible level. In determining feasibility the agency takes into account both technical and economic constraints. Economic feasibility in this case means not a reasonable balancing of social costs and benefits, as most economists would like, but the financial capability of the industry to bear the costs without a substantial number of firms being forced to shut down.

The agency states in the preamble to the cotton dust standards:

In the case of the cotton dust standard, the evidence in the record indicates that the costs of compliance are not overly burdensome to industry. Having determined that the benefits of the proposed standard are likely to be appreciable, OSHA is not obligated to carry out further exercises toward more precise calculations of benefit which would not significantly clarify the ultimate decision.[13]

From the economist's perspective, mandating health and safety regulations for workers according to the financial capability of the industry in which they happen to work is far less intelligent than attempting to maximize worker health and safety given the opportunity costs of providing it and the willingness of workers, employers, and the public to pay for it.

11. The original standard set an exposure level of 1,000 micrograms of dust per cubic meter, equivalent to approximately 500 micrograms of *respirable* dust per meter.

12. Occupational Safety and Health Act of 1970, sec. 6(b)(5), 84 Stat. 1594.

13. Occupational Safety and Health Administration, "Occupational Safety and Health Standards: Cotton Dust," p. 27379. Actually this statement or one like it has been in almost all of the health standards that the agency has promulgated in the last few years.

Furthermore, the former policy does not always provide a greater degree of health and safety protection for a given hazard since cost-benefit analysis may demand control beyond the financial capability of an industry to pay for it.

Pressure to examine costs and benefits in the same context before promulgating regulations has been applied to the Occupational Safety and Health Administration by all three branches of government: the Executive Office of the President in the form of executive orders and reviews by the Council on Wage and Price Stability and the Council of Economic Advisers; the Congress in the form of directions to the Department of Labor to review the costs, benefits, and effects of the cotton dust standard and its alternatives; and the courts in the form of the Fifth Circuit Court of Appeals' ruling in the benzene case, which held that the agency should try to quantify benefits and promulgate standards that are "reasonably necessary."[14]

In the past, particularly in the proposal for the occupational noise standard, the Occupational Safety and Health Administration has argued that it would be unfair and perhaps illegal to subject workers in different industries to unequal risks of the same hazard. The departure from a uniform standard in the final cotton dust regulations thus surprised many observers. However, this breakthrough may not be the step toward cost-effectiveness that it first appeared to be since the risk of byssinosis, given constant dust levels, also varies with each cotton processing stage.

The Occupational Safety and Health Administration has stated:

Of course, the Agency does not view the economic and technological feasibility of reducing dust exposure in a vacuum. It is primarily concerned with the health of weavers, and the record supports the conclusion that a permissible exposure limit of 750 $\mu g/m^3$ will provide weavers as safe an environment as their co-workers in other textile operations exposed to 200 $\mu g/m^3$.[15]

In the preamble to the final regulation the agency also explicitly rejected using cost-effectiveness analysis as a basis for varying the standard, as the Council on Wage and Price Stability had recommended in its post-

14. This case was later affirmed by the Supreme Court, with the cost-benefit issue being a central point of contention. *Industrial Union Department, AFL-CIO, Petitioner*, v. *American Petroleum Institute, et al.;* and *Ray Marshall, Secretary of Labor, Petitioner*, v. *American Petroleum Institute, et al.*, 48 U.S.L.W. 5022 (Sup. Ct. 1980), *aff'd*, 581 F.2d 493 (5th Cir. 1979).

15. Occupational Safety and Health Administration, "Occupational Safety and Health Standards: Cotton Dust," p. 27360.

hearing comments.[16] The safety and health administration explained its rejection:

That model assumed a ceiling amount, as the most the industry could afford, to be spent for compliance costs and indicated the marginal basis for allocation of such expenditure. However, OSHA has no desire to be punitive or to impose on industry all that it could afford.[17]

However, the agency appeared to be implicitly endorsing just such a concept when it said:

OSHA agrees with the reasoning of the North Carolina Department of Labor that optimal worker protection would be served by concentrating the textile industry's technical and economic resources on achieving 200 $\mu g/m^3$ in yarn manufacturing as rapidly as feasible, rather than diverting substantial resources to eliminating dust exposure in weaving.[18]

In the report to Congress on cotton dust that was completed almost a year after the standard was issued the Department of Labor concluded:

By ignoring these differences [in costs and incidence], any across-the-board standard imposes unnecessarily high costs to comparatively low-risk segments of the industry. Varying the exposure levels can offer workers essentially the same health protection, but at substantial cost savings.[19]

Tables 1, 2, and 3 attempt to explain what influenced the Occupational Safety and Health Administration in setting the final variable exposure levels. Table 1 presents the annual cost per employee of the three control levels on which we have cost data in each of the five sectors. Cost per employee is used as a rough approximation of financial capability.[20] The costs for the exposure levels finally adopted range from slightly over $100

16. "Comments of the Council on Wage and Price Stability before the Occupational Safety and Health Administration on the Proposed Standard for Exposure to Cotton Dust," Council on Wage and Price Stability Report 250, June 20, 1977. Also see John Morrall, "The Cost and Benefits of the Proposed Standards for the Control of Cotton Dust," *Review of Industrial Management and Textile Science*, vol. 17 (Spring 1978), which draws heavily on the Council on Wage and Price Stability filing.

17. Occupational Safety and Health Administration, "Occupational Safety and Health Standards: Cotton Dust," p. 27379.

18. Ibid., p. 27360.

19. Department of Labor, "Report to the Congress: Cotton Dust—Review of Alternative Technical Standards and Control Technologies" (May 14, 1979), pp. 8–9.

20. Also note that health and safety expenditures are properly considered labor costs and, to the extent that risk differentials and working conditions improve, may partially substitute for wages (and to the extent they do not, may reduce employment).

Table 1. Annual Cost per Employee of Three Control Levels for Respirable Cotton Dust

Dollars

Industry segment	500 micrograms per cubic meter	200 micrograms per cubic meter	100 micrograms per cubic meter
Cotton warehousing	120[a]	1,306	1,306
Cottonseed oil production	6,550[a]	8,700	8,700
Yarn manufacturing	276	1,078[a]	2,790
Fabric manufacturing	104[b]	1,782	4,872
Waste processing	259	422[a]	686

Source: Calculated from U.S. Department of Labor, "Report to the Congress: Cotton Dust—Review of Alternative Technical Standards and Control Technologies" (May 14, 1979), tables II-2, III-2, III-4, III-6, pp. 35–36, 48, 52, 61.

a. Indicates the control level chosen by the Occupational Safety and Health Administration in the final standards.

b. Indicates the upper bound estimate for the 750 micrograms per cubic meter level set for fabric manufacturing in the final standards.

per employee for fabric manufacturing to $6,550 for the cottonseed oil industry. No clear pattern emerges that explains the levels chosen.

In table 2, which shows the expected prevalence of byssinosis among new workers for the different levels, a pattern does emerge. Predicted byssinosis prevalence ranges from 8 percent for fabric manufacturing to 23 percent for yarn manufacturing. There appears to be a definite attempt to equalize the risk among sectors and aim for an incidence rate of around 10 percent.[21]

Table 3 presents the annual marginal cost of each byssinosis case avoided per year in five sectors. Several factors stand out. First, in the nontextile sectors tightening the standards from 500 to 200 micrograms of allowable cotton dust per cubic meter would have provided more protection at less cost per case avoided. The weighted average marginal costs for the three sectors in moving to 200 micrograms per cubic meter is about $10,200—only slightly more than the $7,194 cost for yarn manufacturing at the same level and similar to the $10,118 for fabric manufacturing at the 500-microgram level.[22] Second, reducing the fabric manufacturing standard to 500 micrograms from the chosen 750 micrograms

21. The weighted average byssinosis rate for the nontextile sectors that are subject to the standard of 500 micrograms per cubic meter is 10 percent, about the same as the weighted average rate for the five textile sectors.

22. Presumably the level of 750 micrograms per cubic meter actually chosen would have cost less, but reliable data are not available since this level was not considered in the Research Triangle Institute's "Inflationary Impact Statement."

Table 2. Predicted Byssinosis Prevalence Rates among New Workers for Various Levels of Respirable Cotton Dust

Percent

Industry segment	Current level[a]	750 micrograms per cubic meter	500 micrograms per cubic meter	200 micrograms per cubic meter	100 micrograms per cubic meter
Cotton warehousing	15.0	15.0	15.0	9.0	4.0
Cottonseed oil production	21.0	14.0	9.0[b]	4.0	2.0
Yarn manufacturing	23.0	23.0	23.0	12.0[b]	7.0
Fabric manufacturing	7.8	7.3[b]	6.8	6.1	3.1
Waste processing	11.0	11.0	8.0[b]	4.0	2.0

Source: Same as table 1.
a. As last measured in 1970–71.
b. Indicates the control level set by the Occupational Safety and Health Administration.

Table 3. Annual Incremental Costs of Meeting Three Control Levels of Respirable Cotton Dust per Case of Byssinosis (All Grades) Avoided per Year

Dollars

Industry segment	500 micrograms per cubic meter	200 micrograms per cubic meter	100 micrograms per cubic meter
Cotton warehousing	n.m.[a]	20,143	n.a.
Cottonseed oil production	53,469[a]	40,952	n.a.
Yarn manufacturing	n.m.	7,194[a]	34,042
Fabric manufacturing	10,118[b]	261,040	129,113[c]
Waste processing	9,920[a]	3,333	15,596

Source: Calculated from Department of Labor, "Report to the Congress: Cotton Dust," tables III-2, III-4, III-6, pp. 48, 52, 61.
n.a. Not available.
n.m. Not meaningful. No benefit from controls is expected.
a. Indicates the final control level adopted by the Occupational Safety and Health Administration.
b. Indicates the control level closest to the 750 micrograms per cubic meter adopted by the administration, which did not estimate control costs for the level adopted.
c. Calculated relative to 500 micrograms per cubic meter since marginal costs relative to 200 micrograms per cubic meter are declining.

per cubic meter appears to make sense—even without cost data for the 750-microgram level—since the average cost at 500 micrograms per cubic meter is only $10,118. Third, the annual cost per case avoided each year for the cottonseed oil sector ($53,469) appears to be out of line with the other sectors.

A variable standard is more cost-effective than a uniform one; however, the most cost-effective mix does not seem to have been reached, and there is evidence that the final mix was chosen to minimize the differences in risk of byssinosis among sectors.

Cost-Effective Alternatives

In addition to varying standards across sectors to equalize marginal costs and marginal benefits, standards can be made more cost-effective by allowing greater flexibility in how given levels of protection are met. Thus performance standards are generally thought to be more cost-effective than design standards. What is not always appreciated is that so-called performance standards may be of different degrees. A pure performance standard may be concerned only with health effects, a less pure standard with the dust one breathes, and an even less pure one with only the ambient dust level. The last example describes the Occupational Safety and Health Administration's current approach; the agency does maintain that the cotton dust standard is a performance standard.[23]

Ideally, cotton dust should be reduced only to the extent that the reduction also reduces byssinosis cost-effectively. The Occupational Safety and Health Administration also regulates byssinosis by requiring a medical surveillance program. Although medical removal of workers is not mandated by the cotton dust standard, the agency has said it may add it to the regulations. Currently, an employee at risk may request a respirator or a transfer to less dusty areas; there is a presumption that the request will be granted.

The agency is counting on medical screening, respirators, and safe work practices to virtually eliminate the remaining cases of chronic byssinosis.[24] Medical surveillance is not used more than it is because the agency is concerned that the industry would not be able to transfer additional workers at risk to "clean" jobs.[25] Thus the Occupational Safety and Health Administration determined that employers can transfer the approximately 10 percent of new workers each year who are expected to contract byssinosis. The agency has assumed that if 20 percent of all cotton processing workers are new each year, the maximum number of employees that would have to be transferred to a dust-free environment each year would be 9,342, or about 2 percent of the total cotton process-

---

23. The Occupational Safety and Health Act in fact states, "Wherever practicable, the standard promulgated shall be expressed in terms of objective criteria and of the performance desired." 84 Stat. 1594.

24. Department of Labor, "Report to the Congress: Cotton Dust," p. 44.

25. Ibid., p. 45.

ing work force. This number includes employees who might choose to wear respirators, which, if properly worn, can reduce exposure levels from one-fifth to one one-hundredth, depending on the type of respirator.[26]

It is also estimated that 4,698 new employees will be protected each year by engineering controls. The average cost of engineering controls per byssinosis case avoided is $42,767, compared with the cost of $555 for medical surveillance, monitoring, and respirators.[27] Additional costs should be included for the medical surveillance program—for example, the cost to the employer and the employee of transferring workers at risk and the compensation paid to employees that is necessary to make them indifferent to wearing respirators. It is not likely that these costs would approach the $42,212 per employee difference between the average cost of engineering controls and a medical surveillance program.

The crucial question is, on what basis did the Occupational Safety and Health Administration decide that 2 percent rather than 3 percent of the labor force each year could be accommodated by a medical surveillance program? (The 4,698 workers who are to be protected by engineering controls represent only 1 percent of the labor force.) That decision may have cost up to $200 million per year.

It is unlikely, of course, that the agency asked this question. A basic tenet of the agency and of occupational health professionals is that engineering controls should always be used where feasible and that personal protective devices should only be relied on as a last resort. There are good reasons for this preference as long as costs are not considered (and health professionals have few incentives to consider costs). The reasons are: (1) it is more difficult for the agency to determine whether workers are wearing respirators properly than to measure ambient dust levels; and (2) the Occupational Safety and Health Act includes no enforcement mechanisms to ensure that employees follow safe work practices.

However, in the case of cotton dust, the Occupational Safety and Health Administration has determined that a medical surveillance program can be effective in preventing irreversible health impairment and relies on it to provide two-thirds of the benefits of the cotton dust stan-

26. Occupational Safety and Health Administration, "Occupational Safety and Health Standards: Cotton Dust," p. 27386. Employees may choose the type of respirator they want.

27. Ibid., p. 27380. Engineering controls are estimated to cost about $201 million annually and all other compliance provisions about $5 million.

dard.[28] It thus appears that the agency has lost an opportunity to establish a much more cost-effective pure performance standard. It could have promulgated a standard that simply stated that no employer shall allow an employee to progress to the advanced stages of byssinosis. An agency-sanctioned medical surveillance program could have been the enforcement mechanism. Employers could then have complied with the regulation by using cost-effective mixtures of engineering controls, work practices, respirator programs, medical transfer programs, safer grades of cotton, and more synthetic blending—factors that reduce the incidence of byssinosis but that do not necessarily reduce cotton dust levels.

Costs and Benefits

The previous discussion has assumed that the benefits of regulating cotton dust or byssinosis justify the costs. Although it appears that the Occupational Safety and Health Administration may not have selected the most cost-effective alternative, it is important to examine the relationship between the costs and benefits of the alternative finally selected.

According to the Department of Labor's report to Congress, the average cost of the final standard per case of byssinosis avoided is $8,658.[29] This is really the cost per case avoided each year. The Department of Labor found this number by dividing the annual cost of compliance by the total number of cases that would be avoided in steady state equilibrium, which would occur after a complete turnover of the labor force. Thus, either the annual cost of compliance should be added up until the steady state is reached and then divided by the steady state reduction in byssinosis, or the annual cost of compliance should be divided by the reduction in byssinosis prevalence among the annual new entrants to the work force. I have chosen the latter method to correct the Department of Labor estimate.

Assuming that the industry each year acquires new workers that make up 20 percent of the total cotton processing industry, as estimated in the standards' preamble, and not counting the cost of the nonengineering provisions, the average cost per case avoided is about $42,200 in 1977

28. Furthermore, the agency relies on medical surveillance, safe work practices, and respirators to control byssinosis completely in the cotton ginning industry, where the predicted byssinosis prevalence rate is 17 percent.

29. Department of Labor, "Report to the Congress: Cotton Dust," table VI-1, p. 28.

dollars. Two crucial questions need to be answered. Is this cost biased and is it a reasonable amount for society to pay?

My tentative conclusion is that the amount may be biased downward but that technological breakthroughs such as washing cotton or new forms of harvesting could reduce costs substantially. The following factors may have biased the cost per case downward:

1. The Occupational Safety and Health Administration chose the lowest of three cost estimates discussed in the preamble of the standards. The higher estimates were based on the agency's "Inflationary Impact Statement" and were about 36 percent and 83 percent higher than the lowest estimate (adjusted for 1977 prices).

2. The agency uses an estimate that there are 467,000 workers at risk, excluding those in cotton ginning, but does not cite any reference. The "Inflationary Impact Statement," citing a 1971 Bureau of Labor Statistics study and adjusting statistics for workers in the textile industry working only with synthetics or in finishing stages, estimates that only about 273,000 workers were actually exposed to cotton dust in 1971. Since 1971, employment in the textile industry has declined by 10 percent, and the movement toward synthetics has continued. These factors may bias downward the cost per case by 75 percent.

3. The byssinosis prevalence rates may be high by an undetermined amount since other studies have found lower rates, dust levels probably have been falling since the 1960s, and medical surveillance and respirator programs established since 1971 may have reduced the incidence of byssinosis.

4. The estimates are in 1977 dollars; thus they may be biased downward by about 20 percent at today's prices.

5. From one-half to two-thirds of the byssinosis cases are at the grade ½ level (occasional chest tightness on Mondays) and probably should not be counted in benefit estimates. The Department of Labor's report to Congress does not count these cases in its calculations of dollar benefits. This factor may bias the dollar costs downward by 50 percent.

6. The benefits in terms of reduced incidence will not be evident until a year or two after the expenditures on engineering controls are made. Employers have been given four years to comply with the requirements for engineering controls. This time gap may bias costs downward by about 10 percent.

The following factors may have biased the cost per case upward:

1. Workers already employed may benefit from the lower dust levels

attained. Although this seems plausible, I have not seen any medical evidence for this proposition.

2. The estimated compliance costs, which are based on a static technology, may decline with technological improvement. Real costs could decline by 5 to 10 percent per year for five years because of this factor. Thus, with strong technological progress, costs may be overstated by about 50 percent.

Another factor may create a bias either upward or downward. The Occupational Safety and Health Administration has estimated that 20 percent of the cotton processing labor force each year are new workers. According to the agency this is a conservative estimate based on the monthly data the Bureau of Labor Statistics collects. What is really needed are data on new workers who stay long enough to be in danger of grade one byssinosis. This number may or may not be 20 percent of the labor force per year.

When the quantifiable biases are multiplied by the estimate of $42,200 per case, the result is $134,000 per case. Since the unquantified biases and the factor with an unknown bias are on either side, there is no reason to believe that about $135,000 is not the best estimate. However, the range of uncertainty is probably $30,000 to $300,000.

The answer to the second question of whether this cost is reasonable requires an assessment of the amount society is willing to pay to avoid a case of byssinosis. There are, of course, several identifiable groups in society willing to pay for a reduction in byssinosis.[30] First, the willingness of workers to pay should be considered. Presumably workers are unwilling to pay much since they could avoid the risk of byssinosis by wearing respirators or choosing another job.[31] On the other hand, employers probably are willing to pay for a reduction in byssinosis. However, they already have the incentive to do so because of workmen's compensation costs, possible declines in productivity, and increases in sick leave. Thus these costs have probably already been internalized in the industry's cost and wage structure. Finally, the public may be willing to pay a considerable amount to reduce the risks of byssinosis. This willingness could be attributed to the public's altruism and compassion for disadvantaged

30. For a more complete discussion on the benefits to society of reducing occupational illness, see John Morrall, "OSHA and U.S. Industry," in R. Lanzillotti, ed., *Economic Effects of Government Mandated Costs* (University Presses of Florida, 1978).

31. Recall that the benefits accrue to new workers hired and that the risks of byssinosis have been well publicized.

workers in southern textile mills and the public's desire to reduce medical expenses that are furnished through taxes or insurance to byssinosis victims.

The Department of Labor in its report to the Congress on cotton dust estimated that the medical and lost productivity costs of grades one and two of byssinosis were about $44,000.[32] The estimate was derived by tracing the byssinosis-related costs of a new worker for forty years on the job and then fifteen years into retirement. Arbitrary, but perhaps reasonable, assumptions were made about lost work days accumulating up to thirty days per year, early retirements, medical costs, and even the administrative costs of government-funded medical assistance programs. Over the fifty-five-year period lost worker earnings, medical costs, and administrative costs were increased at annual compound rates of 4, 3, and 2 percent, respectively. Then the entire stream was discounted back to the present at a 4 percent "social rate of discount."[33] Clearly this procedure gives a biased estimate, especially when compared with estimates for the cost side that use a 10 percent discount rate, which is the rate used in this paper and in the Department of Labor report itself.[34] Although it is correct to inflate the value of lost earnings for assumed future productivity improvements, there is little rationale for inflating medical costs and administrative costs indefinitely over a period of fifty-five years.[35]

Clearly, a value-free and good workable rule is to treat both costs and benefits the same and to discount both by the same social rate of discount.[36] After all, just as a dollar today is worth a lot more than a promise

32. The Department of Labor study also estimated costs for grade three byssinosis but people with this stage of the disease were all retired workers who had worked in textile mills before byssinosis was recognized in the United States as an occupational disease. It is doubtful that medical surveillance and work awareness would allow the disease to progress to this grade today, even in the absence of a new standard.

33. See Department of Labor, "Report to the Congress: Cotton Dust," pp. 93–96, for these calculations.

34. For example, discounting an even benefit stream for fifty-five years at 4 percent rather than 10 percent produces a total benefit estimate almost two and a half times larger.

35. One could make a case, based on official predictions, that energy costs that are about 25 percent of annual compliance costs should be increased in real terms by up to 7 percent per year.

36. Robert S. Goldfarb, in "A Missing Link in the Social Rate of Discount Literature," *Journal of Public Economics*, vol. 6 (October 1976), pp. 309–12, proposes that one way to deal with the problem of agencies overstating the benefits of projects that they would like to see undertaken (a problem that has been well documented for the U.S. Army Corps of Engineers) is for the central authority to set

of a dollar paid to you ten years from today, a case of byssinosis avoided today is a lot more desirable than avoiding it ten years from now, especially since there is a nonzero probability of finding a cure for byssinosis.

Conclusion

The cost of the cotton dust standard appears to be quite high—perhaps $135,000 per byssinosis case avoided. The quantifiable benefits when properly discounted are probably about $20,000 per case avoided. It is difficult to know whether there are other benefits not yet quantified equal to the $115,000 difference that society will have to pay to reduce byssinosis prevalence, since evidence on society's willingness to pay to avoid morbidity equivalent to byssinosis is not available.

Even without this information, criticism of the cotton dust standard is valid, since there were more cost-effective alternatives available than the one chosen—even though the standard promulgated was more cost-effective than the across-the-board standard originally proposed. The current standard was probably chosen to minimize the differences in risk among sectors, not to minimize costs for a given level of byssinosis prevalence.

Furthermore, the Occupational Safety and Health Administration could have provided the same amount of benefits at a fraction of the costs if a pure performance standard had been promulgated. The agency could simply have stated that no employer shall allow any employee to advance to a harmful stage of byssinosis. The employer then would have been free to find the most cost-effective way of preventing byssinosis.[37]

---

higher social discount rates for agencies that are most likely to overstate benefits. Allowing agencies to discount benefits by a lower rate than cost is not in this spirit. (Note also that intergenerational benefits and irreversible harm to the environment are not being considered.)

37. The question of an enforcement mechanism remains, however. A fine set per case of byssinosis equal to society's willingness to pay to avoid a case of byssinosis would not only be cost-effective but would also maximize net benefits.

Cotton Dust:
A Regulator's View

MORTON CORN

THE Supreme Court recently followed the court of appeals in upholding almost in its entirety the cotton dust standard issued by the Occupational Safety and Health Administration. The upholding of a standard by the courts is not a judgment about the correctness of the regulatory approach. Rather it indicates the views of an objective third party charged with relating governmental activity to the laws and, I believe, current public opinion about the issues involved. The views expressed here about the regulatory approach to the development of the cotton dust standard existed before the standard was proposed and finally set.

The Occupational Safety and Health Act of 1970

The Occupational Safety and Health Act contains a clear statement about the issuing of standards. Section 6(b)(5) of the act says:

The Secretary, in promulgating standards dealing with toxic materials or harmful physical agents under this subsection, shall set the standard which most adequately assures, to the extent feasible, on the basis of the best available evidence, that no employee will suffer material impairment of health or functional capacity even if such employee has regular exposure to the hazard dealt with by such standard for the period of his working life. Development of standards under this subsection shall be based upon research, demonstrations, experiments, and such other information as may be appropriate. In addition to the attainment of the highest degree of health and safety protection for the employee, other considerations shall be the latest available scientific data in the field, the feasibility of the standards and experience gained under this and

109

other health and safety laws. Whenever practicable, the standard promulgated shall be expressed in terms of objective criteria and of the performance desired.[1]

The controversial phrase in this section is "on the basis of the best available evidence." What is the best available evidence? The review of available data by the Occupational Safety and Health Administration and the National Institute for Occupational Safety and Health provided information for the initial assessment made in the standard's original proposal, and the hearing record provides the public's view of the government's interpretation of the best available evidence. The directive states that *no* employee will suffer material impairment of health or functional capacity. This rationale differs from the threshold limit values set by the American Conference of Governmental Industrial Hygienists, which state that "nearly all employees will not suffer material impairment if exposed to the agent at the concentration indicated forty hours per week, fifty weeks per year for forty years."[2] The concept of threshold limit values anticipates that some individuals will be affected; the directive of the government does not.

History of Cotton Dust Regulation

The respiratory symptoms associated with byssinosis have been present in the U.S. mills since the mechanization of the cotton textile industry in the 1830s. Today between 250,000 and 800,000 U.S. workers risk contracting byssinosis each year because of their exposure to cotton dust. The first cotton dust standard was promulgated in 1964 under the Walsh-Healey Public Contracts Act of 1936. This standard set a cotton dust exposure limit of 1,000 micrograms per cubic meter. The dust referred to was the total amount of cotton dust in the air, also known as raw cotton dust. The British Occupational Hygiene Society recommended setting a standard requiring a maximum exposure level of 500 micrograms per cubic meter. The dust referred to by the society was dust without the so-called fly—large particles removed by a wire screen. In 1974 the American Conference of Governmental Industrial Hygienists reduced their threshold limit values, on which the 1964 standard had been based, to 200

1. Occupational Safety and Health Act, 84 Stat. 1594.
2. Threshold limit values for chemical substances in workroom air, adopted by the American Conference of Governmental Industrial Hygienists in 1980 (ACGIH, P.O. Box 1937, Cincinnati, Ohio 45201).

micrograms per cubic meter, the dust being measured with a vertical elu-triator that removed large dust particles roughly equivalent to the fly of the British standard.

Medical Evidence

Before the final cotton dust standard was promulgated medical evidence clearly documented a disease state associated with inhalation of cotton dust; however, classification of disease and the population at risk were not well defined. There were widely diverging estimates of the number of persons suffering from symptoms classified in different ways. The disease was classified as chronic or advanced byssinosis, as chronic obstructive lung disease, and as chronic bronchitis and emphysema. Although "brown lung" has been a term synonymous with disabling respiratory disease used by textile workers, the clinical nature of the disease was not delineated consistently. It was difficult for the Occupational Safety and Health Administration to sort out the definitions of disease present in the exposed population. However, it was evident that excess disease existed among the population most at risk. The work of Dr. Arend Bouhuys (see the paper by James Merchant in this volume) suggested that approximately 35,000 employed and retired textile workers were currently disabled. His study population suggested 200,000 workers currently at risk in the mills and 235,000 retired textile workers no longer employed in the industry.[3]

There was little evidence on the record associating the degree of disablement or impairment of the population at risk with the concentration of dust in the mill. Indeed, there seemed to be a good deal of evidence that the severity of the symptoms decreased progressively as cotton processing advanced from stage to stage—from the processing of the raw cotton to the final manufacturing operations. There were suggestions that a disease-provoking agent, still to be identified, was present in the raw cotton and that processing operations, including washing, removed it. It was also suggested that efforts at control could be delayed until the agent was identified.

The relationship of airborne dust to the disease was further complicated by the lack of evidence on the size of dust particles causing the

3. Arend Bouhuys and others, "Byssinosis in the United States," *New England Journal of Medicine*, vol. 277 (July 27, 1967), pp. 170–75.

symptoms. If, indeed, cotton dust was an immunologic reagent, any particle size of cotton dust in the human respiratory tract could cause an immunologic response. There seemed, however, to be some evidence that the finer cotton dust, which could be inhaled, was associated with byssinosis; this explained the efforts to eliminate fly, or large particles, in Britain and the use of elutriators to remove the large particles in the United States. The relationship between dust particle size and the risk associated with inhaled cotton dust is still uncertain.

The dose-response curve associated with cotton dust (that is, the relationship between cotton dust exposure and byssinosis prevalence) suggested that even individuals exposed to very low concentrations of cotton dust who were sensitive to the dust would experience symptoms of early stages of byssinosis. Data at that time suggested that respirable cotton dust might start affecting individuals at concentrations only slightly higher than concentrations of suspended background dust (fifty to sixty micrograms per cubic meter in rural areas). This information shifted the focus of regulatory efforts from the regulation of suspended cotton dust to prevent physical impairment or disease to the regulation of suspended cotton dust to the extent technically feasible.

Feasibility Considerations

It was already evident that the Occupational Safety and Health Administration would have to recommend the lowest feasible level of appropriately size-segregated cotton dust because even at that level, persons exposed would experience symptoms. The agency had to consider, however, whether the conditions in the cotton industry could be engineered to achieve the recommended level of cotton dust.

The cotton processing industry is an old one, housed in large, old buildings. It had suffered economically before cotton dust regulation had become an issue and had only begun to regain its economic viability. The industry also had been charged to control another major occupational health hazard in its facilities, namely noise. Because of all these factors, cotton dust regulation in textile facilities would be very expensive.

The Occupational Safety and Health Administration had enough medical evidence to document the effect of cotton dust on the work population. However, the agency had to infer from the information available a specific dust concentration that could be achieved through engineering controls in the industry. This was not easy, and furthermore, the burden of proof was on the government to show that such engineering was feasible. Also, the government would gain credibility if it could show that the cost of regulation would not cripple the industry. Early estimates of costs to the textile industry of cotton dust control ranged from $500 million to $1 billion. Extremely high dollar costs had also been presented to the agency by contractors charged with estimating the cost of controlling noise in the textile industry.

The agency decided that the standard would not take effect immediately throughout the entire industry and that the industry would pay for engineering controls (depending on the extent of engineering needed and the cost) over a period of up to seven years from promulgation of the standard.

The pay-back period was controversial. The government essentially was saying that eventually all those exposed to cotton dust would be exposed to the same average dust concentration—an exposure level deemed unsafe, but one that could be technically achieved. However, since the industry cannot afford to achieve this level at the same rate in all its sectors, employees will have to endure exposure to unacceptable levels of cotton dust for different periods of time.

To discover workers' response to this approach, meetings were held with union representatives and others close to cotton processing workers. Meetings were also held with the managers of textile companies. It was agreed that a sequential approach to control was feasible. During the interim period, before engineering controls had been put into place in all industry sectors, protection would be provided through respirators, even though testimony at hearings had determined that respiratory protection programs, to be effective, require fittings, instruction, and enforcement. (Some people cannot even be fitted properly at all with respirators.) The strain of wearing respirators eight hours a day and the difficulty encountered by those who do have some respiratory impairment also clearly highlighted respirators as only an interim solution. But during the variable period of implementation, respirators as well as medical surveillance would be required and carefully monitored.

Permissible Exposure Limit

The permissible level of exposure to cotton dust was selected on the basis of evidence that different stages of the manufacturing process present varying degrees of risk. The initial proposal called for a permissible exposure level of 200 micrograms of vertical elutriated cotton dust per cubic meter for all segments of the cotton industry. The final standard established a permissible exposure level of 200 micrograms per cubic meter for yarn manufacturing, 750 micrograms per cubic meter for slashing and weaving operations, and 500 micrograms per cubic meter for all other processes in the cotton industry and for nontextile industries in which workers are exposed to cotton dust. The standard also has specific provisions for environmental and medical surveillance, engineering controls, work practices, respirators, employee training, and signs and record-keeping. The initial proposal of an exposure level of 200 micrograms per cubic meter for the entire industry was rejected because achieving a uniform exposure level throughout the industry was not technically feasible. The Occupational Safety and Health Administration concluded that the exposure limit set for slashing and weaving—750 micrograms per cubic meter —corresponded to a byssinosis prevalence in that sector of less than 10 percent. The cost of complying with a standard of 200 micrograms per cubic meter in weaving operations alone could have cost up to $1.3 billion; it was also not clear that the lower exposure level could be achieved with present technology.

Summary

To establish the cotton dust standard the Occupational Safety and Health Administration has had to participate in certain trade-offs, which are now being hotly debated. Despite the congressional directive, a feasible permissible exposure limit could not be found at which no worker would suffer any material impairment or adverse effect. Maximum cotton dust exposure levels were selected according to what was technically and, to some extent, financially feasible. The cotton dust standard epitomizes, I believe, a rational approach to regulation in which all factors are carefully weighed to produce a compromise in effective controls for worker protection, one deemed to be feasible for the affected industry.

Part Three

Saccharin: A Scientist's View

CLIFFORD GROBSTEIN

THERE IS a necessary and growing involvement of scientists in policy issues that demand analysis and understanding of relevant scientific data. The past decade has brought an avalanche of issues in this category. Science in what I call the policy mode is the developing response. I think this mode of science eventually will be recognized as a third major kind of scientific activity. Basic science is oriented toward new understanding, and applied science focuses on new instrumental technology. Science in the policy mode is oriented toward more effective social policy. It draws on both basic and applied science but adds a dimension of its own.

Although this kind of science cannot be ignored in policy analysis, it is rarely decisive in policymaking, in part because available scientific knowledge almost never exactly fits the given issue. What is relevant frequently comes from several disciplines whose perspectives are not easily integrated and whose members have little incentive to focus on the issue. The relevant information generally is of little intrinsic interest to the discipline, is too narrow in focus to be basic, and makes too small a contribution to actual implementation to be called applied. Relevant information often is concerned with safety, health, alternative solutions, and even aesthetics and long-term values. Little time or money will be spent on information relating to such considerations until the information becomes essential to decisionmaking. Then, since sound scientific investigation takes time, policymakers often find themselves frustrated and inadequately guided by objective facts. They plaintively seek, in the words of one senator, a one-armed scientist who cannot respond to questions with "on the one hand . . . but on the other hand." However, scientists who involve themselves in controversial policy diminish their usefulness if they do not stubbornly adhere to the primacy of scientific fact. A decisional crisis cannot create a scientific conclusion out of inadequate data.

117

Saccharin as a food additive is not one of the most profound public issues. The issue has, however, become one of the noisiest and, in the process, something of a bellwether in the area of food safety policy. The issue may be formulated by a disarmingly simple question: can saccharin safely be added to foods as a nonnutritive sweetener? The key word here is safely, which I will discuss later. Without the issue of safety the question becomes one of simple fact: is saccharin added to foods as a nonnutritive sweetener? The answer, of course, is yes. Part 1 of the National Academy of Sciences–National Research Council 1978 report on saccharin and food safety policy noted that use of saccharin in foods in the United States increased from 1.3 million pounds in 1961 to 6.4 million pounds in 1977, an average increase of 10.5 percent per year.[1] Much of the increase occurred after the Food and Drug Administration banned the use of cyclamates as a nonnutritive sweetener in 1969. In 1976, 1.3 million pounds of saccharin went into cosmetics, pharmaceuticals, tobacco, cattle feed, and other substances. Soft drinks and tabletop sweeteners accounted for more than 80 percent of saccharin use (2.9 million pounds and 1.2 million pounds, respectively). Most of the remainder was added to fruits, premixes, juices, candy, gum, jellies, and other foods.[2]

Although saccharin consumption is widespread, it is by no means equally distributed among the population. Reliable data on consumption by particular individuals or groups are hard to come by. The National Academy of Sciences assessment, however, on the basis of a consumption study done by the Market Research Corporation of America, noted that "women are greater users of saccharin than are men" among the estimated 50 million to 70 million American saccharin consumers.[3] Included among the consumers are estimated to be about 80 percent of the one million or so diabetics and about one-third of the children under ten years of age.

How *safe* is this pattern of consumption? Safety is not a simple concept; in particular it has a subjective as well as an objective component. Scientists always seek objective data on which all informed individuals can agree. Risks posed by a pattern of saccharin consumption can be assessed objectively if one can determine the frequency of a harmful effect causally

1. National Academy of Sciences, National Research Council Institute of Medicine and Assembly of Life Sciences, Committee for a Study on Saccharin and Food Safety Policy, *Saccharin: Technical Assessment of Risks and Benefits*, pt. 1: *Saccharin and Its Impurities* (Washington, D.C.: NAS, 1978), p. 2-2.

2. Ibid., pp. 2–5.

3. Ibid., pp. 2–8.

linked to saccharin. The frequency measures risk to an *average* individual. Individuals vary, however, both in susceptibility to risk and in willingness to accept risk. Different groups may also show different degrees of risk aversion. Risk, therefore, is subject to objective measurement and scientific study. Safety, on the other hand, must be specified in terms of individual and group values and can only be registered by consensus or other political mechanisms.

Risk and Saccharin Consumption

What risk is associated with saccharin consumption? At the moment the issue centers on the risk of bladder cancer, although this has not always been the focus of concern. Pure saccharin is a substituted benzene ring compound, synthesized as an unanticipated by-product at Johns Hopkins University in 1879.[4] It was at first thought possibly useful as a food preservative or an antiseptic. Its outstanding characteristic, however, was its high potency in stimulating taste receptors for sweetness—350 times more potent by weight than ordinary sugar. Moreover, the substance undergoes little or no chemical change in the body and hence yields no energy (calories). This makes saccharin a nonnutritive sweetener and a potential substitute for ordinary sugar when sugar is undesirable—for example, because of its high calorie yield or the difficulties it causes diabetics. Saccharin was used as a sugar substitute as early as 1907.

Concern about the possible toxicity of saccharin had surfaced well before 1907, with occasional reports of appetite loss and gastrointestinal upset. In 1912 saccharin was banned from foods but was reinstated when a sugar shortage developed during the First World War. After the war, toxicologic studies on saccharin effects on animals began to appear. Early lifetime or shorter studies gave little cause for alarm. In 1951 lymphosarcomas were reported in animals exposed to saccharin, but the result was discounted because incidence also was high in untreated controls.[5] In 1955 the Committee on Food Protection of the National Academy of Sciences–National Research Council reviewed the existing scientific data

4. Constantin Fahlberg and Ira Remsen, "On the Oxidation of O-toluene Sulphonamide," *Chemische Berichte,* vol. 12 (1879), pp. 469–73.

5. O. Garth Fitzhugh, Arthur A. Nelson, and John P. Frawley, "A Comparison of the Chronic Toxicities of Synthetic Sweetening Agents," *American Pharmaceutical Association Journal,* Scientific Edition, vol. 40 (1951), pp. 583–86.

on saccharin and offered the opinion that "the maximal amount of saccharin likely to be consumed is not hazardous."[6]

In the early 1960s the use of saccharin (and cyclamates) increased, leading the Food and Drug Administration to again consult the National Academy of Sciences. A report from the latter in 1968 differed from the 1955 evaluation only in suggesting further study of possible cancer-inducing effects of saccharin, since by 1968 testing methodologies had significantly improved.[7] In 1970 another National Academy of Sciences report affirmed that moderate saccharin consumption probably did not create risk. Nonetheless, the report called for comprehensive toxicologic testing and for epidemiologic studies on diabetics and pregnant women.[8] It also suggested exploring possible toxic interactions between saccharin and other substances being consumed.

Subsequent studies involved chronic administration of saccharin to rats over two generations—a toxicologic procedure introduced to detect low-level environmental toxins that might require cumulative exposure to saccharin or exposure at particular stages of the life history. In several such studies results suggested that saccharin significantly increases the frequency of bladder cancer in second-generation male rats when administered at 5 percent of the food intake.[9] Although interpretation of the results was complicated by possible effects of impurities and the high dosage levels, these results for the first time seriously posed the question whether saccharin added to human food is likely to increase the incidence of bladder cancer.

This question should be answered most cogently by studies of human populations. Such studies are the business of epidemiology, the discipline dealing with the incidence of human disease. In the welter of variables in

6. National Academy of Sciences, Committee on Food Protection, "The Safety of Artificial Sweeteners for Use in Foods" (NAS, 1955).

7. National Academy of Sciences, Committee on Food Protection, Ad Hoc Committee on Nonnutritive Sweeteners, "Nonnutritive Sweeteners: An Interim Report to the Food and Drug Administration, U.S. Department of Health, Education, and Welfare" (NAS, 1968).

8. National Academy of Sciences, Committee on Food Protection, Ad Hoc Committee on Nonnutritive Sweeteners, "Safety of Saccharin for Use in Foods" (NAS, 1970).

9. Wisconsin Alumni Research Foundation, "Preliminary Report: Chronic Toxicity Study—Sodium Saccharin," paper presented at Harrison House, Glen Cove, N.Y., April 26–28, 1972.

human populations the epidemiologist looks for significant correlations between a suspected factor and disease incidences as a clue to causes of disease and possible prevention. In the case of saccharin, changes in bladder cancer incidence during the period of increasing saccharin use as well as increased incidence among either heavy saccharin users (diabetics) or workers in saccharin production plants are possible correlations to be studied. The approach is limited, however, by the usually complex causal backgrounds of human disease. Bladder cancer incidence, for example, is known to be increased by smoking, caffeine, and in certain occupations.[10] Moreover, chemically induced cancer has a long latency, effects appearing as much as ten to forty years after initial exposure. Statistical, epidemiologic approaches to a complex causal background, therefore, may miss weak carcinogens exerting small effects, especially if there are unrecognized oppositely acting influences (anticarcinogens). Although epidemiology is the most direct approach to risk assessment of a substance like saccharin, it is insensitive to low-level effects and requires cautious interpretation of both positive and negative borderline results. Moreover, it can only be applied *after* problems have arisen.

The 1978 National Academy of Sciences report includes a detailed analysis and evaluation of existing epidemiologic studies of saccharin.[11] The report concludes the following.

1. Significant changes in incidence of bladder cancer in relation to the time period of changing saccharin consumption patterns are not detectable. However, interpretation of the negative finding is complicated by limitations of methodology, particularly in separating saccharin effects from those of, for example, cigarette smoking. Smoking also is known to affect bladder cancer incidence—and its frequency has been changing in the population over the same interval.

2. Studies on diabetics, who as a group consume a lot of saccharin, show no positive correlation between saccharin consumption and bladder cancer. However, the negative finding is not regarded as persuasive for the general population because diabetics are not typical in genetic background or metabolic characteristics; the studies give no data on individual saccharin consumption; and smoking habits and occupational exposures were not examined as possible confounding factors.

10. National Academy of Sciences, *Saccharin: Technical Assessment,* p. ES-7.
11. Ibid.

3. Studies of comparisons between saccharin consumption by people already diagnosed as having bladder cancer and consumption by people free of the disease neither support nor refute an association between saccharin and bladder cancer. Most such studies conducted in the past are regarded as noninterpretable on methodological grounds. Two studies that do meet methodological criteria for reliability gave seemingly opposite results. One found a statistically reliable but small excess of saccharin users among bladder cancer patients when compared with a group of patients without cancer that were carefully matched for other characteristics. A second study found no such excess. Given the small difference in the actual results, the methodological differences between the two studies make a decision between the conflicting possible interpretations impossible.

Thus, available direct epidemiologic data on human populations do not really answer the questions whether saccharin added to foods has in the past altered incidence of bladder cancer, and whether such addition is likely to do so in the future.

Given the inconclusiveness of the epidemiologic data on humans, one is forced back to consider the animal results. The National Academy of Sciences committee that reviewed all available animal data concluded that "saccharin is a bladder carcinogen in male rats," as demonstrated by two-generational studies but not by one-generational studies. In reaching this conclusion the committee considered that effects were produced only by high saccharin dosages, that is, 5 percent or 7.5 percent of the diet. The question arises whether so high a dose might induce general toxicity of which the bladder tumors are a secondary consequence. The committee found no convincing evidence that this was the case and concluded that the high dosage was legitimate and necessary to demonstrate weak activity of the material under test. The committee also approved the two-generational approach, finding that it had not produced reproductive toxicity and may well indicate particular susceptibility of fetuses in female rats. From the absence of a demonstrated correlation between dose level and tumor incidence, the committee concluded that, given a weak effect, a modified experimental design might show such a correlation but that the fact that such a correlation was not shown does not vitiate the conclusion that saccharin induces bladder cancer in rats.

What does the conclusion about rats imply about the risk of saccharin to humans? Here one enters a difficult area for regulatory decision about saccharin or any other suspected human toxin.[12] There are two strong arguments for assuming that a substance that produces tumors in rats will also produce them in humans. The first may be called a theoretical argument since it stems from a generalization based on much comparative biological data. It asserts that fundamental metabolic processes are very similar in all organisms and certainly in groups as closely related as mammals. Since tumor production is thought to involve fundamental metabolic processes of this kind it is unlikely that what induces tumors in rats will not do so in humans. The second argument may be called empirical since it rests on specific comparisons rather than a generalization. It notes that of the known human carcinogens almost all have been shown also to be carcinogenic for one or more animal species. The fact that the converse statement cannot be made is due to unwillingness, for obvious reasons, to test suspected or known carcinogens on humans.

Against these two arguments must be set a third, also empirical. Although the generalization that there is a correlation between human and animal effects is sound, there are many specific instances of quantitative differences in response between species. Several mechanisms accounting for such differences can be cited—for example, varying permeability to the active substance, varying metabolic conversion of precursor to the active substance, and varying inactivation by detoxifying mechanisms. Such variations make it difficult to make simple extrapolations from one species to another, particularly concerning quantitative effects. Saccharin appears to be a weak bladder carcinogen in rats, and it may be a weaker or stronger one in humans, but it cannot legitimately be labeled as totally innocuous. Thus the National Academy of Sciences committee concluded: "Saccharin must be viewed as a potential carcinogen in humans" but "the state of the art in extrapolation does not permit confident estimation of the potency of saccharin as a cause of cancer in humans."[13]

Tests that do not involve whole animals are another general source of information for assessing carcinogenic effects. These tests are often referred to as short-term because, if successful, they make unnecessary the

12. S. Weinhouse, "Problems in the Assessment of Human Risk of Carcinogenesis from Chemicals," in H. H. Hiatt, J. D. Watson, and J. A. Winsten, eds., *Origins of Human Cancer,* Cold Spring Harbor Conferences on Cell Proliferation, vol. 4, book C: *Human Risk Assessment* (Cold Spring Harbor, New York: Cold Spring Harbor Laboratory, 1977), pp. 1307–09.

13. National Academy of Sciences, *Saccharin: Technical Assessment,* pp. ES-4, ES-10.

heavy cost in time and money of either epidemiologic or animal studies.[14] Short-term tests vary in character but generally are carried out on laboratory-contrived systems rather than on whole animals. They depend on responses that are assumed to be aspects of the actual process of cancer formation, aspects that can be demonstrated both more conveniently and more quickly than the whole process. Most such tests are based on genetic change—on the partially validated assumption that carcinogenesis involves modification of the cell's replicative macromolecules. On the basis of that assumption a mutagenic agent inducing genetic change may be expected to be carcinogenic and vice versa. Empirically there is a substantial but not complete correlation between agents inducing the two kinds of cellular change.

Saccharin had been tested in twenty-one short-term assays at the time the National Academy of Sciences report was completed. Sixteen of the assays were negative and five were positive. The committee concluded that "because saccharin appears to be a carcinogen of low potency, the variations in findings might be expected." The results were seen as "compatible with the *in vivo* carcinogenic effects" but not providing "definitive information on the interpretation of risks to humans."[15]

Extrapolating information on human risk from animal data for regulatory purposes is complicated for additional reasons. When a substance is administered to a group of animals and increases the frequency of tumors it is referred to as carcinogenic or cancer-inducing. It must be remembered, however, that the carcinogenetic process is not completely understood; evidence suggests that it is a complicated process consisting of many steps.[16] Experimental studies in animals have shown that (1) the initiating substance (precarcinogen) usually is chemically altered within the body before it can begin inducing cancer (when it becomes an ultimate carcinogen); (2) the active compound generally interacts with macromolecules within the cell—often with DNA—possibly thereby initiating a first genetic change; (3) other substances, so-called cocarcino-

14. Joyce McKann and Bruce N. Ames, "The Salmonella-Microsome Mutagenicity Test: Predictive Value for Animal Carcinogenicity," in Hiatt, Watson, and Winsten, eds., *Origins of Human Cancer.*

15. National Academy of Sciences, *Saccharin: Technical Assessment,* p. TS-4.

16. Isaac Berenblum, "Historical Perspective," in Thomas J. Slaga, Andrew Sivak, and Rosewall K. Boutwell, *Carcinogenesis: A Comprehensive Survey,* vol. 2: *Mechanisms of Tumor Production and Cocarcinogenesis* (Raven Press, 1978), pp. 1–10.

gens, may be necessary to begin or facilitate the initiatory steps; (4) the initial changes are often followed much later by alterations in the affected cell or cells and the descendant cells before a clinically evident tumor appears; and (5) the appearance of such a tumor, sometimes years after the initial change, often depends on substances, called promotors, that by themselves cannot initiate the first genetic change.

These facts imply that cancer's onset may consist of many steps and causes and that the substances that increase tumor incidence in animals (or humans) may not all do so in the same way. Saccharin, for example, is unusual among chemical carcinogens in that it does not undergo chemical change in the body and does not appear to attach directly to genetic material. In addition, it has been reported to act as a promotor under certain circumstances in which another carcinogen acts as an initiator. Should a distinction be made for regulatory purposes among precarcinogens, ultimate carcinogens, cocarcinogens, and promotors?

The argument for making such distinctions centers on the matter of quantitative extrapolations from animal data for humans. There is substantial evidence, for example, that moderate to high levels of radiation cause cancer in animals and humans. There has, however, been a long and still unresolved debate about the effects of low levels of radiation. Observations of low-level radiation exposure require long periods of time and many cases to be statistically reliable. Because suitable data have been unavailable, the debate has focused on how to extrapolate effects to zero radiation exposure and especially on whether a minimum threshold of effect exists above zero exposure. Many scientists argue that whatever the truth may prove to be, a cautious position must assume absence of a threshold, since if this is an error it is on the safe side. Similar caution is urged with respect to chemical carcinogens. However, the argument might be different for precarcinogens and promotors. Actual carcinogens might, for example, resemble radiation, which also is assumed to act by inducing genetic change, and might be subject to inactivators or antagonists that are effective only up to some threshold concentration level. If this is true, extrapolation of animal data to assumed lower exposure levels in humans would be different for carcinogens and promotors, though both might be related to increased cancer incidence in animal tests.

The National Academy of Sciences food safety committee considered this matter and decided against making a regulatory subclassification of carcinogens along these lines. The committee reasoned that although the experimental literature on carcinogenesis justifies and requires such distinction, the significance and mechanisms of the several causes of different stages of carcinogenesis, particularly for humans, are still not well enough understood to be introduced into regulation. Given the still rudimentary knowledge of the nature of chemical carcinogenesis, it would be confusing and possibly harmful to design regulatory strategies to fit concepts still being evaluated and possibly yet to be modified by laboratory studies. Although regulatory judgment on carcinogenicity should take the state of knowledge into account, it necessarily must lag behind the theoretical forefront of that knowledge just as it must err on the side of caution in areas of factual uncertainty.

The National Academy of Sciences report recorded the conclusion that "further laboratory studies to establish the carcinogenicity of saccharin are not needed under existing law."[17] This conclusion referred to the adequacy of the data bearing on the ability of saccharin to increase bladder cancer incidence in male rats. According to both the Food and Drug Administration's general mandate and the specific mandate of the Delaney clause (contained in the Food Additives Amendment of 1958), regulatory attention to these data is required by the evidence at hand. However, the report also noted, "research leading to a better understanding of methods for qualitative and quantitative extrapolation, *in utero* exposure, and the mechanisms of cancer promotion would be highly desirable."[18] In short, if saccharin is to remain in the American diet, and recent congressional action suggests that it will—at least for a while—more research on the effects of saccharin is essential. The Food and Drug Administration/National Cancer Institute Interagency Saccharin Working Group has in progress a major epidemiologic study on the significance of saccharin in human bladder cancer. The National Academy of Sciences report suggests additional epidemiologic studies. Also, industrial sources have begun a series of studies intended to quantify rats' response to saccharin to determine whether *in utero* exposure is critical and to establish whether saccharin acts directly as a primary carcinogen or exerts influence in some other way. It is hoped that these research efforts will provide a more informed base for regulatory action.

17. National Academy of Sciences, *Saccharin: Technical Assessment*, p. ES-5.
18. Ibid.

Regulatory Policy and Health

As the scientific study of cancer has progressed, the number of cancer's possible causes has increased. During the past fifty years scientists have advanced as alternative hypotheses chemical induction, viruses, mutation, reversion to embryonic states, failure of immune recognition, and other mechanisms. As results pour in none of these has been excluded; in fact, the accumulating data suggest that all may be involved. Cancer more and more is considered to be a collection of diseases with overlapping pathological features but with conceivably different etiologies and underlying mechanisms.

The trend of epidemiological data in recent years has laid greater and greater stress on external factors as etiologic agents in human cancer. This emphasis results from the finding that the pattern of incidence of different cancers varies in different locales and cultures and that groups moving from one locale or culture to another conform in incidence pattern, given time, to their adopted site rather than to their site of origin. This points to important effects of local environmental factors, whether physical, chemical, nutritional, or more generally biological and social. Concern in general has been increasing about the consequences of environmental change and the effects of the dispersion of chemical and physical agents developed by modern technology. Particularly regarded with suspicion are radiation and a variety of chemicals.

This legitimate concern is easily exaggerated. Despite the increase in certain kinds of cancer, notably of the lung, an epidemic or imminent catastrophe is not apparent. Indeed, incidence of stomach cancer, for example, appears to be declining. Overall, there is no striking evidence that our way of life now is much more carcinogenic than it was at the century's beginning, although the lag in expected effect does not exclude the possibility that at the end of this century epidemiological data will reflect effects of high levels of cancer-inducing substances in the last decade or two.

The main point, however, is that because of the multiplicity of new suspected carcinogens that are being introduced into our way of life and because of the possibility that they interact synergistically in unknown but possibly complex ways, it is becoming less and less feasible to deal with the carcinogen problem on an empirical, item-by-item basis. Efforts are now being made to improve testing programs both technically (developing short-term screening tests) and administratively (centralizing federal testing responsibility to feed information to all regulatory agencies concerned with carcinogenicity). Such procedures are essential but can only be expensive temporary measures. What is needed is (1) a more complete and deeper understanding of the biology of carcinogenesis; (2) a theory of chemical carcinogenesis that makes it possible to forecast carcinogenic potency from molecular structure; (3) more knowledge of interactions, particularly synergistic ones, between various carcinogenic effects, including natural background factors such as radiation; (4) more detailed information on genetic and developmental variation in human populations that affect carcinogenic susceptibility. Until the last two are acquired the setting of tolerance levels for individual weak carcinogens is almost entirely guesswork.

Rather than devote too much time and energy to assessing individual weak carcinogens, it may be more productive to develop strategies to reduce carcinogenic burden, that is, the aggregate carcinogenic impact of life-styles and resultant environments on populations and subpopulations. Such strategies would simultaneously reduce exposure to many carcinogenic agents. For example, there is reason to believe that the substitution of mechanical refrigeration for chemical preservatives may be a factor in reduced incidence of stomach cancer. Similarly, chemical pesticides almost certainly add more to carcinogenic burden than would more extensive use of biological pesticides.

The necessity for item assessment and regulation, with all of their cost and nuisance, would be far less if the design of technical devices and systems included more input based on criteria for health. When short-term economic benefits alone are considered in relation to a projected technology, the long-term loss may register not only in health care dollars but also in increased morbidity, shortened life span, and often ghastly deaths. Sound food safety policy cannot, therefore, be based solely on improved detection of weak carcinogens. It requires an overall assessment of how food habits, food production, and food delivery systems affect health. From this perspective saccharin is a minor component of a much larger and more pressing problem.

One cannot rely on either fundamental scientific or technological approaches to detect or cope with the larger problem of food safety in a complex, technology-based society. Scientific and technical competence are required but this competence must be exercised in the context of broad socially defined purposes. Science in the policy mode, to return to my opening theme, is not primarily oriented to strengthening knowledge as a value in itself or to extending instrumental mastery over nature. It is directed toward decisionmaking that will integrate all of our aspirations. Saccharin must be sweet but also safe in all its uses. Attaining this goal requires more than accurate measurement of either sweetness or carcinogenicity. It requires sound judgment to face the residual uncertainty that will always exist when dealing with real world phenomena. These can be assessed and influenced but never fully forecast or totally controlled.

Saccharin:
An Economist's View

OLIVER E. WILLIAMSON

THIS PAPER explains the rudiments of a new approach to regulation—the decision process approach. This approach was evolved during the deliberations of the National Academy of Sciences Committee for a Study on Saccharin and Food Safety Policy.[1] Although the decision process approach focuses on the recent (and continuing) saccharin controversy, the same general approach can be applied to most food safety issues and can help fashion a more rational regulatory policy in nonfood areas as well.

The National Academy of Sciences committee made operational what Herbert Simon has recently referred to as procedural rationality, as distinguished from substantive rationality.[2] Whereas substantive rationality takes the definition of the problem as given and refers to the "extent to which appropriate courses of action are chosen," procedural rationality

This paper draws extensively on my involvement in the National Academy of Sciences Committee for a Study on Saccharin and Food Safety Policy. Research on this paper was facilitated by a grant from the National Science Foundation. I also acknowledge the help I received from Sherwin Rosen, who commented on an earlier version of this paper, and from Howard Kunreuther, Peter Linneman, Elena Nightingale, Victor Goldberg, Richard Posner, Roger Noll, and seminar presentations at the Industrial Organization Workshop and the Information, Decision, and Control Workshop held at the University of Pennsylvania.

1. National Academy of Sciences, National Research Council Institute of Medicine and Assembly of Life Sciences, Committee for a Study on Saccharin and Food Safety Policy, *Food Safety Policy: Scientific and Societal Considerations*, pt. 2 (Washington, D.C.: NAS, 1979).

2. Herbert A. Simon, "Rationality as Process and as Product of Thought," *American Economic Review*, vol. 68 (May 1978, *Papers and Proceedings, December 1977*), p. 9.

131

deals with how complex public policy issues are structured. It ensures that the relevant dimensions are identified and ordered and that indirect consequences are described in a way that can contribute to a well-considered public policy.

Although procedural rationality is a logically anterior rationality exercise, it has received nowhere near the attention that has been directed at substantive rationality. This is unfortunate, since self-conscious attention to structure can often yield deep insights. Indeed, "solving" a problem once the dimensions and qualitative properties have been carefully organized is frequently trivial. But how can the necessary structuring be accomplished? The decision process approach is one way.

Following are a brief history of the saccharin issue, a description of different ways to approach food safety policy, and an explanation of the decision process approach.

The Saccharin Dilemma

The Food and Drug Administration did not take steps to remove saccharin from the food supply until a Canadian study of two generations of rats disclosed an increase in bladder cancer among male (especially second-generation) rats. As a consequence of both the general safety requirement of the Food Additives Amendment of 1958 and the Delaney anticancer clause contained in that amendment, the commissioner of the Food and Drug Administration concluded that "saccharin may no longer be approved as a food additive."[3] The Delaney clause reads, in part: "No additive shall be deemed safe if it is found to induce cancer when ingested by man or animal, or if it is found, after tests which are appropriate for the evaluation of food additives, to induce cancer in animal or man."[4] Inasmuch as the law prohibited the Food and Drug Administration from taking the benefits of saccharin (or any other food additive) into account, the commissioner could only permit the continued consumption of saccharin if it could be shown to be an effective over-the-counter drug.[5]

3. U.S. Department of Health, Education, and Welfare, Food and Drug Administration, "Saccharin and Its Salts: Proposed Rule Making," *Federal Register,* vol. 42 (April 15, 1977), pt. 3, p. 20002.

4. 72 Stat. 1786.

5. Food and Drug Administration, "Saccharin and Its Salts," p. 20002.

The proposed saccharin ban was controversial, particularly since an acceptable saccharin substitute did not exist. Cyclamates had been banned by the Food and Drug Administration in 1969,[6] and the possibility of developing a nonnutritive sweetener "that is safe, economical, and esthetically acceptable for widespread use" was judged to be remote.[7] Congressmen reportedly received more mail on saccharin than on any issue since the Vietnam war. Public Law 95-203 was passed in November 1977 and provided for a moratorium during which period the National Academy of Sciences was asked to review federal food safety policy, with special emphasis on saccharin.

The National Academy of Sciences Committee for a Study on Saccharin and Food Safety Policy was divided into two panels. Panel 2 had the task of devising a rational policy for food safety into which saccharin could be fitted. Concurrently, panel 1 was to assess the risks and benefits of saccharin. The principal study on which the risk projections relied was the Canadian rat study. Epidemiological evidence relating to saccharin consumption in World War II failed to establish a conclusive risk in humans of bladder cancer.[8] In addition, although a plausible case could be made for the health benefits of saccharin—including its use as a weight control measure, for diabetes, in the prevention of dental caries, and in the preparation of pediatric drugs—the studies that had been done on these matters were judged to be unsatisfactory. Panel 1 concluded that "no study that meets the current criteria for an adequate clinical trial has been conducted explicitly to examine the effectiveness of saccharin in the control of weight or diabetes."[9]

Panel 1 also was reluctant to include nonhealth benefits as a part of its assessment, observing that "there is no system for obtaining an overall estimate of benefit. This is pertinent because many of the benefits attributed to saccharin are subjective, for example, improvements in taste

6. Ibid., p. 19997.
7. National Academy of Sciences, National Research Council Institute of Medicine and Assembly of Life Sciences, Committee for a Study on Saccharin and Food Safety Policy, *Saccharin: Technical Assessment of Risks and Benefits*, pt. 1: *Saccharin and Its Impurities* (NAS, 1978), p. 4-29.
8. Ibid., pp. 3-81, 3-82. The two best epidemiological studies of saccharin reviewed in the National Academy of Sciences report (see ibid., pp. 3-84 through 3-92) were conflicting. One study reported that the risk of bladder cancer in males is increased (by a factor of 0.6) by the use of nonnutritive sweeteners. The other study reported no statistically significant effect for either sex.
9. Ibid., p. 4-37.

or psychological well-being. As such, benefits are evaluated in different terms than risks."[10] The possibility that demand curves reflect perceived benefits of all kinds was evidently dismissed. This may reflect a failure to appreciate the way in which demand curves suggest relevant benefits. There were only two economists on the panel, and many of the biomedical scientists were unmoved by and skeptical of economic analysis. One panel member expressed his concern by saying, "The decisionmaking process should not be modified by economic considerations." But it was not merely that economics was thought to be an unwanted intrusion into a biomedical domain. Had the demand curve for saccharin been well defined, and if it could have been argued that it accurately reflected health benefits and health hazards (or if demand could have been disaggregated to include subsets of the population that were believed to be least well informed and most susceptible to hazards), use of demand curves to characterize benefits would have been easier to accept. However, the aversion to demand curve valuation of benefits was understandable, given the fact that neither aggregate nor disaggregated demand curves for saccharin were known or could be estimated with confidence.

Approaches to Food Safety Policy

I have designated five alternative conceptual approaches to the food safety issue, of which the saccharin issue is a part. Four will be considered here and the fifth in the following section.[11]

The Food and Drug Administration Approach

This approach divides the world into safe and unsafe parts. Although Richard Merrill recognizes that this is a somewhat arbitrary position, he regards it as supportable and observes that the legal standards governing the regulation of food additives are mandatory.[12]

10. Ibid., p. 4-4.
11. There is a sixth approach: the liability approach. Thus anyone can market anything with undisclosed hazards, but victims are entitled to compensation if they successfully sue for damages. The problem with this approach emerges when causality is difficult to establish—as unresolved liability for radiation-induced cancer demonstrates. The problem is even more pronounced for weak carcinogens such as saccharin that have long latency periods. And of course the liability approach is weakened even more by supplier bankruptcy and fly-by-night suppliers.
12. See the paper by Merrill in this volume.

To the extent that regulatory agencies influence the rules under which they operate, and they often do, the mandatory rules defense should be challenged. If the rules are defective, if the agency is in the best position to recognize this, and if the agency has made no concerted effort to correct the rules, the agency must then be comfortable with them. This seems to have been the case with the Food and Drug Administration and saccharin. Thus, although Merrill asserts that the rules on food additives are supportable, his main arguments in favor of the agency's recommendation to ban saccharin are that the agency had no choice and that the regulatory climate was unfavorable to any other decision. This is not an adequate basis for sound public policy.

The Food and Drug Administration believes that food additives containing any carcinogenic hazard, however small, should be banned, regardless of the additive's benefits. This was an extreme position even when the Delaney clause was passed, when "there were only a few known [and very potent] carcinogens—soot, radiation, tobacco smoke, and β naphthylamine."[13] Since then the capacity to detect chemicals in food in quantities as small as parts per trillion has been perfected. According to Elena Nightingale and Frederick Robbins, "The significance of these tiny amounts in carcinogenesis is unknown. Because of the ability to detect minute concentrations of substances, absolute safety may be an impossible goal."[14] Absolute safety nevertheless seems to have been the goal of the five people who signed the minority statement in the National Academy of Sciences' report on food safety policy and saccharin (the panel 2 report). As the president of the National Academy of Sciences, Philip Handler, interprets the minority statement, "Only a zero probability of cancer is acceptable; if that probability is greater than zero, the substance should be deemed of high risk and removed from the food supply."[15] This position is consistent with a literal reading of the Delaney clause and was the position of the Food and Drug Administration's commissioner in April 1977 when he proposed the saccharin ban.

Traditional Food and Drug Administration views on net benefit assessment surfaced early in panel 2's deliberations. As already noted, some of

13. Richard Wilson, "Risk Caused by Low Levels of Pollution," *Yale Journal of Biology and Medicine,* vol. 51 (January–February 1978), p. 48.

14. Elena O. Nightingale and Frederick C. Robbins, "Food Safety Policy: Scientific and Societal Considerations," *Impact* (1979), p. 3.

15. Letter of transmittal, Philip Handler to Joseph A. Califano, Jr., February 28, 1979, National Academy of Sciences, *Food Safety Policy,* p. 3.

the panel's biomedical scientists believed that the usual food safety decision process should remain unmodified by "economic" considerations. Instead, "scientific" factors should govern, and all-or-nothing decisions should be dictated by the evidence. That this view did not prevail within panel 2 moved Fred Abramson, a signer of the minority statement, to express embarrassment over the "casual attitudes toward science" reflected in the report.[16] As Joshua Lederberg has observed, however, "the literal language of the Delaney Amendment . . . has no scientific justification."[17] Grobstein's reference to science in the policy mode plainly extends the reach of science beyond that which Abramson would entertain.

Abramson's narrow conception of science is nonetheless the prevailing mentality among many physicians and much of the health regulatory establishment in formulating health policy. Richard Neustadt and Harvey Fineberg observe that physicians "often think simplistically . . . [and regard] health [as] an absolute value."[18] Neustadt's and Fineberg's analysis of the swine flu decision disclosed that "doctors . . . rarely think in probabilistic terms and, if asked, dislike it. . . . As scientists accustomed to thinking about experiments and 'truth,' they were uncomfortable expressing subjective estimates"[19]—to say nothing of making net benefit assessments. Instead, physicians seem to favor worst-case scenarios. Indeed, reference was made during panel 2's discussions to a saccharin catastrophe if a ban were not adopted. Such a siege mentality contributed to the swine flu fiasco.

The Risk Classification Approach

The dictum that the law should be fair has obvious appeal. One way to ensure fairness is to adopt the standard that similar risks should be treated similarly. This view was expressed often during panel 2's delibera-

16. Statement by Dr. Fred P. Abramson in *Saccharin Ban: Oversight,* Hearing before the Subcommittee on Health and the Environment of the House Committee on Interstate and Foreign Commerce, 96 Cong. 1 sess. (Government Printing Office, 1979), pp. 23–25. Of the five signatories of the minority report, three were biomedical scientists.

17. Joshua Lederberg, "A System-Analytic Viewpoint," in *How Safe Is Safe? The Design of Policy on Drugs and Food Additives,* Academy Forum Series (National Academy of Sciences, 1974), p. 80.

18. Richard E. Neustadt and Harvey V. Fineberg, *The Swine Flu Affair* (GPO, 1978), p. 88.

19. Ibid.

tions and is the core of Peter Hutt's scheme for reforming food safety decision rules.[20]

Stage one of Hutt's scheme involves a risk assessment. He argues that a uniform basis for scaling risks should be adopted—a relatively uncontroversial proposal. The cutting edge in Hutt's program arises at stage two, the risk classification stage, which is discussed below. The possibility that risks of each kind can be reduced is addressed at stage three of Hutt's program. Introduced at this stage is a sensitivity to cost-benefit considerations.

In the distinctive second stage of Hutt's proposal he suggests that food risks first be classified into high, moderate, and low risk categories. All high risk items would be banned, all moderate risk items would be flagged with warnings, and all low risks would be disregarded.[21] Although Hutt does not offer his own criteria for risk classification, he is evidently sympathetic with the standards suggested by Richard Wilson. Thus, Hutt observes:

> Perhaps the most difficult aspect of classifying food risks into high, moderate and low risks is in determining the appropriate dividing lines. Professor Wilson has suggested that, based on linear extrapolation from animal testings, a risk higher than 10^{-2} (1 in 100) should be banned, a risk lower than 10^{-5} (1 in 100,000) should be regarded as trivial, and a risk between those two levels should be the subject of public education, warning, and efforts at reduction.[22]

I have four problems with this approach. First, a classification based strictly on probabilities implicitly assumes that losses are constant for all items both within and across risk classifications. Suppose that the risk of an adverse outcome associated with the use of item i is p_i and that the loss, in the event that the unwanted outcome materializes, is L_i. The expected loss, then, from using i (at normal levels) is $p_i L_i$. Now if L_i is constant for all items, the hazard can be described by reference to p_i alone. If, however, L_i is not constant for all items, the risk classification proposed by Hutt would presumably lead to the banning of items that produce trivial losses and to the continued consumption of items that result in significant losses. This is unsatisfactory.

20. Peter Hutt is a legal specialist on food and drug regulation. He served as general counsel to the Food and Drug Administration in the early 1970s.

21. In his proposal Hutt also encourages measures that would reduce the likelihood of adverse outcomes, thus permitting items to be shifted from higher to lower risk categories. Peter B. Hutt, "Unresolved Issues in the Conflict Between Individual Freedom and Government Control of Food Safety," *Food Drug Cosmetic Law Journal*, vol. 33 (October 1978), pp. 584–85.

22. Ibid., pp. 582–83.

A second problem with comparable risks receiving comparable treatment is that benefits are ignored. Ignoring benefits would be acceptable only if benefits were identical. But since they are not, judgments about acceptable risks depend on an item's benefits as well. For example, a drug that has a high probability of producing severe side effects but that also has lifesaving qualities is apt to be judged by many physicians and users as carrying an acceptable risk.[23] By contrast, an item that involves low risk but negligible benefit, possibly because a good substitute is available, lacks redeeming value and ought not to be consumed. Regulation on the basis of risk alone cannot make these distinctions.[24]

A third problem with the risk classification approach is that it implicitly assumes that all members of the population are identical. Thus if individuals (or distinguishable subsets) are represented by j, then p_{ij} represents the probability that an unwanted side effect will occur when item i is used by individual j; L_{ij} is the attendant loss; and B_{ij} is the benefit realized by individual j. The Hutt approach suppresses the benefits and treats probabilities and losses as though these were independent of the user characteristics.

Finally, the risk classification approach seems to presume that probabilities are known within an order or two of magnitude.[25] While this may often be true, at times this possibility is debatable. Thus the agreed range of the number of bladder cancers attributable to saccharin varied from zero to 10^3, but some placed the upper bound higher than this. Possibly

23. This raises the anomaly of physicians apparently being willing to make probabilistic judgments in treating individual patients but, as indicated earlier, being reluctant to accept risks in formulating public policy when a "zero risk" alternative is described.

24. Note, however, that Hutt does allow for substitutes at stage three of his proposed regulatory process.

25. Simon's experience as chairman of a National Academy of Sciences committee on air quality studies is germane. He observes that it was easy to formulate a subjective expected utility model of the problem, but that this was not helpful: "There is a production function for automobiles that associates different costs with different levels of emissions. The laws governing the chemistry of the atmosphere determine the concentrations of polluting substances in the air as a function of the level of emissions. Biomedical science tells us what effects on life and health can be expected of the pollutants. All we need do is to attach a price tag to life and health, and we can calculate the optimum level of pollution control. There is only one hitch. . . . None of the relevant parameters of the various 'production functions' are known—except, within half an order of magnitude, the cost of reducing the emissions themselves." Simon, "Rationality as Process and as Product of Thought," pp. 13–14.

worst case probabilities could be used when such disputes arise. This, however, might invite exaggerated estimates. The risk classification approach, in its apparent appeal to so-called hard numbers, invites litigation by those to whom worst case scenarios appeal.

Although the risk classification approach is a definite improvement over the Food and Drug Administration's approach, it is seriously defective in remediable ways. It prepares the way for the economic approach.

The Net Benefit Approach

The economic approach assesses risks in net benefit terms. This requires definition of both direct and indirect benefits and costs. Gross benefits are ordinarily taken as the area under the demand curve, but most members of both National Academy of Sciences panels doubted that this was an appropriate benefit measure. Their doubt was partly explained by lack of familiarity with net benefit analysis, and also reflected concern that this procedure assigned excessive weight to monetary valuations and that consumer preferences reflected ignorance or were shaped by advertising and ought not to be respected. Furthermore, a good estimate of the demand curve for saccharin had not been made (although it could have been had an appropriate study been sponsored).

Indirect health benefits and costs will, of course, be reflected by the demands of knowledgeable consumers. As noted earlier, however, the committee doubted consumers' knowledgeability. Separate estimates of health benefits could nevertheless have been attempted. But although the committee was prepared to enumerate the sources of health benefits and costs, the data base did not permit these to be quantified; nor was the committee keen to make such an effort. Aside from subsidized medical care, indirect third-party effects are not obvious in the case of food additives.[26] For reasons that the Food and Drug Administration has presumably found congenial, it has been prohibited, under legislative mandate, from considering benefits at all. However, although the net benefit approach to food safety policy is conceptually superior to both the Food and Drug Administration and risk classification approaches, and although cost-benefit analysis can and often does help to organize issues (most of the defects in the risk classification approach result from bene-

---

26. The prospect that cancer patients would receive subsidized medical care is a possible third-party effect that distorts perceived demand. Greater risks would be taken than would otherwise be the case if such subsidized care were not available.

fit-cost omissions and mistakes), the economic approach also has short-comings. Four are especially notable.

First, cost-benefit analysis is abused too often and thus has earned a bad name. Second, policymakers sometimes lose control when complex issues are settled by technicians. Third, cost-benefit analysis sometimes encourages premature quantification. Fourth, the aggregation features of cost-benefit analysis are suspect.

The abuses of net benefit analysis are legion—abuses by the U.S. Army Corps of Engineers working on the Tennessee-Tombigbee Waterway through Mississippi and Alabama being a recent example.[27] Richard Cooper, previously the chief counsel to the Food and Drug Administration, flatly states that cost-benefit analysis "is not viable" and cites his experience working on the National Energy Plan, in which there was "hardly any economic projection for which an econometrician and his friendly computer couldn't be found to provide support."[28] Using incomplete data to deal with complex issues leaves too much latitude in which cost-benefit calculations can be tilted to reflect the inclinations of interested parties rather than the outcome of dispassionate analysis.

Decisionmakers are also concerned that decisionmaking will be appropriated by technicians who engage in premature quantification and arbitrary aggregation. Another concern is that cost-benefit analysis of food safety requires the valuation of human lives in monetary terms, which many people find distasteful.[29] Risk-benefit assessment is a possible resolution of this problem.[30] This involves a two-stage analysis in which health consequences are evaluated first (the risk assessment). Trade-offs between health benefits and health hazards can thus be expressed in terms such as a "quality adjusted life year,"[31] which avoid the need to place monetary value on health. All other economic consequences are assessed in the second stage. No explicit aggregation of stages one and two is attempted. Instead, both parts are reported and

27. See Wayne King, "Army Engineers Under Attack for Their 'Dig We Will' Zeal," *New York Times,* February 4, 1979. More generally, see Aaron B. Wildavsky, *The Politics of the Budgetary Process* (Little, Brown, 1974).

28. Richard M. Cooper, "The Role of Regulatory Agencies in Risk-Benefit Decision-Making," paper delivered at the midyear animal drug meeting of the Animal Health Institute, Key Biscayne, Florida, October 26, 1978, p. 12.

29. Food Safety Council, *Principles and Processes for Making Food Decisions,* December 1978, p. 41.

30. Ibid., pp. S-3 to S-8.

31. Richard Zeckhauser and Donald Shepard, "Where Now for Saving Lives?" *Law and Contemporary Problems,* vol. 40 (Autumn 1976), pp. 5–45.

the final disposition is left to the policymakers. Risk-benefit assessment is thus less dispositive than benefit-cost analysis. But not everyone is comfortable with it. Sheldon Samuels believes that risk-benefit assessment is a "cosmetic version of cost-benefit analysis" and that "most attempts at determining the socially acceptable risk by these methods really amount to exercises in determining the economically acceptable."[32]

The Information Approach

Suppose that two equally effective and identically priced additives are on the market, one risky and the other not. It would seem that disclosure of the hazards associated with the risky product is the best way to drive it out of the market. However, the success of disclosure would depend on whether (1) the probability of the unwanted consequence crosses some threshold level of sensitivity;[33] (2) exposure to the additive is voluntary; (3) some users are children; (4) the incentives for intelligent risk-bearing are undistorted by the prospect of subsidized medical care; (5) the number of hazards is low in relation to the capacity of individuals to keep hazard warnings straight; and (6) the expense of disseminating information is low.[34] If, after these factors are considered, the quickest and cheapest way to eliminate the risky product (that everyone agrees should vanish) is to ban it, why not?

The principal objection is that to do so is an infringement of consumer sovereignty.[35] After all, most risky choices violate one or more of the above conditions. The consumption of peanut butter, for example, in-

32. Sheldon W. Samuels, "Determination of Cancer Risk in a Democracy," *Annals of the New York Academy of Sciences,* vol. 271 (1976), p. 423.

33. For a discussion of some of the experimental and empirical findings on this question, see Howard Kunreuther and others, *Protecting Against High Risk Hazards: Public Policy Lessons* (Wiley, 1978).

34. The list is not exhaustive. For a discussion of other factors that some observers believe are relevant to safety assessments, see William Lowrance, *Of Acceptable Risk* (Los Altos, Calif.: N. M. Kaufman, Inc., 1976), chap. 4.

35. See Kenneth Arrow for a discussion of paternalism and its hazards. He observes that paternalism involves "a firm assertion that a significant fraction of the people are judged by their peers to be incompetent to handle their own affairs, to understand themselves so poorly that the necessarily imperfect and impersonal knowledge that remote experts have of them is better control than they can have over themselves." Kenneth J. Arrow, "Government Decision Making and the Preciousness of Life," in Laurence R. Tancredi, ed., *Ethics of Health Care,* Papers of the Conference on Health Care and Changing Values, Institute of Medicine, November 27–29, 1973 (National Academy of Sciences, 1974), pp. 44–45.

volves a risk of exposure to aflatoxin, a very potent carcinogen. Voluntary assumption of risk is permitted for peanut butter, so why not for food additives?

The food safety policy committee was plainly distressed by anomalies of this kind. It reasoned that unless there were compelling reasons to do otherwise, carcinogenic hazards ought to be considered in a symmetrical way. The easiest symmetrical rule, but a very crude one, would be to ban all hazards or ban none (and rely entirely on warnings). The risk classification approach is symmetrical in terms of its three-way probability classification, but it is also defective for reasons already explained. The net benefit approach, while more discriminating, also has objectionable features. This brings us to the decision process approach.

The Decision Process Approach

Although both of the economists on panel 2 prepared memoranda dealing with cost-benefit analysis, and although Richard Zeckhauser discussed risk-benefit assessment with the panel, members were unwilling to adopt either of these assessment technologies.[36] This did not, however, imply a rejection of a rational approach to food safety issues. It reflected, rather, a sense that the problems and the data were not yet quantifiable and that a more primitive approach was needed to deal with issues. What was needed was a procedure that was orderly and comprehensive—requiring decisionmakers to confront rather than suppress the difficult issues—yet that neither forced unwarranted quantification nor precluded judgment.

Self-conscious attention to procedure is important for two reasons: it has significant rationality ramifications, and it has an important bearing on fairness. Simon's distinction between substantive and procedural rationality, to which I referred earlier, arises in connection with the former.

Procedural rationality deals with "the effectiveness, in light of human cognitive powers and limitations, of the *procedures* used to choose actions."[37] Complex public policy issues are especially troublesome. When dealing with these, there is a constant danger "that attention directed to a single facet of the web will spawn solutions that disregard vital consequences for the other facets."[38] Although saccharin would seem to be

36. My own efforts are set out in a memorandum to the panel, May 25, 1978. Sherwin Rosen's discussion appears in a draft, September 1978.
37. Simon, "Rationality as Process and as Product of Thought," p. 9.
38. Ibid., p. 13.

a relatively comprehensible issue, panel discussions were frequently piecemeal, and "solutions" were repeatedly offered that neglected or suppressed important dimensions. Procedural assistance is evidently needed when such difficulties arise. Simon counsels that such assistance should be in two parts: ordering the issues on the public agenda in a rational way, and appropriately attending to indirect consequences.[39] Such an abstract statement of procedural purposes needs, however, to be made operational. Simon does not indicate how procedural rationality should be implemented. The decision process approach is one possibility.

Attention to process is also important for reasons that relate to fairness. As Zeckhauser observes, many analysts "dismiss too quickly the significance of having an equitable and widely accepted process."[40] In many societal decisions, the procedure by which the decision is made may be as important as the efficiency assessment: "How people feel about the society in which they live matters a tremendous amount."[41] Lederberg makes a similar point when he observes that "one of the axial conflicts of modern life [is] that there are many who value *equality* of access to [health] care . . . and the *equality* of exposure to risk even higher than the absolute benefits."[42] More generally, the point is this: perceptions that the process by which decisions are reached is open and that the interests of affected groups, especially disadvantaged ones, are not arbitrarily aggregated are important to the acceptability of a procedure.

The Food Additive Decision Tree

The decision process approach sets out issues in a comprehensive, hierarchical way that leaves policymakers in control and yet discourages arbitrary or capricious decisionmaking. The decision process approach somewhat resembles risk-benefit assessment but is less formal, breaks problems down more completely, and allows for judgments to be made at different stages of analysis. It makes both use and user distinctions, which permits differential hazards and benefits to be recognized. Rather, therefore, than impose a single, uniform policy on all uses and users, a discriminating policy can be devised instead.

The basic analytical aid of the decision process approach is the decision tree. Figure 1 illustrates the basic decision tree for evaluating food

39. Ibid.
40. Richard Zeckhauser, "Procedures for Valuing Lives," *Public Policy,* vol. 23 (Fall 1975), p. 446.
41. Ibid., p. 459.
42. Lederberg, "A System-Analytic Viewpoint," p. 92.

Figure 1. Decision Tree for Evaluating Food Additives

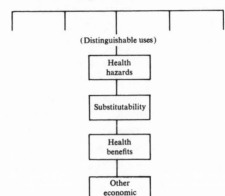

additives. Decisions to approve, ban, or otherwise restrain the use of a food additive can be made at any stage in the hierarchy. Consideration of additional factors would be unnecessary if decisions could be reached on the basis of factors analyzed early on (in the categories of the hierarchy) or if further assessment would be unduly speculative. Figure 2 illustrates a more complete food additive decision tree, which is composed of the following attributes.

1. *Hierarchical ordering.* The tree breaks down the food additive issue into parts and orders these sequentially. This calls attention to issues according to their relative importance and also eliminates the need for a comprehensive study if a decision can be reached on the basis of high priority considerations. The order in which issues are addressed has both substantive and procedural significance. Failure to reach a consensus on ordering might indicate perceived procedural unfairness.

2. *Conservatism.* Traditional values are featured early in the decision tree. This ensures that no drastic changes will be introduced without according great weight to the traditional way of dealing with the issues. Since there are obviously benefits in protecting the food supply from problematic hazards, the evaluation of food additives should give prominent and early attention to hazards.[43]

3. *Equity and efficiency.* Because of the tension between equity and

43. This is not, of course, an immutable characteristic of decision process analysis. If traditional values are thought to be inappropriate—because of societal changes or reassessments—these could be assigned a lower position in the hierarchy.

Figure 2. Food Additive Decision Tree

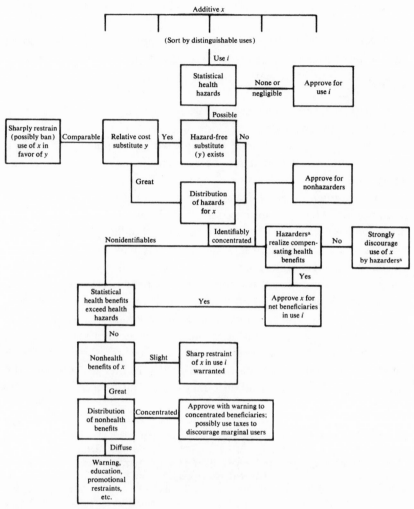

a. Those who are subject to hazards.

efficiency in health care and the importance of equity in health procedures, efficiency appears late in the sequence. The concern here is that efficiency should not serve special interest groups at the expense of people with less power.

4. *Completeness and openness.* Decisions ought not to be made arbitrarily or capriciously. That is, relevant dimensions of a problem ought

not to be suppressed without explanation. The food additive decision tree forces decisionmakers who would foreshorten analysis to do so openly and presumably with reason.[44]

5. *Substitutability.* The evaluation of a food additive can often be ended early if decisionmakers know of good substitutes. The tree addresses substitutability early and encourages solution by substitution whenever feasible.

6. *Health benefits.* To ban a substance for which no good substitutes exist and for which health hazards are more than offset by health benefits is ludicrous and makes trouble for any food safety policy. An analysis of health effects is essential for the resulting policy to be rational and acceptable.[45]

7. *Discrimination.* When feasible, the different uses and users of a food additive should be taken into account. An additive may pose greater hazards when used in one way than in another. Similarly, the hazards or benefits of an additive used in a particular way may vary among distinguishable members of the population. A uniform policy that does not recognize distinctions among uses and users may be unnecessarily crude.

8. *Augmentation.* Although the food additive decision tree is reasonably comprehensive, it is not exhaustive. Augmentation is possible when special features or follow-on opportunities are thought to exist. If, for example, special user characteristics (such as income or ignorance) are found to be significant to the decision or if remedies can be found by supporting research on substitutes, they can be introduced easily. Deci-

44. This need be no more than a statement such as "I have gone this far and no further because I have no confidence in processing this issue in a more refined way for the following reasons." Reasons could include poor data at lower levels of the decision hierarchy, or limitations of the regulatory process. Whatever the reasons, the dilemmas should be exposed. (Conceivably data shortcomings can be overcome or a more refined regulatory process devised to make further processing feasible in the future.) As Nightingale and Robbins observe, "Balancing of risks and consideration of benefits already implicitly enter into current regulatory decisions—as is the case with nitrites. It is probably better to consider them explicitly." Nightingale and Robbins, "Food Safety Policy," p. 8.

45. Stephen Breyer and Thomas Erlich, in a joint letter to David Hamburg, propose the following simple test of effectiveness: "The decision, when implemented, must, on balance, save lives." National Academy of Sciences, *Food Safety Policy,* p. SC-20. This is a somewhat narrow definition of health benefits but reveals a widely held belief. The public outcry that greeted the proposed saccharin ban, which was viewed as irrational, and the congressional request that the National Academy of Sciences review the saccharin issue partly resulted from the ban's neglect of health benefits.

sions, moreover, are not final. Policymakers can reprocess information using the decision tree as they receive new information.

More generally, the food additive decision tree has the property of being a "decision aid" rather than a "decision made." This and the attributes described above were responsible for the general approval given it when I first presented the decision tree to selected members of the National Academy of Sciences food safety policy committee and a group of economists.[46] And although opinions on panel 2 about the decision tree's utility varied, it was generally agreed that the decision process approach helped to structure issues.[47] A separate chapter of the panel's final report describes the decision tree schema.

Applications

Three brief and incomplete applications of the decision process approach follow. At best they are suggestive. The first application is hypothetical, involving a food coloring, the second involves saccharin, and the third, peanut butter.

Food coloring. Suppose that there is a dye, D_1, which animal tests have recently shown to have carcinogenic potential. The same tests do not disclose any hazards for a substitute dye, D_2, which is only slightly more expensive. Except as food coloring, D_1 and D_2 have no food uses (for example, they have no special taste, nutrient, or known health benefit properties). Working through the decision tree, it is possible to ascertain that (1) D_1 poses statistical health hazards; (2) D_2 is a hazard-free substitute; and (3) D_2 is only slightly more expensive than D_1.

If warnings would not be subject to the limitations noted in the section on the information approach, a warning should be made against the consumption of D_1; otherwise it should be banned. At this point it would be possible to end the evaluation that has been made using the decision tree, since further processing of information would add nothing.

---

46. Robert M. Solow chaired the October 18, 1978, meeting at which I first presented the food additive decision tree. Participants included Kenneth J. Arrow, Rashi Fein, Thomas C. Schelling, Jeffrey Harris, Peter Temin, and Paul Joskow. Members of the food safety policy committee present were Don Price, Sherwin Rosen, Sheldon W. Samuels, and myself. Richard Sheffler was present in his capacity as staff director of the Ad Hoc Committee on Economics of Food Safety. National Academy of Sciences, *Food Safety Policy,* p. H-4.

47. The minority dissent in panel 2's report appears to be less about the decision tree (chap. 4) than about its applications (chap. 9).

Termination of the decision tree exercise does not, however, imply that no further analysis is warranted. For example, if banning is contemplated and if the hazards posed by D_1 are small, it might be argued that inventories of D_1 should be sold with hazard warnings rather than destroyed. Policymakers might also be concerned about unemployment and factories left idle. The more severe and concentrated these effects, the stronger the case would be for redeployment relief.

Saccharin. The saccharin issue is no different from any other food safety issue. However, it does pose more complex problems because of saccharin's interesting health benefits.

Saccharin has several distinguishable uses. It is used as a nonnutritive sweetener for diet purposes (for diabetics and to control obesity), in dentifrices, and in pediatric drugs. Saccharin is at worst a weak carcinogen. Its potency is one-millionth that of aflatoxin, a substance produced by certain fungi and found in molding peanuts and certain grains.[48] The ingestion of saccharin in dentifrices, for example, is negligible, as is the statistical health hazard of using saccharin as a dentifrice. Approval of saccharin as a dentifrice is indicated.

The statistical health hazard of using saccharin to control weight may be small but not clearly so negligible. Since saccharin is the only nonnutritive sweetener currently permitted in the U.S. food supply—cyclamate was banned in 1969—the distribution of hazards becomes important. The risk of using saccharin as a sweetener is thought to be concentrated in children and fetuses of pregnant women.[49] Whether the health benefits more than compensate for the risk is problematical. At the least, obstetricians should counsel patients against consumption, and parents should be advised to restrict consumption among children. The remainder of the population could be warned against high consumption but be allowed to continue using saccharin as a weight control measure (benefit).[50]

The decision tree can also be used to evaluate saccharin's use by

48. U.S. Congress, Office of Technology Assessment, *Cancer Testing Technology and Saccharin* (GPO, 1977), p. 22.
49. National Academy of Sciences, *Food Safety Policy,* p. E-1.
50. Whether a significant number of saccharin users actually lose weight is unknown. Many users evidently increase caloric intake from other foods when sugar is replaced by a nonnutritive sweetener. Plainly, however, the potential for losing weight without sacrificing sweets is increased when saccharin is available. Saccharin may also enhance a sense of well-being among those who maintain their caloric intake by using it—and surely improved quality of life is a significant health benefit.

diabetics and in pediatric drugs. The main point, however, is that the food additive decision tree breaks problems down and processes issues in a way that exposes the relevant dimensions and makes possible a rational resolution. The more that is known about the benefits and risks, the more quantitative, hence complete, these assessments can be.

Peanut butter. Aflatoxin content in peanut butter is not supposed to exceed fifteen parts per billion.[51] There are nevertheless individual samples that exceed this level. Since aflatoxin is a potent carcinogen (a million times more potent than saccharin), it presents a statistical health hazard. No good substitutes for peanut butter exist, nor does it have any special health benefits. Peanut butter is, however, an inexpensive source of protein. Although there are other cheap sources of protein (for example, soybeans), they are not taste substitutes. The possibility that protein deficiencies would arise among children in low-income groups thus counsels against the hasty banning of peanut butter.

Aflatoxin is also present in animal feeds (especially corn) and thus shows up in both meat and dairy products. Even if peanut butter were banned, what could be done about these products? The distressing fact is that aflatoxin hazards can never be eliminated; they can only be reduced. This suggests that efforts to improve the screening technology for detecting aflatoxin are needed. How far these efforts should go is a net benefit issue for which the decision tree yields no specific help.

Relation of the Decision Process Approach to the Food Safety Policy Report

As with most committee decisions, final reports reflect compromise. The final report of panel 2 of the National Academy of Sciences food safety policy committee was no exception. Although the panel found the decision process approach congenial and devoted a large portion of a chapter to the development of the food additive decision tree, the crucial chapter dealing with current policy issues and recommendations came out in favor of using a modified risk classification approach to assess saccharin.

This, in my judgment, was a mistake. As I have already shown, the dictum that similar risks should be treated similarly is fundamentally flawed. The popular appeal of risk categories, however, cannot be denied.

51. National Academy of Sciences, *Food Safety Policy*, p. 3-35.

Fortunately, the risk classification approach recommended in the report is much more flexible than Peter Hutt's scheme.[52]

Panel 2's use of risk categories goes beyond assignment of three levels of risk (high, medium, and low) to allow for the possibility of limiting or discontinuing use. "In some cases, this may mean assessing the objective [health?] or perceived [economic?] benefits so as to weight them against risks."[53] Furthermore, "the range of regulatory options for a given risk category should be broad so that the option selected can be carefully matched to the particular case. In many instances an option lying between total discontinuance of use and unrestricted use may be optimal either temporarily or indefinitely."[54]

Assigning a substance to a risk category does not automatically lead to policy consequences but is just the first step. The analysis also entails distinguishing among uses and users and allows for health and other benefits. Evidently the main justification for the initial risk classification is its appeal to the public and to nonspecialists who have less appreciation for the nuances of the more comprehensive—and crucial—decision process analysis that follows.

Conclusion

As matters stand now, if a food additive poses a demonstrated carcinogenic risk, however small, it is banned—without regard for health benefits, substitutability, use and user incidence, economic consequences, and the possibility that less extreme regulatory measures might be effective. Some characterize this tradition as science and resist any changes in the regulatory process. But as Lederberg observes, regulation governed by or, more generally, in the spirit of the Delaney amendment lacks scientific justification.[55] The time has come for the Food and Drug Administration to engage seriously in science in the policy mode. The National Academy of Sciences food safety policy report offers the administration the opportunity to initiate major and overdue regulatory reform.[56]

52. Hutt, "Unresolved Issues."
53. National Academy of Sciences, *Food Safety Policy,* p. 9-16.
54. Ibid., p. 9-17.
55. Lederberg, "A System-Analytic Viewpoint," p. 80.
56. Whether the Food and Drug Administration will seize the opportunity remains to be seen. Food safety is an emotional issue. An unsympathetic Food and

Procedural rationality in general and the decision process approach in particular are responsive to the spirit of Eli Devons's remarks about the role of the economist.[57] Devons concludes with the observation that "there are many complex problems of policy to which the economist does not know the answer. . . . On such questions there might be more understanding by the public of the issues involved if economists exercised self-restraint and confined themselves to attempting to *explain the nature and complexity of problems,* rather than providing conflicting and widely divergent solutions."[58]

Whatever its impact on food safety reform, the decision process approach can usefully be applied to regulatory reform more generally. Although there is a widely held view that regulation is perversely administered to benefit those who are regulated (and evidence to support this position), this is not an inevitable outcome. As has recently been shown, some rather simple policy guidelines at the Federal Communications Commission have had a positive impact on regulatory outcomes.[59] If piecemeal policy guidelines can have a significant impact, the prospects for the decision process approach, which is more systematic and comprehensive than guidelines, are surely much better.[60]

Drug Administration commissioner and his staff could easily frustrate reform by adopting a "white knight" posture when Congress considers whether existing food safety policy should be modified.

57. Eli Devons, *Essays in Economics* (London: Allen and Unwin, 1961), chap. 2.

58. Ibid., p. 46; emphasis added.

59. Margaret F. Barton, "Conditional Logic Analysis of FCC Decisionmaking," *Bell Journal of Economics,* vol. 10 (Autumn 1979), pp. 399–411.

60. I do not, however, think that use of the decision process approach will lead to a regulatory scheme along the lines of "total carcinogenic burden," a concept presented by Grobstein at the end of his paper in this volume. Although the decision process approach provides a systematic way to evaluate a variety of substances, it does not preclude the need for item-by-item assessment.

Saccharin:
A Regulator's View

RICHARD A. MERRILL

GIVEN the current legal standards that govern the regulation of food additives and the Food and Drug Administration's historical handling of the issue, the agency's 1977 decision to propose a ban on saccharin was inevitable. Although some soft drink enthusiasts question the conclusion that saccharin is a carcinogen—albeit a weak one—in laboratory animals, that verdict has been confirmed by every scientific body that has reviewed the data. No independent observer has seriously suggested that, in the face of the evidence and the Food and Drug Administration's previous interpretation of the law, the agency could have refrained from initiating proceedings to ban saccharin from food.

The proposed ban elicited a reexamination of current food safety policy. Many critiques, including the National Academy of Sciences study, have brought useful insights to the debate over this policy.[1] Nevertheless, it is fair to question whether the handling of the saccharin issue is representative of current policy. I believe a good case can be made that current regulation, despite its complexity, yields correct decisions in the majority of cases and at less expense than would accompany more elaborate decision-making approaches.

Several features of the saccharin controversy remove it from the ordinary run of food safety decisions, which themselves are unlike many other health-focused decisions made by regulatory agencies. Decisions about the

---

1. National Academy of Sciences, National Research Council Institute of Medicine and Assembly of Life Sciences Committee for a Study on Saccharin and Food Safety Policy, *Food Safety Policy: Scientific and Societal Considerations*, pt. 2 (Washington, D.C.: NAS, 1979).

153

safety of common foods have an immediacy that regulatory decisions about other substances and activities do not. Food is consumed by every person every day. Eating is associated with pleasure and ritual in our society and is often viewed as a respite from unpleasant activities. Public concern about and interest in foods run high.

Saccharin provokes special interest because it has made possible an entire category of foods—low-calorie versions of traditional foods whose existence depends on saccharin's continued use. Although some individuals may have become attached to saccharin's distinctive flavor, which sugar cannot duplicate, the absence of a substitute nonnutritive sweetener is the primary reason for the public's resistance to the ban. These features may simply demonstrate that saccharin is perceived as providing special benefits, although those benefits are difficult to describe or quantify. More important, the benefits are associated with an ingredient already in use, not one being considered for approval. A new food substance would not generate the same intense feelings, even if it could be shown that such a substance had potential benefits matching those of saccharin.[2]

Factors That Influence Food Safety Decisions

To place the Food and Drug Administration's action on saccharin in context, it is useful to identify the factors that influence most food safety decisions. These factors undoubtedly have counterparts in other regulatory agencies. Not all are influential in every case.

1. *Legal standards.* The legal criteria for food safety decisions are a product of statutory requirements, agency regulations, and precedent (previous decisions applying the same statutory provision in similar contexts). Present law, however, affords the agency some flexibility both in its choice of criteria for making decisions and in the timing of its decisions.

2. *Procedural requirements and court challenges.* The Food and Drug Administration's decision on saccharin was influenced very little by procedural requirements. Furthermore, the agency accepted as unavoidable

2. Other food substances besides saccharin are distinctive: sodium nitrite, the curing agent that provides the flavor and color of bacon and other pork products, and peanuts, which, obviously, are the source of peanut butter. Not surprisingly, Food and Drug Administration efforts to restrict sodium nitrite have provoked opposition similar to that mounted against the proposed saccharin ban. One could also expect resistance if the agency tried to prevent the marketing of peanuts containing any detectable amounts of aflatoxin, a potent carcinogen.

the prospect of court challenges to whatever decision it reached. If the agency had ignored the results of the Canadian study that showed that saccharin caused bladder cancer in second-generation rats or tried to avoid banning saccharin while conceding that it caused cancer in animals, it would have been sued and probably ordered to commence the process to withdraw approval.

3. *History of the substance in question.* The Food and Drug Administration's past decisions about a substance can influence both the timing and outcome of its final decision. In the case of saccharin, by 1977 the agency had narrowed the issues requiring resolution to the single question of carcinogenicity. It had also come under increased pressure to decide that question conclusively.

4. *Regulatory climate.* In early 1977, the agency was emerging from three years of intense and critical oversight by a Democratic Congress of a Republican-administered agency. Congressional hearings and reports had dramatized the agency's alleged failures to protect the public from unsafe products. Consumer groups and the Washington-based press had criticized the agency for its handling of polychlorinated biphenyls in fish, polybrominated biphenyls in Michigan livestock, the food color Red No. 2, diethylstilbestrol, and many other well-publicized health hazards.

5. *Adequacy of scientific and other data.* Saccharin is unusual because it has been tested extensively. Even new food additives are not usually subjected to as much testing in animals. No other approved additive has been the focus of several epidemiological studies, as saccharin has, including a recent $1.5 million study commissioned by the Food and Drug Administration and conducted by the National Cancer Institute. Saccharin's notoriety, the commercial interests supporting and attacking its use, and the shared concern of the U.S. and Canadian governments have produced a large body of data about saccharin's safety. Yet the study results have been hotly contested; they leave questions unanswered; and they have taken more than a decade to conduct. A more elaborate set of criteria for decisionmaking than present law prescribes might have generated more data, but with greater delay.

Clifford Grobstein's paper in this volume describes the scientific data on the safety of saccharin. Because procedural issues did not significantly influence the Food and Drug Administration's decision, I will not discuss this element. Strident criticism of the agency before 1977 helped create a regulatory climate in early 1977 that predisposed agency officials to view the Canadian rat study as a true key to saccharin's continued approvability and to credit preliminary reports that the final results would demonstrate carcinogenicity. The two primary determinants of the Food and Drug Administration's decision—the history of its previous actions on saccharin and legal standards governing food safety—warrant further elaboration.

A History of the Food and Drug Administration's Regulation of Saccharin

A recurring problem for health regulatory agencies is determining when scientific data are adequate to provide a basis for definitive judgment; a lack of data often explains delays in decisions.[3] Yet an agency cannot postpone a decision indefinitely without weakening its credibility. The regulatory history of saccharin illustrates this point.

The Food and Drug Administration had been asked to take a position on saccharin's safety on many occasions before 1977, perhaps in part because the scientific data are more extensive for saccharin than for other food ingredients. This does not mean that saccharin presents unusual risks; it simply indicates that saccharin has been on the agency's public agenda for many years.

Even before the 1906 Pure Food and Drugs Act was enacted, saccharin was being used as a nonnutritive sweetener in human foods.[4] Within five years, government officials were pressed to express an official view on saccharin's safety. In 1912, saccharin was banned from food but a sugar shortage in World War I soon prompted lifting of the ban.[5]

Saccharin's growing popularity as a cheap sugar substitute after World War II prompted the Food and Drug Administration to reexamine its

3. To avoid taking unpopular regulatory actions regulators often delay making a decision initially, which can sometimes be done without any public explanation. This has been the Food and Drug Administration's response to reports that black pepper causes cancer in animals. If an issue becomes volatile, an agency may convene a group of experts to evaluate fresh evidence on safety—a technique the Food and Drug Administration and the U.S. Department of Agriculture have used with sodium nitrite. Persistent, highly visible issues often dictate a request for advice from some outside body, such as the National Academy of Sciences or the National Cancer Institute. The Food and Drug Administration relied on these two organizations in its deliberations on saccharin and cyclamate, respectively.

4. 34 Stat. 768 (repealed 1938).

5. National Academy of Sciences, National Research Council Institute of Medicine and Assembly of Life Sciences, Committee for a Study on Saccharin and Food Safety Policy, *Saccharin: Technical Assessment of Risks and Benefits* (NAS, 1978).

safety. The agency referred the issue to the National Academy of Sciences in the first of what became a series of attempts to enlist scientific support for regulatory positions. In 1955, the academy's Committee on Food Protection reviewed the literature and decided that up to one gram per day of saccharin was safe. When the Food Additives Amendment was enacted in 1958, manufacturers continued to use saccharin in the belief that it was "generally recognized as safe" (GRAS). The Food and Drug Administration ultimately included saccharin on its so-called GRAS list.[6] Thus saccharin came into widespread use without formal approval as a food additive.

Use of both saccharin and cyclamate increased sharply during the early 1960s, and in 1967 the agency asked the National Academy of Sciences to review the safety of both sweeteners. An ad hoc subcommittee of the Committee on Food Protection was formed to conduct this review.[7] A year later, the committee reported that adult consumption of one gram or less of saccharin per day should present no health hazard. This judgment, though operationally identical, was slightly more cautious than the one reached a decade earlier. The committee observed that existing scientific studies were inadequate for determining whether saccharin might cause cancer, a possibility the committee suggested seriously for the first time. It recommended that the necessary long-term studies be conducted.

In 1970, the issue of saccharin's safety assumed new importance when the Food and Drug Administration banned cyclamate—the only other artificial sweetener—based on reports suggesting that the substance seemed to be a carcinogen in laboratory animals. The cyclamate ban gave ammunition to those who believed saccharin had never been adequately tested, particularly since in one of the incriminating cyclamate studies the test animals had also been fed saccharin.

The cyclamate experience taught the Food and Drug Administration two lessons. One was that it could not allow judgment of important ingredients to depend on a single controversial study that raised, but did not resolve, doubts about their safety. The agency concocted a new regulatory category—"interim food additives"—in which ingredients once generally accepted as safe could escape banning until more or less defini-

6. 21 C.F.R. pt. 182, 23 Fed. Reg. 9511 (1958), 24 Fed. Reg. 9368 (1959).
7. National Academy of Sciences, Committee on Food Protection, Ad Hoc Committee on Nonnutritive Sweeteners, "Nonnutritive Sweeteners: An Interim Report to the Food and Drug Administration, U.S. Department of Health, Education, and Welfare" (NAS, 1968).

tive evidence became available. The second lesson was that any attempt to classify artificially sweetened products as drugs to escape the Delaney anti-cancer clause (contained in the Food Additives Amendment of 1958) would not be credible. The agency had initially tried to characterize cyclamate-sweetened fruits and similar products as drugs for use by diabetics, but it later retreated in the face of congressional accusations that it was ignoring the law.

Following its cyclamate ban, the Food and Drug Administration once more asked the Food Protection Committee to review the data on saccharin's safety. A second ad hoc committee issued a report within the year in which it generally confirmed the conclusions of the former study, but urged that long-term studies be conducted to determine saccharin's possible carcinogenicity.[8] Because saccharin was not an approved food additive but rather was used as a generally recognized as safe ingredient that required no approval, the agency could not legally demand such studies. The agency itself began a two-generation study of rodents and at about the same time learned that a similar study had been undertaken for the sugar industry by the Wisconsin Alumni Research Foundation.

Pending completion of the long-term tests recommended by the National Academy of Sciences, the agency proposed in 1971 to delete saccharin from the generally recognized as safe list and establish an interim food additive regulation that would limit use in general purpose foods to ensure that adult consumption would not exceed one gram per day. In February 1972, the Food and Drug Administration made final its proposal to transfer saccharin to interim food additive status and limit its use to foods for special dietary use.[9] Later that year the agency received the results of the Wisconsin Alumni Research Foundation study, which found that rats fed a diet of 5 percent saccharin developed bladder tumors not unequivocally characterized as cancerous.

In June 1972, the agency once more asked the National Academy of Sciences to review the available studies on saccharin, including the WARF study and its own recently concluded study. Early the next year, the agency extended the interim food additive regulation for saccharin until it re-

8. National Academy of Sciences, Committee on Food Protection, Ad Hoc Committee on Nonnutritive Sweeteners, "Safety of Saccharin for Use in Foods" (NAS, 1970).
9. "Title 21—Food and Drugs, Chapter 1—Food and Drug Administration, Department of Health, Education, and Welfare, Subchapter B—Food and Food Products, Part 121—Food Additives: GRAS and Food Additive Status Procedures," *Federal Register,* vol. 37 (December 2, 1972), pp. 25705–08.

ceived the National Academy of Sciences report. On December 10, 1974, the academy reported that, based on existing studies, the carcinogenicity of saccharin could not conclusively be determined.[10] It suggested that a contaminant, orthotoluene sulfonamide, contained in most commercial-grade saccharin might be responsible for the excess tumors observed among the dosed animals in the WARF and Food and Drug Administration studies. Earlier that year, the Health Protection Branch of the Canadian government had begun a third long-term study involving fetal exposure *in utero* to commercial-grade saccharin, to saccharin free of orthotoluene sulfonamide, and to this substance alone.

In 1975 the Food and Drug Administration again extended the interim food additive regulation for saccharin through 1976, by which time it expected to have received the findings of the Canadian study. In public statements the agency implied that the only unresolved safety question was that of carcinogenicity and that a decisive answer would be possible when the Canadian study was completed. In January 1977 the Food and Drug Administration once more extended saccharin's interim approval, stating that it would act promptly after evaluating the results of the Canadian study, which were expected in the near future. Within a few days of this announcement the agency received a preliminary report on the Canadian study findings. In March, three agency scientists met in Ottawa with scientists from Canada and Great Britain and two independent research laboratories to evaluate the study. After reviewing the tissue slides, the group agreed that saccharin had induced cancer in the second-generation male animals tested.

On March 9, 1977, the Canadian government announced that saccharin could no longer be used in foods in that country. The same day, the Food and Drug Administration announced that it would soon publish a proposal to withdraw its interim food additive regulation for saccharin. This decision reflected the unanimous agreement among the agency's scientists that the Canadian results were reliable. At this time the agency did not seriously consider possible alternatives to a ban. To have suggested that further testing of saccharin was necessary would have invited ridicule in the press and from Congress, whose own General Accounting Office had previously castigated the agency for delaying action on saccharin. Another referral to the National Academy of Sciences also was considered out of the ques-

10. National Academy of Sciences, Committee on Food Protection, Ad Hoc Committee on Nonnutritive Sweeteners, "Safety of Saccharin and Sodium Saccharin in the Human Diet" (NAS, 1974).

tion. Furthermore, the legal requirements applicable to food additives seemed to afford no choice. Indeed, it was only reluctantly that the agency's Bureau of Drugs considered permitting the marketing of saccharin as an over-the-counter drug. Surprising as it may now seem, one of the Food and Drug Administration's main concerns was that its announcement about saccharin's cancer-causing properties might panic consumers. Accordingly, the agency's statement repeated language from the Canadian press release, which emphasized the high doses that the test animals had been fed. Ironically, this emphasis on the relative dose levels —the agency stated that a person would have to drink 800 cans of soft drinks to consume the amount of saccharin that had been fed to the rats in the Canadian study—seriously weakened the credibility of the agency's basic conclusion, which was that saccharin could no longer be considered safe for humans.

On April 15, 1977, the agency published a proposal to prohibit use of saccharin in foods and in cosmetics, but held open the possibility of permitting the sweetener to be marketed as a single-ingredient drug— ostensibly for use by diabetics as a sweetener—if proponents could show that saccharin met the drug efficacy requirements of the Federal Food, Drug, and Cosmetic Act.[11] In proposing to ban the use of saccharin in foods, the agency offered as legal justification both the Delaney clause and the general safety standard of the Food Additives Amendment of 1958.

In November 1977, Congress enacted legislation that prohibited the Food and Drug Administration from terminating its approval of saccharin for at least eighteen months.[12] The legislation directed the secretary of health, education, and welfare to arrange for the studies recently conducted by the National Academy of Sciences. The moratorium law also imposed a requirement—to be implemented by the Food and Drug Administration—that foods containing saccharin bear a warning about the possible cancer risk. This requirement was included in the law at the Food and Drug Administration's urging. The agency entertained the faint hope that such a provision might ultimately defeat the legislation, and it also believed that some warning was ethically mandatory. But the agency never considered labeling alone to be a sensible response to the long-term risk saccharin poses.

11. U.S. Department of Health, Education, and Welfare, Food and Drug Administration, "Saccharin and Its Salts: Proposed Rule Making," *Federal Register,* vol. 42 (April 15, 1977), pt. 3, pp. 19996–20010.
12. Saccharin Study and Labeling Act, 91 Stat. 1451.

The Legal Framework for Food Additive Regulation

By the early spring of 1977 the Food and Drug Administration had concluded that it had no credible option under the law but to ban saccharin from food. By regulating saccharin as a food additive since 1972, the agency had made it subject to the Delaney anticancer clause, which prohibits the agency from approving as safe any food additive found to induce cancer in humans or in laboratory animals. Through statements to the press and to Congress and by its repeated referrals to the National Academy of Sciences, the agency had made the issue of carcinogenicity the decisive test of saccharin's acceptability. To understand the agency's thinking it is helpful to be familiar with the statutory framework within which the agency regulates food safety. The governing law is the Federal Food, Drug, and Cosmetic Act of 1938,[13] which includes several amendments. The food safety requirements of the act are, therefore, an aggregate of provisions enacted over thirty years, most of them drafted to regulate a distinct category of food constituents, such as food additives. The law's categorization of food constituents according to their origin or use rather than the risks that they pose has been criticized and misunderstood.

The present law is indeed complex, but this reflects the complexity of the subject and the tendency of Congress to address only one problem at a time. As interpreted by the Food and Drug Administration, the law reflects often inchoate judgments about the political feasibility of regulating different categories of food constituents, judgments that in some instances withstand risk-benefit analysis. Congress has clearly concluded that the Food and Drug Administration should not have the same authority over all substances found or used in human food.

History of Food Safety Legislation

The first federal statute governing food safety, the Food and Drugs Act of 1906, declared unlawful (that is, adulterated) any food that contained "any *added poisonous* or other added deleterious *ingredient which*

13. 52 Stat. 1040 (hereafter referred to as the Food, Drug, and Cosmetic Act). See generally Richard A. Merrill, "Regulating Carcinogens in Food: A Legislator's Guide to the Food Safety Provisions of the Federal Food, Drug, and Cosmetic Act," *Michigan Law Review,* vol. 77 (1979), p. 171.

may render such article injurious to health."[14] The 1906 law did not deal with hazards posed by constituents that were not added to food. While the term "added" was not defined, it was understood to include substances intentionally incorporated as ingredients or advertently used during processing.

In writing the 1938 Federal Food, Drug, and Cosmetic Act, Congress wanted to expand the 1906 law's controls over potentially toxic substances in food. Section 402(a)(1) of the 1938 act thus declares adulterated any food that "bears or contains any poisonous or deleterious substance which may render it injurious to health . . ." without apparent limitation of "added" substances.[15] But Congress then qualified this standard by appending the following clause: "[I]n case the substance is *not an added substance* such food shall not be considered adulterated under this clause if the quantity of such substance in such food does not *ordinarily render it injurious* to health."[16] The 1938 act thus retained the 1906 act's distinction between substances that are added and those that are not, but made the latter subject to Food and Drug Administration regulation for the first time. The legal standard applicable to the latter category has remained unchanged since 1938. The "ordinarily injurious" test determines whether a nonadded substance adulterates food. This test is less rigorous, that is, it is more permissive of potentially toxic constituents, than other food safety provisions of the act.[17]

Because the act does not define "added," however, the Food and Drug Administration has exercised broad discretion in determining which food constituents fall under the "ordinarily injurious" test. In general, the agency has interpreted the concept of "added" broadly,[18] bringing most food constituents, including environmental contaminants, under the "may render injurious" test or under one of the even more stringent standards subsequently enacted for specific classes. The result is that only un-

14. 34 Stat. 770; emphasis added.

15. 52 Stat. 1046.

16. 21 U.S.C. sec. 342(a)(1) (1976); emphasis added.

17. The distinction between added and nonadded constituents is often difficult to apply and, in some people's view, irrational. See Peter Barton Hutt, "Unresolved Issues in the Conflict Between Individual Freedom and Government Control of Food Safety," *Food Drug Cosmetic Law Journal*, vol. 33 (October 1978), p. 558. The distinction can result in the application of different standards to the same food, depending on the form in which the food reaches consumers. For example, apples are sold and eaten in their natural state and are also "added" in the production of other products, such as applesauce.

18. See "Poisonous or Deleterious Substances in Food: Notice of Proposed Rule-Making," *Federal Register*, vol. 39 (December 6, 1974), p. 42743.

processed foods of natural origin, that is, agricultural commodities, are subject to the standard that forbids marketing if they contain substances that *ordinarily* render food harmful.

From the outset Congress recognized that certain added substances required more comprehensive control than could be achieved by court enforcement under the "may render injurious" test. Thus, in section 406 of the 1938 Food, Drug, and Cosmetic Act Congress empowered the Food and Drug Administration to establish tolerances for added "poisonous or deleterious" substances whose occurrence in food "cannot be avoided" or whose use is "required" to produce the food. Apparently, Congress recognized the utility of some potentially toxic substances or placed a high value on foods from which such substances cannot practicably be eliminated. Pesticide residues provided the example cited in the legislative history.

Section 406 has become the legal basis for the Food and Drug Administration's regulation of environmental contaminants of food, such as aflatoxin. The legal standards governing the agency's decisions about this category of food constituents contrast sharply with those applicable to food additives. In setting a tolerance for a contaminant, the agency considers two criteria: (1) the level of the substance at which consumption will not pose a health risk, and (2) the extent to which occurrence of the substance can be controlled by good manufacturing practice. Although not explicitly sanctioned by the Food, Drug, and Cosmetic Act, the agency also considers a third criterion, the capability of analytical methods to measure a particular contaminant.

Section 406 implies that no contaminant may exceed the level that poses a health risk; however, the lowest achievable level of some contaminants exceeds the level that can be considered risk free. For example, *no* level of exposure to aflatoxin, a potent carcinogen, can be considered safe for all individuals. The Food and Drug Administration has declined, however, to adopt a "no threshold" rationale for regulating carcinogenic contaminants (such as aflatoxin) of important agricultural commodities. The agency considers the value of the food, as well as the extent to which its occurrence can be controlled. Thus, in regulating unintended food contaminants the agency weighs the risk against some benefits.

Amendments Enacted after 1938

The three legal standards originally contained in the 1938 act have been elaborated by several subsequent amendments. Each of these amendments deals with a specific category of added food constituents and establishes a system under which the Food and Drug Administration is empowered—by administrative order or regulation—to limit the use or the occurrence of such constituents in or on food.

The first of these amendments was the Pesticide Chemical Residues Amendment of 1954, now section 408 of the Food, Drug, and Cosmetic Act.[19] This provision parallels the Environmental Protection Agency's authority, under another statute, to approve pesticides for use in the United States. Section 408 says that a raw agricultural commodity shall be deemed adulterated if it bears any residue of a pesticide that does not conform to a tolerance established by the Environmental Protection Agency and outlines an elaborate procedure for the establishment of tolerances. The standard for establishing pesticide tolerances contrasts sharply with the criteria Congress subsequently applied to other categories of added constituents, such as food additives and color additives. Section 408 instructs the Environmental Protection Agency to limit the amount of residue on a raw commodity "to the extent necessary to protect the public health," but adds that the agency "shall give appropriate consideration, among other relevant factors . . . to the necessity for the production of an adequate, wholesome, and economical food supply."[20] Thus, the standard for regulating potentially toxic pesticide residues explicitly permits some consideration of benefits.

In 1958 Congress recognized another category of added constituents of food requiring special treatment. The Food Additives Amendment, section 409 of the Food, Drug, and Cosmetic Act, establishes a licensure scheme for substances intended for use as ingredients in formulated foods. The amendment also covers substances that may come in contact with food, such as packaging materials, and which "may reasonably be expected to result" in becoming a component of food.[21] This amendment does not apply, however, to (1) substances whose use in food is generally recognized as safe (GRAS) by qualified experts, or (2) substances that either the Food and Drug Administration or the Department of Agriculture had sanctioned for use in food before 1958. The amendment was designed to focus the Food and Drug Administration's attention on substances not previously used in food.

The agency may permit the use of any food additive that is "safe"—a standard described in the legislative history as requiring reasonable cer-

19. 68 Stat. 511.
20. 68 Stat. 511–12.
21. 72 Stat. 1784.

tainty that no consumer of a food containing the additive will suffer harm. The agency must also satisfy itself that the additive, when used at levels shown to be safe, will achieve its intended technical effect (that is, that a preservative will preserve). Beyond this requirement, the Food Additives Amendment does not require any evidence of benefit before an ingredient may be approved. Nor, according to the agency's consistent interpretation, does the law permit demonstrable benefits to outweigh any significant health risk.

The famous Delaney clause is part of the Food Additives Amendment of 1958.[22] The clause prohibits the Food and Drug Administration from approving as safe any food additive found to induce cancer in humans or in laboratory animals. From the beginning the agency has characterized the Delaney clause as redundant. Assuming that no level of exposure to an animal carcinogen can be considered safe for all consumers and believing itself constrained to ignore the benefits of any additive, the agency has insisted—as in the case of saccharin—that the basic provisions of the Food Additives Amendment would bar approval of a carcinogenic additive even if the Delaney clause had not been enacted.[23]

Because the Delaney clause was drafted to limit the agency's approval authority under section 409 (the Food Additives Amendment), it technically applies only to substances that fall within the statutory definition of food additive.[24] Thus users and manufacturers of food constituents have an obvious incentive to try to escape that definition, for example, by fitting products into the excepted category of ingredients already approved by the Food and Drug Administration or the Department of Agriculture before 1958.

In 1960 Congress addressed the more limited problem of substances used to color foods (as well as to color drugs and cosmetics). The Color Additive Amendments of 1960 require the Food and Drug Administration to approve as safe any color used in food; they contain no exceptions for colors that may be recognized as safe or that were sanctioned for use before 1960.[25] A second Delaney clause prohibits the approval of any food color that has been shown to induce cancer in humans or in laboratory animals.

22. 72 Stat. 1786.
23. The agency position is outlined most recently in its proposed saccharin ban; Food and Drug Administration, "Saccharin and Its Salts."
24. See 21 U.S.C. sec. 321(s) (1976).
25. 74 Stat. 397.

The most recent modification of the food safety provisions of the original Food, Drug, and Cosmetic Act occurred as part of the Animal Drug Amendments of 1968.[26] After 1958, drugs given to animals that are sources of human food were regulated under a combination of statutory provisions: (1) drugs—administered directly to animals—that "could reasonably be expected" to leave residues in human food were regulated under both the new drug approval section and the Food Additives Amendment, and (2) compounds incorporated directly into animal feeds were regulated under the Food Additives Amendment alone.[27] In 1967 Congress tried to simplify the procedure for evaluating animal drugs by prescribing a unified licensure system in a new section 512 of the Animal Drug Amendment.[28] Under this system, no animal drug likely to leave residues in edible tissue of livestock may be used without prior Food and Drug Administration approval.

The standard governing approval of animal drugs has two main elements. First, an animal drug that is not already recognized as safe and effective must be shown to be safe and effective for the target animal. Second, any residue likely to remain in human food must meet the safety criteria of the Food Additives Amendment, with one notable exception. Although the Delaney clause precludes the direct addition to human food of any carcinogenic food additive, the Food and Drug Administration may approve a carcinogenic animal drug if it is satisfied that its use will not result in detectable residues in edible animal tissue. That is, the agency may ignore residues that cannot practically be detected. Although this is not a risk-benefit formula, Congress obviously enacted this limited "exception" to the Delaney clause because it was impressed by the economic benefits of drugs used to promote animal growth.

The Saccharin Decision

The Food and Drug Administration's proposal in 1977 to ban saccharin did not result from careful comparison of saccharin's risks and benefits. The Food, Drug, and Cosmetic Act, however, was only partially

26. 82 Stat. 342.
27. See *Animal Drug Amendments of 1967*, H. Rept. 875, 90 Cong. 1 sess. (Government Printing Office, 1967); *Animal Drug Amendments of 1968*, S. Rept. 1308, 90 Cong. 2 sess. (GPO, 1968).
28. 21 U.S.C. sec. 360(b) (1976).

responsible for the agency's narrow focus and its relatively perfunctory analysis of the effects of its proposed action. The Delaney clause made legally unnecessary, though not politically irrelevant, quantification of saccharin's risks or reexamination of the relevance of animal experiments as evidence of human risk. Extrapolation from animals to man has become such a well-established premise of toxic chemical regulation, however, that it is inconceivable that the agency could have made saccharin the pretext for reexamining it. Furthermore, it was the Food Additives Amendment, not the Delaney clause, that obviated any consideration of benefits.

When the agency acted, not only was its vision restricted by the law, but its attention—and that of the observant public—had progressively become focused on the single issue of carcinogenicity. The possibility that saccharin induced cancer had been raised in the mid-1960s, and it had grown stronger as successive studies and National Academy of Sciences reports explored the role of the contaminant orthotoluene sulfonamide (OTS). By 1977 the agency had as much as said: "If the Canadian study rules out OTS as the culpable agent [which it did], saccharin will have to be banned." Subsequent claims that the agency's proposed ban came as a surprise are simply not credible.

The issue confronting the Food and Drug Administration was, thus, a narrow one. At the same time, it had available a relative abundance of data, accumulated at considerable expense over more than a decade. In addition, many vocal critics were impatient for decisive action. During the previous year the General Accounting Office had issued a report sharply criticizing the agency for delaying a decision on saccharin.[29] Members of Congress and consumer advocates hounded the agency to get the problem solved. It would have taken unusual fortitude to postpone a decision, much less consider alternative action, in the face of the Canadian study results.

To be sure, saccharin's fate was dictated by the legal standards Congress prescribed in 1958 for food additives. Had saccharin been a pesticide or an environmental contaminant, the Food and Drug Administration could have considered other criteria and conceivably have concluded that the substance should not be banned. The risk posed by saccharin probably does not exceed that of some pesticides that are permitted on foods or that

29. U.S. General Accounting Office, *Need to Resolve Questions on Saccharin, Food and Drug Administration, Department of Health, Education, and Welfare: Report of the Comptroller General of the United States* (GAO, 1976).

of many environmental contaminants. It is appropriate to observe, however, that the authors of the National Academy of Sciences food safety study were not able to agree on the optimum regulatory treatment of saccharin.[30] Nevertheless, it can be argued that saccharin was the victim of an irrational law that applies different criteria to different categories of food constituents.

The current law gave the Food and Drug Administration no real choice about how to regulate saccharin. The agency can delay a decision when the scientific data, though suggestive of risk, are still incomplete. It may limit the level at which an additive is used or possibly require a label warning for an additive to which small numbers of consumers might be allergic. But in the final analysis, the Food Additives Amendment is binary; ultimately it allows only approval/disapproval decisions.

Consequences of Changing the Current Food Safety System

Several proposals have been suggested for revising the current law. Most of them would eliminate the current legal categories, substitute some sort of risk-benefit formula for the no-risk approach of the Food Additives Amendment, and give the Food and Drug Administration a greater variety of methods for controlling food constituents. This section identifies some difficulties with these recommendations.

Eliminating the present law's categories and giving the Food and Drug Administration broader authority to make rational judgments about which constituents should be permitted, restricted, or banned would increase the agency's power and reduce that of Congress. The agency's authority is an extension of congressional power. In the food safety area, as in others, regulatory policy is a product of both legislative prescription and administrative decision. Under a law as old as the Food, Drug, and Cosmetic Act, the agency's power to interpret and rationalize overlapping and sometimes inconsistent statutory provisions gives it a major role in policy formation. The agency clearly has not hesitated to manipulate legal categories and criteria to facilitate decisions that seemed sensible.[31] But the agency's role

30. National Academy of Sciences, *Food Safety Policy.*
31. The agency's performance is analyzed in Merrill, *Regulating Carcinogens in Food;* and Richard Kingham, "Statutory and Administrative Theories by Which FDA Avoids Applying the Delaney Clause" (unpublished manuscript, November

as coauthor of food safety policy is constrained by more or less well-articulated congressional judgments. The current law is not haphazard. The statutory categories may reflect the sedimentary history of food safety legislation, but they also represent legislative decisions about when the agency should be able to limit or ban a substance or a food. In short, the statutory categories embody risk-benefit judgments by Congress. It is no accident that the most permissive standard applies to basic agricultural products, such as fruits and vegetables. Congress has similarly allowed the agency some discretion in regulating pesticides and environmental contaminants because it appreciated their utility or recognized the inability of processors to eliminate them. Congressional estimates of the importance of foods in these categories may not always withstand quantitative analysis, but the judgments were consciously made. A system that authorized the Food and Drug Administration to make independent judgments on an individualized basis would thus diminish congressional control.

The present law's categories also dictate the kinds of disagreement about food constituents that are relevant. Since the law permits only safety to be considered in regulating a substance, the Food and Drug Administration can avoid spending resources to examine the benefits of its use. Similarly, those who make the substance or market food containing it are spared the expense of assembling supporting data. The law's narrow focus may be dysfunctional, of course, if consideration of other criteria would produce better decisions. The point is, however, that any proposal to expand the criteria that the agency must consider should take account of the resulting increased expense of the regulatory process.

Any proposed reform of the present system must be translatable into law—that is, it must be capable of functioning in an arena where par-

---

10, 1977). An example of the agency's procedures is its approval of the nutrient selenium for addition to animal feed, despite evidence that its administration is associated with an increase in liver cancer in laboratory animals. The agency's rationale was that the high experimental dosages of selenium produced a pathologic change in the animals, which in turn led to cancer. This kind of secondary action, the agency argued, did not satisfy the "induce cancer" language of the Delaney clause. See Department of Health, Education, and Welfare, Food and Drug Administration, "Selenium in Animal Feed: Proposed Food Additive Regulation," *Federal Register*, vol. 38 (April 27, 1973), pp. 10458–460; and "Part 121—Food Additives: Subpart C—Food Additives Permitted in Feed and Drinking Water of Animals or for the Treatment of Food-Producing Animals: Selenium in Animal Feed," *Federal Register*, vol. 39 (January 8, 1974), pp. 1355–358.

ticipants are disposed to insist on adherence to fixed standards and to invoke every procedural right to protect their interest. This does not mean that every food safety decision results in litigation, or would do so under another system. But every significant decision should be made on the assumption that litigation is probable. The difficulty of achieving a consensus on food safety policy in the abstract makes it clear that no important decision involving a substance whose risks are uncertain or remote and whose benefits are obvious and immediate will fail to provoke controversy.

The legal system favors consistency and predictability at the expense of discretion and judgment. It also imposes on decisionmakers procedures that complicate any substantive mandate. Every criterion to be weighed becomes the focus of expensive testing and ultimately the subject of testimony, cross-examination, and judicial review. The time it takes to reach a decision is a function of the required legal procedures and the scope of the issues to be explored. Accordingly, if, for example, the Food and Drug Administration were mandated to consider the availability of substitute sweeteners before acting on saccharin, the administrative process would have to generate information about the safety and utility of all such substances and solicit participation by those responsible for their development and sale.

This portrait depicts the present system for regulating food safety and forecasts the consequences of any revised formula for decisionmaking that is not accompanied by fundamental changes in legal procedures. Critics of the Food and Drug Administration's saccharin decision seldom acknowledge the duration and cost of the administrative process before 1977. Fewer still recognize that the agency's proposed saccharin ban began a legally mandated process involving a lengthy administrative trial and subsequent court review, postponing any final agency decision for at least two years. Expanding the agency's criteria for making decisions and giving it a wider range of remedies might or might not improve its ultimate decisions, but such changes would without question lengthen the process and increase its cost.

Part Four

Waterborne Carcinogens: A Scientist's View

DAVID G. HOEL *and* KENNY S. CRUMP

IN THE EARLY 1900s public water works plants in the United States began to use chlorination as a means of controlling bacteria in water supplies. The method was effective and has apparently dramatically reduced outbreaks of waterborne infectious diseases such as typhoid fever. In more recent years, chlorination has also been found to result in the formation in water of potentially harmful compounds such as trihalomethanes. These compounds are evidently formed by a reaction between chlorine and organic material in water. In addition, the widespread manufacture and use of synthetic organic compounds have resulted in trace amounts of many of these compounds finding their way into drinking water supplies.

Questions have been raised about what the presence of such chemical impurities in drinking water implies for human health. Because the concentrations of these impurities are generally quite low, health concerns have focused on their potential carcinogenic effects. Harris observed higher cancer rates among people in Louisiana whose drinking water comes from the Mississippi River and suggested that impurities in the river water were responsible.[1] This initial study was challenged by DeRouen and Diem, but since then a number of other epidemiological studies have found significant correlations between the quality of drinking water and cancer incidence.[2] In 1974 and 1975, concurrent with the en-

1. R. H. Harris, "The Implications of Cancer-causing Substances in Mississippi River Water," report submitted to James A. Moreau, councilman-at-large (New Orleans, 1974).
2. T. A. DeRouen and J. E. Diem, "The New Orleans Drinking Water Controversies: A Statistical Perspective," *American Journal of Public Health*, vol. 65 (October 1975), pp. 1060–62.

actment of the National Safe Drinking Water Act, the Environmental Protection Agency tested drinking water samples from about 150 different locations in the United States through the National Organics Reconnaissance Survey and the Region 5 Organics Survey.[3] A number of organic compounds were identified in drinking water, including chloroform and other trihalomethanes. The National Cancer Institute subsequently determined through its animal bioassay program that chloroform was carcinogenic.[4] Concerns raised by these and other studies prompted the Environmental Protection Agency to sponsor a study by the National Academy of Sciences on the health effects of drinking water.[5]

Water utilities could reduce concentrations of organic compounds in drinking water by implementing certain processes for treating water. One of the most promising of such processes is treatment with granular activated carbon.[6] Studies by the Environmental Protection Agency indicate that granular activated carbon can remove trihalomethane precursors as well as other chemical pollutants from water supplies. However, before initiating a comprehensive water treatment program with granular activated carbon or a similar process, it would be helpful to balance the cost of different processes being considered against the health benefits that would be derived from them. The first step in identifying these health benefits is to determine to what extent water impurities affect human health. In this paper we will review the concentrations of organic chemicals in water; discuss the possible carcinogenic risks these chemicals pose; estimate human carcinogenic risks posed by exposures to low levels of water pollutants on the basis of experimental animal cancer data and epidemiological studies; consider the problems inherent in these two sources of evidence; and discuss the uncertainties involved in assessing the carcinogenic risks of drinking water.

3. U.S. Environmental Protection Agency, Office of Toxic Substances, *Preliminary Assessment of Suspected Carcinogens in Drinking Water: Report to Congress* (EPA, 1975), apps. 1 and 5.

4. N. P. Page and U. Saffioti, "Report on Carcinogenesis Bioassay of Chloroform" (Bethesda, Md.: U.S. National Cancer Institute, 1976).

5. National Academy of Sciences, Safe Drinking Water Committee of the National Research Council, *Drinking Water and Health* (Washington, D.C.: NAS, 1977); National Academy of Sciences, Panel on Low Molecular Weight Halogenated Hydrocarbons of the Coordinating Committee for Scientific and Technical Assessments of Environmental Pollutants of the National Research Council, *Nonfluorinated Halomethanes in the Environment* (NAS, 1978).

6. Environmental Protection Agency, *Preliminary Assessment of Suspected Carcinogens in Drinking Water*, pp. 41–42.

Organics in Drinking Water

Until recently organic pollutants in water were primarily measured by crude nonspecific parameters such as biological oxygen demand, total organic carbon, or carbon oxygen demand. However, new developments in computer-assisted gas chromatography and mass spectrometry have generated a flood of new information about concentrations of specific organic chemicals in water. Before 1970 only about one hundred different organic compounds had been discovered in water. Today between four hundred and five hundred organic compounds have been identified in drinking water alone.[7] However, although approximately 90 percent (by weight) of the volatile organic compounds—including trihalomethanes—in drinking water have been identified and quantified, these represent only 10 percent of the total organic content in water. Of the nonvolatile compounds that make up approximately 90 percent of the total organic content in drinking water, only 5 percent to 10 percent have been identified.[8] Presumably thousands of the more than 2 million identified organic compounds are present in drinking water.

The National Organics Reconnaissance Survey and the Region 5 Organics Survey were initial efforts by the Environmental Protection Agency to determine the extent of organics, trihalomethanes in particular, in drinking water. In the reconnaissance survey samples of both raw water and finished water from eighty water utilities were analyzed to determine the concentrations of the four trihalomethanes (chloroform, bromodichloromethane, dibromochloromethane, and bromoform), carbon tetrachloride, and 1,2-dichloroethane. These eighty utilities were selected to provide a representative sample of the U.S. drinking water utilities that chlorinate their water. In the region 5 survey, raw and treated water from eighty-three utilities in the Environmental Protection Agency's fifth region were analyzed for the presence of methylene chloride, polychlorinated biphenyls, and certain pesticides and phthalate esters in addition to the six volatile organic compounds considered in the reconnaissance survey. Concentrations of volatile organics determined from these two surveys are

---

7. Lawrence H. Keith, *Identification and Analysis of Organic Pollutants in Water* (Ann Arbor Science Publishers, 1977).

8. National Academy of Sciences, *Drinking Water and Health*, p. 492.

Table 1. Average and Maximum Concentrations of Trihalomethanes in Raw and Finished Water (from the National Organics Reconnaissance Survey and the Region 5 Organics Survey)

Micrograms per liter

Substance	Average concentrations				Maximum concentrations, finished water	
	Raw water		Finished water			
	NORS	Region 5	NORS	Region 5	NORS	Region 5
Chloroform	1	1	45	20	311	366
Bromodichloromethane	1	1	14	6	116	31
Dibromochloromethane	1	1	8.5	1	100	15
Bromoform	1	1	2.1	1	92	23

Source: U.S. Environmental Protection Agency, Office of Toxic Substances, *Preliminary Assessment of Suspected Carcinogens in Drinking Water: Report to Congress* (EPA, 1975), apps. 1 and 5.

summarized in table 1. These data show that chlorination creates trihalomethanes, particularly chloroform, in drinking water.[9]

The amount of trihalomethanes in drinking water supplies varies considerably. In the reconnaissance survey data from the water works in Ottumwa, Iowa—one of the least polluted—the only trihalomethane detected was chloroform, at a level of one microgram per liter. At the other extreme, the Huron, South Dakota, water supply and the Miami, Florida, water supply had the highest levels of trihalomethanes discovered in the reconnaissance survey, including chloroform concentrations of over 300 micrograms per liter. Huron receives its water from the James River, and Miami uses ground water contaminated by industrial waste. Concentrations of halogenated compounds and nonvolatile total organic carbon for these two cities are shown in table 2.[10]

Carcinogenic Risk Evaluation from Animal Data

Animal carcinogenesis experiments typically are conducted using a few hundred animals exposed to doses near those that would cause acute short-term effects. Such tests can be carefully controlled and can provide relatively precise information about the excess risk of developing tumors

9. Environmental Protection Agency, *Preliminary Assessment of Suspected Carcinogens in Drinking Water,* apps. 1 and 5.

10. Ibid., app. 1.

Table 2. Concentrations of Volatile Organics and Nonvolatile Organic Carbon (TOC) in Miami, Florida, and Huron, South Dakota, Water Supplies (from the National Organics Reconnaissance Survey)

Micrograms per liter

Substance	Huron	Miami
Chloroform	309	311
Bromodichloromethane	116	78
Dibromochloromethane	49	35
Bromoform	8	3
1,2-Dichloroethane	...	0.2
Carbon tetrachloride	...	...
TOC	12.2	5.4

Source: Environmental Protection Agency, *Preliminary Assessment of Suspected Carcinogens in Drinking Water*, app. 1.

from exposure to the experimental doses. Such risk estimates apply to the specific strain of animals being tested under fully controlled laboratory conditions. An aim of such studies is to obtain information about the risks to humans from possibly much lower environmental doses. The problem of extrapolating these data from animal studies is further complicated by the fact that humans do not live in a carefully controlled laboratory environment but are exposed to a variety of environmental pollutants that may also induce or promote cancer.

There is doubt about whether evidence of carcinogenicity in an animal species has any implications at all for humans. Most of the known human carcinogens have been shown to be carcinogenic in some animal species. It is prudent and probably correct in most cases to presume that a substance that is carcinogenic in some animal species is also carcinogenic in humans under the appropriate circumstances.

Quantifying the carcinogenic risk to humans posed by drinking water on the basis of animal experiment data requires making several judgments for which conclusive scientific evidence is not available. The problem involves extrapolating low environmental doses of potential carcinogens to which humans are exposed from high experimental doses used in animal experiments and transferring risks from the animal strain to humans.

Traditional procedures for evaluating risks from toxic chemicals and drugs and for controlling these risks have been based on finding a concentration level at which no effects are apparent in animals and converting this level to humans by applying a safety factor. There is currently considerable debate about whether a "no-effect level," or threshold, exists for cancer-causing agents.[11] The argument that thresholds sometime exist centers primarily around the idea that physical defenses such as detoxification reactions and immunological responses can protect the body from cancer when very small doses of carcinogens are present. The case against the existence of thresholds is generally made for chemicals that induce cancer through damage to the deoxyribonucleic acid (DNA) of a single cell. It is argued that even a very small amount of a carcinogen can initiate a neoplastic charge in a cell's DNA, which could eventually lead to a malignant cancer. This argument would not necessarily apply to a chemical that promoted the development of a tumor by causing some gross physiological change that predisposes one to cancer. For example, hepatocellular carcinomas are frequently the type of tumor induced in rodents but are rarely implicated in epidemiological studies. It may be that the induction of these tumors requires chemically induced liver damage that would not occur with lower doses of a chemical. If this were the case, the prevalence of hepatocellular carcinomas in an experiment might not indicate risks from low doses.

The National Academy of Sciences safe drinking water committee took the position that if the cancer-causing mechanism is unknown, it is prudent to assume that DNA damage is involved.[12] When this assumption is valid, there is likely to be no threshold dose. In this case any dose level, no matter how low, might cause cancer.

The estimation of this extra risk for a given low dose, using experimental animal data, is known as low-dose extrapolation. In this procedure a mathematical dose-response model is applied to the data with appropriate statistical procedures. It is well known that the result of a low-dose extrapolation depends on the mathematical dose-response function used.[13] Which mathematical function to use cannot be decided solely on the basis of how well the function describes the data, since two dose-response functions can fit experimental data equally well and still predict carcinogenic risks from low doses that are orders of magnitude apart. These differences can best be resolved by using a mathematical function that reflects what

11. For the current status of this debate, see Thomas H. Maugh II, "Chemical Carcinogens: How Dangerous Are Low Doses?" *Science*, vol. 202 (October 6, 1978), pp. 37–41.

12. National Academy of Sciences, *Drinking Water and Health*, pp. 20–21.

13. National Academy of Sciences, Safe Drinking Water Committee of the National Research Council, "Problems of Risk Estimation" (NAS, 1979).

is known or at least plausible regarding the carcinogenic process. The National Academy of Sciences report concluded "that, if there is evidence that a particular carcinogen acts by directly causing a mutation in the DNA, it is likely that the dose-response curve for carcinogenesis will not show a threshold and will be linear with dose at low doses."[14] Statistical procedures for extrapolation based on models that vary linearly at low doses have been suggested for use with the linear model,[15] the one-hit model, and the multistage model.[16] Upper statistical confidence limits on extra risk computed from these three methods are usually in relatively close agreement. When the assumption of low-dose linearity is not valid, these methods are likely to overestimate the true extra risk posed by a carcinogen.

The uncertainties of extrapolating risks from animal species to humans is possibly even greater than those of extrapolating from high doses to low doses within a particular animal species. There are many physiological and biochemical differences between rodents and men that are likely to affect the relative levels of carcinogenic responses. A single human represents about the same number of susceptible cells as two thousand mice. Thus a carcinogen that acts by combining with DNA would have about two thousand times as many receptor sites in a human as in a mouse. The life span of a man is about thirty-five times that of a mouse and consequently a chemical has a longer time in which to produce a cancer in humans than in mice. On the other hand, blood circulates faster in rodents, and they generally have faster metabolic rates. Chemicals may be metabolized to different end products in the two species, and these metabolites are transported to different organs. Storage and excretion rates also vary considerably. All of these differences could have implications concerning differences in cancer formation rates between rodents and humans as well as differences in cancer types.

14. National Academy of Sciences, *Drinking Water and Health,* p. 38. See also K. S. Crump and others, "Fundamental Carcinogenic Processes and Their Implications for Low Dose Risk Assessment," *Cancer Research,* vol. 36 (September 1976), pp. 2973–79.

15. David Hoel and others, "Estimation of Risks of Irreversible, Delayed Toxicity," *Journal of Toxicology and Environmental Health,* vol. 2 (September 1979), pp. 873–87.

16. H. O. Hartley and R. L. Sielken, Jr., "Estimation of 'Safe Doses' in Carcinogenic Experiments," *Biometrics,* vol. 33 (March 1977), pp. 1–30; and K. S. Crump, H. A. Guess, and K. L. Deal, "Confidence Intervals and Tests of Hypotheses Concerning Dose Response Relations Inferred from Animal Carcinogenicity Data," *Biometrics,* vol. 33 (September 1977), pp. 437–51.

In addition to these differences, there are environmental and genetic differences, the implications of which, for cancer risk, are difficult to assess. Whereas animal experiments are carried out under carefully controlled laboratory conditions, humans live in diverse environmental conditions and are exposed to a variety of carcinogens and cocarcinogens. It is possible that a chemical that produces few or no tumors by itself in laboratory animals can, in conjunction with another chemical present in the environment, be highly carcinogenic for humans. Animal experiments are usually conducted on genetically homogeneous strains of animals. In heterogeneous human populations, one would expect much more genetic variability in susceptibility to carcinogenic agents.

Given the present understanding of carcinogenic processes, it is impossible to realistically take into account these kinds of differences. Carcinogenic potency in animals is often converted to potency in humans by crudely relating dose levels in animals to dose levels in humans. In the past this has been done in various ways, for example, by assigning the same carcinogenic potency in both species to a daily dose weight proportional to body weight, a lifetime dose weight proportional to body weight, a dose weight proportional to dietary intake, or a daily dose weight proportional to body weight to the two-thirds power. The first two of these methods are the most extreme, yielding risk estimates that differ by thirty-five-fold when extrapolating from mice to humans.

The National Academy of Sciences safe drinking water committee has specified nineteen human, animal, or suspected human carcinogens and three suspected animal carcinogens that have been identified in drinking water or are suspected of being in drinking water. For each of these compounds for which sufficient data were available the committee calculated the upper 95 percent confidence limit of cancer risk to humans posed by a lifetime exposure to water containing one microgram of the compound per liter. The estimates are based on animal carcinogenicity data. Extrapolation from high dose to low dose was based on a multistage model, which is essentially equivalent to saying that the probability of cancer is proportional to dose at low doses.[17] The conversion of animal dose to human dose was done by calculating daily dose per unit of surface weight. The results of this exercise are shown in table 3, which was included in the National Academy of Sciences report.

Other water contaminants have since been determined to be carcinogenic. The insecticide toxaphene, a suspected water contaminant, was

17. Crump and others, "Confidence Intervals and Tests of Hypotheses."

Table 3. Categories of Known or Suspected Organic Chemical Carcinogens Found in Drinking Water

Compound	Highest observed concentrations in finished water (micrograms per liter)	Estimate of lifetime cancer risk from each microgram per liter consumed daily (upper 95 percent confidence limit)
Human carcinogen		
Vinyl chloride	10	4.7×10^{-7}
Suspected human carcinogens		
Benzene	10	i.d.
Benzo(a)pyrene	d.	i.d.
Animal carcinogens		
Dieldrin	8	2.6×10^{-4}
Kepone	n.d.	4.4×10^{-5}
Heptachlor	d.	4.2×10^{-5}
Chlordane	0.1	1.8×10^{-5}
DDT	d.	1.2×10^{-5}
Lindane (γ-BHC)	0.01	9.3×10^{-6}
$-$BHC	d.	4.2×10^{-6}
PCB (Aroclor 1260)	3	3.1×10^{-6}
BTU	n.d.	2.2×10^{-6}
Chloroform	366	1.7×10^{-6}
$-$BHC	d.	1.5×10^{-6}
PCNB	n.d.	1.4×10^{-7}
Carbon tetrachloride	5	1.1×10^{-7}
Trichloroethylene	0.5	1.1×10^{-7}
Diphenylhydrazine	1	i.d.
Aldrin	d.	i.d.
Suspected animal carcinogens		
Bis (2-chloroethyl) ether	0.42	1.2×10^{-6}
Endrin	0.08	i.d.
Heptachlor epoxide	d.	i.d.

Source: National Academy of Sciences, Safe Drinking Water Committee of the National Research Council, *Drinking Water and Health* (Washington, D.C.: NAS, 1977), p. 794.
i.d. Insufficient data to permit a statistical extrapolation of risk.
d. Detected but not quantified.
n.d. Not detected.

listed by the National Academy of Sciences report in a table with non-carcinogens but has recently been shown to be carcinogenic in rodents by a National Cancer Institute bioassay.[18] Similarly, 1,2-dichloroethane, which has been detected in drinking water at a level of 21 micrograms per liter, is not listed in table 3 but has also been shown to be carcinogenic in

18. U.S. Department of Health, Education, and Welfare, National Institutes of Health, *Bioassay of Toxaphene for Possible Carcinogenicity,* National Cancer Institute Technical Report Series no. 37 (Government Printing Office, 1979), pp. 37–40.

a National Cancer Institute bioassay.[19] Undoubtedly, the list of carcinogens in drinking water will grow as more chemicals are identified in drinking water and are tested for carcinogenicity.

Two trihalomethanes, bromodichloromethane and dibromochloromethane, which were identified in the drinking water of 98 percent and 90 percent, respectively, of the utilities surveyed in the reconnaissance survey (at maximum concentrations of 116 micrograms and 110 micrograms per liter) have not been tested for carcinogenicity.[20] Both of these trihalomethanes were shown to be mutagenic in the Ames Salmonella/microsome assay, which suggests that they may also be carcinogenic.[21]

Table 3 reveals a wide disparity in the carcinogenic potency of the chemicals listed. Dieldrin, the most potent carcinogen listed, is two hundred times as potent as chloroform and over two thousand times as potent as carbon tetrachloride. Consequently, concentrations of dieldrin at levels so low as to be undetectable may be more carcinogenic than measured amounts of chloroform or carbon tetrachloride.

Even if one assumes that the estimates of human risks in table 3 represent true human risk, there would still be uncertainty about the total human carcinogenic risk from drinking water. Estimates in table 3 were obtained from controlled animal studies and apply specifically to risks of chemicals in the absence of other carcinogens. Potential synergistic or antagonistic effects may result from simultaneous exposure to many different carcinogens in water and other sources. The magnitude of such effects cannot be predicted from data on individual carcinogens. It may be that synergistic and antagonistic effects are unimportant at low doses. If so, then weighting the risks of chemicals listed in table 3 according to their respective average concentrations in drinking water and adding these weighted risks together would yield an estimate of the total carcinogenic effect of these chemicals. However, this would probably underestimate the total carcinogenic risk from drinking water since the estimate would

19. Department of Health, Education, and Welfare, National Institutes of Health, *Bioassay of 1,2-Dichloroethane for Possible Carcinogenicity*, National Cancer Institute Technical Report Series no. 55 (GPO, 1978), pp. 58–61, 63–64.

20. Environmental Protection Agency, *Preliminary Assessment of Suspected Carcinogens in Drinking Water*, p. 8.

21. Vincent C. Simon and Robert G. Tardiff, "The Mutagenic Activity of Halogenated Compounds Found in Chlorinated Drinking Water," in Robert L. Jolley, Hend Gorchev, and D. Heywood Hamilton, Jr., eds., *Water Chlorination, Environmental Impact and Health Effects*, vol. 2 (Ann Arbor Science Publishers, 1978), p. 419.

not include the carcinogenic potential of the chemicals in drinking water not yet identified or not yet tested for carcinogenicity. (Approximately 90 percent of the total organic content in drinking water falls into this category.) It is quite possible that there are low concentrations of many potent carcinogens in drinking water that have not yet been detected or identified as carcinogens but that may contribute significantly to the total carcinogenic effect of drinking water.

Estimated carcinogenic potencies of low doses of chemicals should be related to studies of these chemicals' mutagenic potential, since a chemical's carcinogenic potential may stem from its mutagenic potential. The mathematical model used for extrapolation in table 3 is derived from the assumption that inheritable changes in a single cell (mutations) trigger cancer. There is greater doubt about whether a chemical is carcinogenic at all at low doses if it is not mutagenic. Simon and Tardiff studied the mutagenic activity of twenty-two halogenated compounds found in the Ames Salmonella assay. Included among the mutagenic compounds were bromodichloromethane and dibromochloromethane (not yet tested for carcinogenicity). The two halogenated compounds not determined to be mutagenic were chloroform and carbon tetrachloride, both of which are carcinogens. Simon and Tardiff favored the view that these chemicals or their metabolites are also mutagenic but that "the metabolites are formed in insufficient amounts or are so unstable that they do not survive long enough [in the Salmonella assay] to penetrate the bacteria and interact with DNA."[22]

Mutagenic activity has also been detected in nonspecific organic concentrates found in drinking water. Loper and others tested organic concentrates in drinking water from Miami, Philadelphia, and New Orleans and found them all to be mutagenic.[23]

Carcinogenic Risk Evaluation from Epidemiological Data

The use of epidemiological data to determine carcinogenic risks from drinking water circumvents the difficulties of extrapolating from high doses to low doses and across species. Epidemiological data are collected di-

22. Simon and Tardiff, "The Mutagenic Activity of Halogenated Compounds."
23. John C. Loper, Dennis R. Lang, and Carl C. Smith, "Mutagenicity of Complex Mixtures from Drinking Water," in Jolley, Gorchev, and Hamilton, eds., *Water Chlorination, Environmental Impact and Health Effects*, pp. 433–50.

rectly from humans, and the populations under study are exposed directly to environmental levels of drinking water contaminants, which eliminates the need to extrapolate downward from artificially high doses. However, epidemiological studies are beset with other problems.

There are two general types of epidemiological studies used for relating human exposure to potentially harmful substances to health effects: ecologic and analytic. Ecologic studies are primarily descriptive, and analytic studies, although generally more difficult to conduct, can be used to test hypotheses. Neither method can establish a direct causal link between drinking water quality and cancer incidence. There are many potentially confounding factors related to exposures to other carcinogens or to possible genetic predispositions to cancer such as occupation, place of residence, ethnicity, and life-style. Thus there is always some doubt about whether an indicated effect results from drinking water or some other factor confounded with drinking water.

Analytic studies may be either prospective studies in which individuals exposed to various levels of a substance are followed and their disease incidence compared, or they may be retrospective studies in which the past exposure of individuals with and without the disease are compared. Because they are expensive and conducted over long periods, prospective studies are seldom used to study induced effects expected to be small in relation to background effects (for example, the induction of cancer from carcinogens in drinking water). Retrospective studies involve comparing differences between diseased individuals' exposure to putative carcinogenic agents and cancer-free control individuals' exposure while controlling the experiment for a number of possible confounding factors, frequently by matching control and diseased individuals. Difficulties with this method include determining an appropriate population from which to select cancer-free individuals and accurately determining exposures that occurred ten or twenty years earlier.

Ecologic studies use aggregate data rather than data from individuals. Usually the data are already available and do not have to be collected. Thus, ecologic studies are often easier and quicker to conduct than analytic studies. Several ecologic studies have related an area-wide health measure, such as county cancer mortality rates, to measures of area-wide water quality. Frequently such data are analyzed through a multiple regression procedure. Water quality and other variables are accounted for by including appropriate terms in the regression equation. These studies suggest relationships that can be investigated further but are also inadequate in several ways. Although prevalence rates would be preferable, ecologic studies often take county death rates as the dependent variable. The county death rates are based on deaths that occur within a county, irrespective of the deceased's place of residence. Thus, for example, counties with medical centers may have higher death rates not attributable to the water quality of that county. In addition, the U.S. population is quite mobile, and the quality of water at a person's residence at his time of death may not resemble the water to which he was exposed ten or twenty years earlier, when the relevant exposures occurred. Frequently, the measure of water quality may be for only a single water utility, which may supply water for only a portion of the county to which the cancer mortality rates apply.

There are additional problems besetting both ecologic and analytic studies related to measuring water quality. Virtually no data were collected before 1970 on the concentrations of specific organics in drinking water. Sophisticated techniques for measuring very small concentrations of organics have become available only recently. Several studies on the potential carcinogenic effect of drinking water have used nonspecific measures of drinking water quality, such as the use of chlorinated water versus nonchlorinated water or the use of surface water versus ground water. With these indirect measurements it is not possible to quantify pollutants such as trihalomethanes in water, but such quantification is needed to estimate the health benefits that can result from reducing trihalomethane concentrations. Further, there is some evidence that these indirect measurements may not be realistic indicators of water quality. The reconnaissance survey revealed a wide variation in the trihalomethane concentrations among water systems that chlorinate water. Also, ground water is not necessarily purer than surface water. Miami uses ground water, but its water supply had the highest concentration of chloroform reported in the reconnaissance survey.[24]

Some of the ecologic studies have used the direct measure of trihalomethane concentrations reported in the reconnaissance and region 5 surveys. However, one-time measurements of water pollutant concentrations may not be reliable measures of water quality over time. Hogan and others compared the two measures of chloroform concentrations for each of the twelve cities covered by both surveys. Although the total concentra-

24. Environmental Protection Agency, *Preliminary Assessment of Suspected Carcinogens in Drinking Water,* app. 1.

tions measured for the twelve cities is almost the same in the two surveys, the differences between the two surveys' determinations for each city range from −62 percent to +182 percent. Since changes of this magnitude can occur within a period of only a few months (both surveys were conducted between November 1974 and April 1975), it is possible that the surveys' results may not indicate trihalomethane concentrations of ten years or more ago.[25]

In 1978, the epidemiology subcommittee of the National Academy of Sciences safe drinking water committee reviewed what it considered to be all of the epidemiological work done on the association between trihalomethane in water supplies and cancer incidence. It reviewed thirteen studies made up of ten ecologic studies and one case-control study that used indirect measures of water quality as well as three ecologic studies that used as the water quality variable trihalomethane concentrations obtained from the reconnaissance and region 5 surveys.[26] The results of nine of these studies for white males and white females are summarized in tables 4 and 5. Three ecologic studies based on indirect measures of water quality are omitted because information was not available on sex-specific associations between water quality and cancer at different anatomical sites.[27] A fourth ecological study was omitted because it did not allow for any confounding factors.[28] The tables show the associations determined between water quality and cancer incidence at five anatomical

25. Michael Hogan and others, "Drinking Water Supplies and Various Site-specific Cancer Mortality Rates," *Journal of Environmental Pathology and Toxicology*, vol. 2 (January–February 1979), pp. 873–87.

26. "Epidemiological Studies of Cancer Frequency and Certain Organic Constituents of Drinking Water—A Review of Recent Literature," study prepared by the Epidemiology Subcommittee of the Safe Drinking Water Committee of the National Research Council (National Academy of Sciences, 1978), as printed in *Oversight on the Federal Safe Drinking Water Act,* Hearings before the House Subcommittee on Health and the Environment of the Committee on Interstate and Foreign Commerce, 95 Cong. 2 sess. (GPO, 1978), pp. 251–83.

27. William S. Carlson and Julian B. Andelman, "Environmental Influences on Cancer Morbidity in the Pittsburgh Region," prepared for the U.S. Environmental Protection Agency, Health Effects Research Laboratory (University of Pittsburgh, 1977); R. A. Mah, G. H. Spivery, and E. Sloss, "Cancer and Chlorinated Drinking Water" (University of California–Los Angeles, 1977); and C. W. Kruse, "Chlorination of Public Water Supplies and Cancer, Preliminary Report: Washington County, Maryland, Experience" (School of Hygiene and Public Health, Johns Hopkins University, 1977).

28. Leland S. McCabe, "Association Between Trihalomethane in Drinking Water (NORS Data) and Mortality," prepared for the Environmental Protection Agency, Water Quality Division (November 1975).

sites. The results recorded in the tables of studies by Page and others, DeRouen and Diem, Harris and others, Alavanja and others, and Hogan and others were obtained directly from these reports.[29] Results for the other studies were obtained from the summaries by the National Academy of Sciences epidemiology subcommittee.[30]

In each geographical area covered by the nine studies an attempt was made to control for possible confounding factors such as ethnicity, race, income, urban or rural status, and employment. There was considerable diversity in the factors considered and the way in which they were accounted for. All of the studies suffered to some extent the shortcomings discussed earlier that are common in epidemiological studies. The general agreement among the studies is probably more significant than the specific results from a single study. There are a total of eighteen significant positive associations recorded for white males versus only a single significant negative association. For white females, there are seven significant positive associations and one negative association. In both tables combined, eight of nine studies show at least one significant positive association, and only one study shows a significant negative association. Among all the associations reported in both tables, including both significant and nonsignificant associations, fifty-two are positive and eleven are negative. (This observation may be biased since some studies apparently reported only a nonsignificant association when there was a significant association at the same anatomical site for some other race or sex category.)

Taken as a whole, these studies suggest a positive association between water quality—trihalomethane concentrations in particular—and cancer

29. Talbot Page, Robert A. Harris, and Samuel S. Epstein, "Drinking Water and Cancer Mortality in Louisiana," *Science* (July 2, 1976), pp. 55–57; Michael Alavanja, Inge Goldstein, and Mervyn Susser, "A Case Control Study of Gastrointestinal and Urinary Cancer Mortality and Drinking Water Chlorination," in Jolley, Gorchev, and Hamilton, eds., *Water Chlorination, Environmental Impact and Health Effects,* pp. 395–409; T. A. DeRouen and J. E. Diem, "Relationships between Cancer Mortality in Louisiana Drinking-Water Source and Other Possible Causative Agents," in H. H. Hiatt, J. D. Watson, and J. A. Winsten, eds., *Origins of Human Cancer,* Cold Spring Harbor Conferences on Cell Proliferation, vol. 4, book A: *Incidence of Cancer in Humans* (Cold Spring Harbor, N.Y.: Cold Spring Harbor Laboratory, 1977), pp. 331–45; R. H. Harris, T. Page, and N. A. Reiches, "Carcinogenic Hazards of Organic Chemicals in Drinking Water," in Hiatt, Watson, and Winsten, eds., *Origins of Human Cancer,* vol. 4, book A, pp. 309–30; and Hogan and others, "Drinking Water Supplies and Various Site-specific Cancer Mortality Rates."

30. National Academy of Sciences, "Epidemiological Studies of Cancer Frequency and Certain Organic Constituents of Drinking Water," pp. 251–83.

Table 4. Sign and Significance of the Relation between Water Variable and Cancer Mortality of White Males in Nine Epidemiological Studies

Study	Study type	Location	Water variable	Anatomical site				
				Gastro-intestinal	Urinary	Lung	Liver	Pros-tate
Page and others	Ecologic (regression)	Louisiana	Percentage of drinking water from Mississippi River	+	+			
DeRouen and Diem	Ecologic (regression)	Louisiana	Percentage of drinking water from Mississippi River	⊕	⊕			
Kuzma and others	Ecologic (regression)	Ohio	Use of surface water	+(S)	+(B)			
Harris and others	Ecologic (regression)	Ohio	Percentage receiving surface water	+	+	⊕	⊕	⊕
Salg and others	Ecologic (regression)	Ohio River	Percentages of surface and prechlorinated water	+(LI)	+(B)			
Vasilenko and Magno	Ecologic (regression)	New Jersey	Percentage not served by individual wells	+(S)	⊖(B)	+		
Alavanja and others	Retrospective (case control)	Upper New York	Chlorinated and non-chlorinated water	+(LI) +(S) +(R)	+(B)	+(and K)		

Study	Method	Population surveyed	Constituent, ppb			
Cantor and others	Ecologic (weighted regression and correlation analyses)	Areas covered by reconnaissance and region 5 surveys	Chloroform, ppb	⊕(K)		⊕
			Nonchloroform trihalomethanes, ppb	⊕(B)		
			Total trihalomethanes, ppb	⊕(S)	⊕	
Hogan and others	Weighted regression	Areas covered by reconnaissance and region 5 surveys	Chloroform, ppb	+(LI) ⊕(B)		⊖
				−(S) ⊖(K)		
				+(LI) ⊕(B)		+
				⊖(S) ⊕(K)		

Sources: Talbot Page, Robert A. Harris, and Samuel S. Epstein, "Drinking Water and Cancer Mortality in Louisiana," *Science* (July 2, 1976), pp. 55–57; T. A. DeRouen and J. E. Diem, "Relationships between Cancer Mortality in Louisiana Drinking-Water Source and Other Possible Causative Agents," in H. H. Hiatt, J. D. Watson, and J. A. Winsten, eds., *Origins of Human Cancer*, Cold Spring Harbor Conferences on Cell Proliferation, vol. 4, book A: *Incidence of Cancer in Humans* (Cold Spring Harbor, N.Y.: Cold Spring Harbor Laboratory, 1977), pp. 331–45; R. H. Harris, T. Page, and N. A. Reiches, "Carcinogenic Hazards of Organic Chemicals in Drinking Water," in Hiatt, Watson, and Winsten, eds., *Origins of Human Cancer*, vol. 4, book A, pp. 309–30; Michael Alavanja, Inge Goldstein, and Mervyn Susser, "A Case Control Study of Gastrointestinal and Urinary Cancer Mortality and Drinking Water Chlorination," in Robert L. Jolley, Hend Gorchev, and D. Heywood Hamilton, Jr., eds., *Water Chlorination, Environmental Impact and Health Effects*, vol. 2 (Ann Arbor Science Publishers, 1977), pp. 395–409; and Michael Hogan and others, "Drinking Water Supplies and Various Site-specific Cancer Mortality Rates," *Journal of Environmental Pathology and Toxicology*, vol. 2 (January–February 1979), pp. 873–87. The results of the other studies are in "Epidemiological Studies of Cancer Frequency and Certain Organic Constituents of Drinking Water—A Review of Recent Literature," study prepared by the Epidemiology Subcommittee of the Safe Drinking Water Committee of the National Research Council (National Academy of Sciences, 1978), as printed in *Oversight on the Federal Safe Drinking Water Act*, Hearings before the House Subcommittee on Health and the Environment of the Committee on Interstate and Foreign Commerce, 95 Cong. 2 sess. (Government Printing Office, 1978), pp. 251–83.

Key to abbreviations and symbols.

ppb Parts per billion.
S   Stomach.
B   Bladder.
LI   Large intestine.
K   Kidney.
R   Rectum.
+   Significant positive association ($p \leq 0.05$).
−   Significant negative association ($p \leq 0.05$).
⊕   Nonsignificant positive association.
⊖   Nonsignificant negative association.

Table 5. Sign and Significance of the Relation between Water Variable and Cancer Mortality of White Females in Six Epidemiological Studies

Study	Study type	Location	Water variable	Gastro-intestinal	Urinary	Liver	Breast
					Anatomical site		
Page and others	Ecologic (regression)	Louisiana	Percentage of drinking water from Mississippi River	+	⊕		⊕
DeRouen and Diem	Ecologic (regression)	Louisiana	Percentage of drinking water from Mississippi River	⊕	⊕		
Kuzma and others	Ecologic (regression)	Ohio	Use of surface water	+(S)	⊕	⊕	⊕
Alavanja and others	Retrospective (case control)	Upper New York	Chlorinated and non-chlorinated water	+(R) ⊕(LI) +(S)	⊖(B)	⊕(and K)	
Cantor and others	Ecologic (weighted regression and correlation analyses)	Areas covered by reconnaissance and region 5 surveys	Chloroform, ppb Nonchloroform trihalomethanes, ppb Total trihalomethanes, ppb	⊖(S)	⊖(K) +(B)		
Hogan and others	Weighted regression	Areas covered by reconnaissance and region 5 surveys	Chloroform, ppb	+(LI) −(S) ⊖(LI) ⊕(S)	+(B) ⊕(B) ⊕(K)	⊖ ⊕	⊕ ⊕

Sources: Page and others, "Drinking Water and Cancer Mortality in Louisiana," pp. 55–57; DeRouen and Diem, "Relationships between Cancer Mortality in Louisiana Drinking-Water Source and Other Possible Causative Agents," in Hiatt, Watson, and Winsten, eds., *Incidence of Cancer in Humans*, pp. 331–45; Alavanja and others, "A Case Control Study of Gastrointestinal and Urinary Cancer Mortality and Drinking Water Chlorination," in Jolley, Gorchev, and Hamilton, eds., *Water Chlorination, Environmental Impact and Health Effects*, vol. 2, pp. 395–409; and Hogan and others, "Drinking Water Supplies and Various Site-specific Cancer Mortality Rates," pp. 873–87. The results of the other studies are in "Epidemiological Studies of Cancer Frequency and Certain Organic Constituents of Drinking Water," pp. 251–83.
    For key to abbreviations and symbols, see table 4.

Table 6. Estimated Extra Lifetime Risks of Tumors from Chloroform for Each Liter of Water Consumed Daily[a]

	Animal to human dose conversion		
Tumors	*mg/kg/day*	*mg/kg/lifetime*	*mg/(kg)²ᐟ³/day*
Renal[b]	4.7×10^{-8}	1.6×10^{-6}	6.1×10^{-7}
	low		*high*
Bladder[c]	5.6×10^{-7}		1.5×10^{-6}

Sources: F. J. C. Roe, "Preliminary Report of Long-Term Tests of Chloroform in Rats, Mice and Dogs" (unpublished paper, London, 1976); and Hogan and others, "Drinking Water Supplies and Various Site-specific Cancer Mortality Rates," pp. 873–87.
a. Assumptions for estimates are described in the text.
b. Upper 95 percent confidence limits.
c. Based on range of regression coefficients from epidemiological study of Hogan and others.

rates. The association may not stem from a causal relationship, since it is possible that water quality is confounded with other factors that were not accounted for systematically or that were inadequately or improperly accounted for in these studies. None of the studies controlled for cigarette smoking, for example. However, because of the diversity in the studies, it seems unlikely that in all of them the level of cigarette smoking would be positively associated with carcinogens in drinking water.

Estimating the Carcinogenic Risks in Drinking Water

We have made the estimates in this section by applying carcinogen potency data from animal studies to estimates of exposure from the reconnaissance survey and by using the ecologic study of Hogan and others.[31] Roe has found that chloroform is carcinogenic in both rats and mice.[32] The National Academy of Sciences study extrapolated data from each of these sources to estimate risks to humans and found the results to be "remarkably consistent."[33] Table 6 shows the results of extrapolating Roe's data on renal tumors in Swiss mice, first from high dose to low dose using the multistage dose-response model,[34] and then to humans, using three different procedures. These calculations are based on the assumptions that a

31. Hogan and others, "Drinking Water Supplies and Various Site-specific Cancer Mortality Rates."
32. F. J. C. Roe, "Preliminary Report of Long-Term Tests of Chloroform in Rats, Mice and Dogs" (unpublished paper, London, 1976).
33. National Academy of Sciences, *Drinking Water and Health,* p. 716.
34. Crump and others, "Confidence Intervals and Tests of Hypotheses."

human weighs 2,220 times as much as a mouse (68 kilograms versus 31 grams) and that a human lives thirty-five times longer than a mouse.

Also recorded in table 6 are comparable estimates of risk calculated from the epidemiological study of Hogan and others.[35] These estimates are calculated from the regression coefficients for bladder cancer, which showed the strongest overall correlation with chloroform concentrations of all the fourteen cancer sites considered. Based on the weighted regression scheme, all of the regression coefficients calculated by Hogan and others for bladder cancer were positive, and three out of four of these were significantly different from zero. The range of estimates in table 6 reflects the range of the sex-specific regression coefficients calculated by Hogan and others using both the reconnaissance and region 5 surveys.

The estimates based on animal data agree with those based on human epidemiological data. It should be kept in mind, however, that the animal data involved renal tumors and the human data involved bladder tumors. Higher incidences of bladder tumors have not been noted in animal bioassays of chloroform.

Table 7 presents comparable estimates obtained from an environmental assessment of chloroform and other halomethanes by a committee of the National Academy of Sciences.[36] The extrapolation procedure of Crump and others was used for these calculations and the animal-to-man conversion was made on the basis of a daily dose weight proportional to body weight to the two-thirds power.[37] These estimates, based on two studies and involving both rats and mice, agree reasonably well among themselves and also with the estimates in table 6.

To estimate the actual carcinogenic risk to humans it is necessary to account for exposure to chloroform in water. Using several sources, the National Academy of Sciences committee estimated average water consumption to be 1.63 liters per day. The reconnaissance and region 5 surveys offer the best data available on the amount of chloroform currently present in chlorinated drinking water. Because the reconnaissance survey was nationwide it may be a better indicator of chloroform levels throughout the country, although the differences in the chloroform levels detected in the two studies are not that great. Therefore, in estimates of the numbers

35. Hogan and others, "Drinking Water Supplies and Various Site-specific Cancer Mortality Rates."
36. National Academy of Sciences, *Nonfluorinated Halomethanes in the Environment.*
37. Crump and others, "Confidence Intervals and Tests of Hypotheses."

Table 7. Low-Dose Lifetime Risk Estimates from Chloroform for a Man Weighing 70 Kilograms (Based on Rodent Studies[a])

Study	Risk estimate	Upper 95 percent confidence limit
National Academy of Sciences		
Rat male (kidney)	1.5×10^{-7}	3.1×10^{-7}
Rat female (kidney)	1.7×10^{-8}	8.5×10^{-8}
Mouse male (liver)	poor fit	1.3×10^{-6}
Mouse female (liver)	1.7×10^{-6}	2.2×10^{-6}
Roe		
Rat female (total)	$3 \quad \times 10^{-7}$	7.5×10^{-7}
Mouse male (liver)	5.5×10^{-8}	4.9×10^{-7}
Mouse male (liver)	2.3×10^{-7}	7.1×10^{-7}

Sources: National Academy of Sciences, Panel on Low Molecular Weight Halogenated Hydrocarbons of the Coordinating Committee for Scientific and Technical Assessments of Environmental Pollutants of the National Research Council, *Nonfluorinated Halomethanes in the Environment* (Washington, D.C.: NAS, 1978), p. 193; and Roe, "Preliminary Report of Long-Term Tests of Chloroform in Rats, Mice and Dogs."
a. Rodents were given an oral dose of 1 microgram of chloroform per day.

of cases of cancer attributable to chloroform in drinking water it is assumed that the average chloroform concentration in drinking water is 45 micrograms per liter, as calculated for the reconnaissance survey (see table 1). This is possibly an overestimate of the true average concentration. No allowance is made for the fraction of people drinking nonchlorinated water, and, since some of the utilities were selected because they represented special pollution problems, utilities surveyed may have higher than average concentrations of chloroform. Assuming that 1.63 liters is the average daily water consumption, that 45 micrograms per liter is the average concentration of chloroform in drinking water, and that a human being has an average life span of seventy years, the range of potencies listed in table 6 translates into a range of risks of from 210 total cancer cases per year to 549 total cases per year. It should be kept in mind that these risks apply to bladder cancer only and do not include risks of other types of cancers resulting from exposure to chloroform.

Since chlorination results in the formation of other trihalomethanes in addition to chloroform, the number of cancers caused by chlorination would be greater than the number caused by chloroform alone. The reconnaissance survey indicates that chloroform constitutes about 65 percent of the total trihalomethane content of drinking water.[38] Although the other

38. Environmental Protection Agency, *Preliminary Assessment of Suspected Carcinogens in Drinking Water,* app. 1.

trihalomethanes have not been tested in animal bioassays for carcinogenicity, mutagenicity tests suggest that they are more carcinogenic than chloroform.

The estimates of overall risk calculated above may reflect to some extent risks posed by trihalomethanes other than chloroform. The regression study of Hogan and others used chloroform concentration as the only water quality variable, although the concentrations of other organics appear to be positively correlated with chloroform concentrations.[39] Consequently, a portion of the risk Hogan's study attributes to chloroform may also be affected by other organics, particularly the other trihalomethanes.

There is even more uncertainty about the total carcinogenic risk posed by all organics in drinking water. The National Academy of Sciences study on drinking water and health (see table 3) lists twenty-two suspected or known organic chemical carcinogens that have been detected in drinking water.[40] The reconnaissance survey tested water in ten cities for the presence of 129 organic compounds, and the region 5 survey included analyses to detect the presence of polychlorinated biphenyls, phthalates, and nine pesticides. The average concentrations of the organics other than the trihalomethanes were quite low compared with the concentrations of chloroform. The concentrations of these chemicals only negligibly add to the carcinogenic risk posed by chloroform alone when coupled with the carcinogenic potency estimates in table 3. For example, even though it is indicated in table 3 that dieldrin is 200 times more potent than chloroform, the average concentration of dieldrin calculated in the reconnaissance survey is less than 0.001 microgram per liter, whereas the average concentration of chloroform in water from the same utilities is 67 micrograms per liter, or over 67,000 times the concentration of dieldrin. Based on the potencies listed in table 3, the greatest carcinogenic risk from a contaminant other than the trihalomethanes, at levels detected in either the reconnaissance survey or the region 5 survey, occurred with the presence of 5.6 micrograms of vinyl chloride per liter of Miami drinking water. This concentration of vinyl chloride has the same carcinogenic potential as 1.3 micrograms of chloroform per liter. However, the Miami water contained 311 micrograms of chloroform per liter.[41]

39. Hogan and others, "Drinking Water Supplies and Various Site-specific Cancer Mortality Rates."

40. National Academy of Sciences, *Drinking Water and Health,* p. 794.

41. Environmental Protection Agency, *Preliminary Assessment of Suspected Carcinogens in Drinking Water,* apps. 1 and 5.

These findings do not mean, of course, that the primary carcinogenic risk from drinking water is from chloroform or even from the other trihalomethanes. They indicate only that, based on the reconnaissance and region 5 surveys and the potencies listed in table 3, the *known* carcinogens other than the trihalomethanes in drinking water do not appear to add significantly to the risk posed by the trihalomethanes.

Suggestions for Further Research

Estimates of the carcinogenic risks posed by contaminants in drinking water based on existing data are largely speculative. The estimates based on animal data agree closely with estimates calculated from the ecologic study done by Hogan and others.[42] Additional case-control studies may further reduce the uncertainty of recent findings. Studies done in the future should use data from populations for which it is possible to exert the most control over potential confounding factors. Smoking habits should be taken into account if at all possible. Ideally, length of exposure should also be taken into account, and water quality variables should involve direct measurements of organics in drinking water.

Further monitoring of the trihalomethanes in selected utilities could help determine the variation over time of trihalomethane concentrations, since one-time measurements may not reflect long-term concentrations.

Major chemicals in drinking water such as bromodichloromethane and dibromochloromethane should be tested for carcinogenicity in animals. These two chemicals are present in drinking water at levels approaching those of chloroform, and mutagenicity tests suggest that they may be more carcinogenic than chloroform.

Further work should be done on the mutagenicity of organic concentrates in drinking water. Whenever it seems meaningful and feasible to do so, mutagenic potencies of organic concentrates should be compared with chemicals whose carcinogenic potency is well documented.

42. Hogan and others, "Drinking Water Supplies and Various Site-specific Cancer Mortality Rates."

Waterborne Carcinogens: An Economist's View

TALBOT PAGE, ROBERT HARRIS, *and* JUDITH BRUSER

THE STUDY described in this paper analyzes the costs and benefits of implementing the amendment to the interim primary drinking water regulations proposed by the U.S. Environmental Protection Agency in February 1978.[1] Specifically, the study considers the costs and benefits of the water supply systems with contamination levels that may require the use of granular activated carbon as a postfiltration adsorbent.

This study builds on and extends the analysis of the regulations conducted by the National Academy of Sciences.[2] In the words of one of the researchers who worked on that study, the study "should be viewed as a guide for the methodology of benefit-cost analysis and not as a complete and definitive study of the proposed EPA regulation of trihalomethanes."[3] The National Academy of Sciences study is insufficient by itself for evaluating the proposed regulations for the following reasons.

1. The only drinking water contaminant the study considered was chloroform; the effects of other chlorination by-products and synthetic organic chemicals were ignored.

2. The surface area adjustment method that was used to estimate

---

1. U.S. Environmental Protection Agency, "Interim Primary Drinking Water Regulations: Control of Organic Chemical Contaminants in Drinking Water," *Federal Register* (February 9, 1978), pt. 2, pp. 5756–80.
2. National Academy of Sciences, Panel on Low Molecular Weight Halogenated Hydrocarbons of the Coordinating Committee for Scientific and Technical Assessments of Environmental Pollutants of the National Research Council, *Nonfluorinated Halomethanes in the Environment* (Washington, D.C.: NAS, 1978).
3. Letter to Victor Kimm, Environmental Protection Agency, from John Cumberland, University of Maryland, August 29, 1978.

the cancer risk associated with chloroform was inconsistent with a method previously recommended by the National Academy of Sciences panel, which yields an estimate of risk approximately three to fifteen times greater than the "upper limit" and "most probable" risk estimates, respectively, derived from the surface area method.[4]

3. The study made no attempt to integrate evidence from epidemiological studies in its derivation of risk estimates.

4. The only methods of contaminant removal considered were granular activated carbon adsorption and aeration—expensive methods that two of the three levels of contamination dealt with in the study would not require.

5. The only benefit considered was reduced number of cancer deaths; the prevention of other adverse health effects (for example, mutations, birth defects, and fetal deaths), reductions in anxiety about the health risks of contaminated drinking water, and improvements in the taste and odor of tap water were not discussed.

6. Two important factors were excluded from the cost-benefit analysis: irreversibility and risk aversion.[5]

A second study, "Analysis of Proposed EPA Drinking Water Regulations," conducted by the U.S. Council on Wage and Price Stability, follows essentially the methodology of the National Academy of Sciences study.[6] The council's study estimates the incremental cost of the regulations in terms of city size and pollution load. Although this study is helpful, it was not designed to develop a methodology but to make realistic estimates of cost per cancer death prevented and from these to draw

4. National Research Council, Environmental Studies Board, *Pest Control: An Assessment of Present and Alternative Technologies,* vol. 1: *Contemporary Pest Control Practices and Prospects* (National Academy of Sciences, 1975), pp. 64–86.

5. Letter, John Cumberland to Victor Kimm, August 29, 1978. "Since chapter 8 referred to above was necessarily limited by data, time constraints, and other guidelines established for the consideration of the panel, some important aspects were necessarily omitted and should be carefully considered in a complete evaluation. Among the additional important considerations which should be evaluated as the basis for any regulation are: (1) benefits of removal of other THMs [trihalomethanes] besides chloroform; (2) benefits of removal of carcinogens which are not THMs; (3) other benefits such as removal of mutagens; (4) consideration of other means of removing THMs such as alternative forms of disinfectants; and (5) inclusion of other means of risk estimation, most importantly inclusion of the epidemiological evidence."

6. Ivy E. Broder, "Analysis of Proposed EPA Drinking Water Regulations" (U.S. Council on Wage and Price Stability, September 1978).

realistic policy recommendations. Nevertheless, the same six limitations of the National Academy of Sciences study also apply to the council's study, suggesting that the council has significantly underestimated the benefits of improving the quality of drinking water.

The study presented here focuses on water supply systems in communities large enough to be affected by the proposed regulations. We have derived the cancer risks associated with organic drinking water contaminants from the evidence of animal and epidemiological studies. We will also deal to some degree with benefits besides prevented cancer deaths.

We realize that this study has shortcomings, particularly with regard to some simplistic assumptions we have made. As more information is developed on the risks of contaminated drinking water, some of these assumptions may need revision. Also, we refer only briefly to irreversibility and social risk aversion. Nevertheless, we believe that this study, at the very least, carries the analysis of the economic evaluation of the proposed regulations a step beyond the analyses done by the National Academy of Sciences and the Council on Wage and Price Stability of the benefits and costs of chloroform reduction in drinking water. In its approach to risk estimates, the methodology of this paper resembles that used by Hoel and Crump in this volume.

Background

Under the Safe Drinking Water Act of 1974, the Environmental Protection Agency is required to regulate contaminants that may be harmful to human health. Under section 1412(a)(2), these contaminants are to be controlled "to the extent feasible . . . (taking costs into consideration)."[7] The congressional intent is preventive; conclusive proof of an adverse health effect is not a prerequisite to regulation.

The Problem

Recent research has demonstrated that organic contaminants potentially harmful to human health are ubiquitous in America's drinking water. Over 700 such contaminants have been identified, yet they represent only about 15 percent of the total weight of organic matter in drink-

7. 88 Stat. 1662.

ing water.[8] Many contaminants cannot be identified or quantified with present analytical methodologies.

Only a small part (less than 10 percent) of the known contaminants has been adequately tested for adverse health effects. A recent listing by the National Cancer Institute identified twenty-three chemicals as known or suspected carcinogens, thirty chemicals as known or suspected mutagens, and eleven chemicals as tumor promoters (that is, substances that are not in themselves carcinogens but that interact with carcinogens and hasten the rate of tumor formation).[9] In addition, some drinking water contaminants are known to be teratogenic (cause birth defects) or fetotoxic (result in fetal deaths or stunted growth).[10]

Although observed concentrations of specific contaminants range from approximately one part per million parts of water to five parts per trillion (lowest detectable level), concentration levels are meaningless without knowledge of potency.[11] Tests on rodents have revealed more than a 100 millionfold range in the potency of carcinogens. This means that one part of one of the most potent carcinogens per trillion parts of water can cause as much cancer in rodents as one hundred parts of one of the weakest carcinogens per million parts of water. Most information about relative potency comes from animal studies. Although there is much to be learned about comparisons between species, animal studies have shown that chloroform, the most prevalent carcinogen in drinking water, is only moderately potent in rodents and that many chemicals in drinking water with much lower concentrations are far more potent. Dieldrin, for example, which is generally present in far lower concentrations than chloroform, is 1,500 times more potent than chloroform in mice and 3,000 times more potent in all rodent species.[12]

8. National Academy of Sciences, Safe Drinking Water Committee of the National Research Council, *Drinking Water and Health* (NAS, 1977), pp. 489–92; and Environmental Protection Agency, Office of Water Supply, "Statement of Basis and Purpose for an Amendment to the National Interim Primary Drinking Water Regulation on a Treatment Technique for Synthetic Organic Chemicals" (EPA, 1978), p. 1.

9. Talbot Page, Robert Harris, and Judith Bruser, "Removal of Carcinogens from Drinking Water: A Cost-Benefit Analysis," Social Science Working Paper 230 (California Institute of Technology, September 1978), app. A.

10. National Academy of Sciences, *Drinking Water and Health*, pp. 489–856.

11. Environmental Protection Agency, "Statement of Basis and Purpose for an Amendment to the National Interim Primary Drinking Water Regulation," pp. 8–13.

12. National Academy of Sciences, *Drinking Water and Health*, p. 794.

Furthermore, the total risk associated with exposure to multiple carcinogens may be far greater than the sum of the risks posed by each chemical individually, because of synergistic interactions between carcinogens. Exposure to tumor promoters might also enhance the carcinogenic effect of chemicals in drinking water. A single promoter has been shown to intensify the effects of a particular carcinogen by a factor of 1,000.[13] In addition, the effects of drinking water contaminants may be magnified by exposure to other carcinogens and promoters—such as those from food, air pollution, and smoking—which is a problem for people living in urban areas or exposed to occupational carcinogens.

It is clear that organic contaminants pose a potential threat to health today and in the future. The effects of exposure to carcinogens have a typically long latency; the time between exposure and the outbreak of clinical cancer symptoms is often as much as twenty to forty years, depending in some cases on the level of exposure. Drinking water contamination has been consistently linked to gastrointestinal and urinary tract cancer, although associations with other sites (for example, lung and brain) have been observed as well.[14] Mutagens are a suspected causal factor in atherosclerosis, and they are capable of causing subtle biochemical changes, some of which may affect individuals' health now in unknown ways and some of which may not be manifested for several generations. Even less is known about the extent to which drinking water contaminants may contribute to fetal deaths, stunted growth, and birth defects, although a recent study suggests these in fact may be caused by water contaminants.[15]

Although researchers are continually trying to estimate the risks to human health posed by these chemicals, such estimates are highly uncertain. Both means of determining cancer risks—animal experiments and human epidemiologic studies—are limited, and the methodologies used to establish mutagenic and teratogenic effects may be even less applicable to man than animal cancer tests.[16] Because of the uncertainties

13. Eula Bingham and Hans L. Falk, "Environmental Carcinogens: The Modifying Effects of Carcinogens on the Threshold Response," *Archives of Environmental Health,* vol. 19 (December 1969), pp. 779–83.

14. See the paper by Hoel and Crump in this volume.

15. J. D. McKinney and others, "Possible Factors in the Drinking Water of Laboratory Animals Causing Reproductive Failure," in Lawrence H. Keith, ed., *Identification and Analysis of Organic Pollutants in Water* (Ann Arbor Science Publishers, 1976), pp. 417–32.

16. National Academy of Sciences, *Drinking Water and Health,* pp. 19–60.

involved, the appropriate question is, is there enough evidence of potential harm to take precautionary action—or is there enough evidence of safety to justify not taking precautionary action?

Sources of Contamination

The major sources of organic contamination are synthetic organic chemicals that enter the water supply by way of municipal and agricultural runoff, industrial discharges, and chemical spills and natural organic matter produced by decomposing plants and animals. When chlorine disinfectants are added to the water, they interact with the natural organic matter and form a host of chlorinated and brominated compounds. The four trihalomethanes—chloroform, bromoform, dibromochloromethane, and bromodichloromethane—are a subgroup of these compounds and are usually the most prevalent organic contaminants that have been identified so far in chlorinated drinking water.

Organic contamination primarily affects surface water, as opposed to ground water, although ground water contamination is becoming an increasingly severe problem. Surface water supplies most urban areas. Although the proposed regulations distinguish between the trihalomethanes and other organics, contaminated surface water usually contains both types of organics.

Regulatory Approach

The proposed regulations consist of two parts, addressing both types of organics. First, a maximum contaminant level of one hundred parts per billion parts of water was proposed for the trihalomethanes, since they are present in the greatest concentrations and can be easily quantified. Second, the treatment technique of granular activated carbon adsorption, or its equivalent, was proposed as a requirement in some cities to reduce synthetic organics as a group. Regulation of individual chemicals was considered infeasible because they are so numerous and because their concentrations and chemical characteristics make detection difficult.

The trihalomethane standard can be met in a variety of ways. Depending on the types and amounts of natural organic matter present, trihalomethane levels may be reduced by using alternative disinfectants; by chlorinating water after coagulation, sedimentation, and sand filtration have removed the natural organic precursors; or by a combination of these methods. These solutions are less costly than granulated activated carbon adsorption. For water supply systems with 250 parts per billion or more of trihalomethanes, however, granular activated carbon adsorption may also be necessary. Granular activated carbon is also able to remove synthetic organics and natural organics other than the trihalomethanes, as well as unpleasant tastes and odors resulting from organic contaminants and their interactions with chlorine.

The proposed regulations are to be applied initially to water systems serving populations of 75,000 or more. Administrative and economic considerations were the primary reasons for this decision. Only 1 percent of the public water systems are in this size range (390 out of 40,000), yet they serve about 52 percent of the population.[17] Decreasing the size of communities subject to the regulations would greatly increase the number of systems involved and thus increase the difficulty of monitoring. Also, due to economies of scale, granular activated carbon adsorption is relatively more expensive (on a cost-per-gallon basis) for smaller systems than for larger systems.

Of the 390 municipal water systems subject to the proposed regulations, an estimated 121 will not meet one or both of the proposed standards. Of these systems, 61 will be required to install granular activated carbon: 11 to meet the trihalomethane standard, 35 to meet the synthetic organics standard, and 15 to meet both standards.[18]

Benefits of Removing Organic Contaminants from Drinking Water

Removal of organic chemical contaminants from drinking water is associated with the prevention of cancer deaths, nonfatal cancer illnesses, and mutagenic, teratogenic, and fetotoxic effects; the reduction of the anxiety caused by knowing that drinking water poses health risks;[19]

17. Environmental Protection Agency, "Interim Primary Drinking Water Regulation," p. 5764.

18. Temple, Barker and Sloane, Inc., "Revised Economic Impact Analysis of Proposed Regulations on Organic Contaminants in Drinking Water," prepared for the Environmental Protection Agency, Office of Drinking Water (July 5, 1978), p. III-2.

19. Page and others, "Removal of Carcinogens from Drinking Water," app. D. Anxiety is listed separately because under both the willingness-to-pay and the lost earnings approaches the component of cost is often excluded.

and improvements in the taste and odor of tap water. Although some of these benefits would probably result immediately after granular activated carbon was installed, their full impact would not be realized until some future time. Since an individual exposed to a carcinogen may bear an increased risk of cancer throughout his lifetime, the benefits of granular activated carbon may not be fully realized until all persons exposed to drinking water contaminants are no longer living (assumed in this study to be seventy years from now).

The number of nonfatal cancer illnesses which might be prevented annually will depend on the extent to which various cancer sites are affected. The number of these illnesses prevented annually might equal half the number of cancer deaths, although this estimate is uncertain.

The Risk of Cancer Posed by Organic Contaminants in Drinking Water

Cancer causes approximately 365,000 deaths annually in the United States, and about 650,000 new cases of cancer (excluding skin cancer) are detected each year. Gastrointestinal and urinary tract cancer, to which organic drinking water contaminants have been most consistently linked, constitute about 30 percent of all cancer illnesses and deaths, or about 200,000 new cancer cases and 115,000 deaths each year.[20]

Although the extent of excess cancer associated with organic contaminants is unknown, considerable evidence suggests the range of possible risk. Since this study considers the expected benefits and costs of efforts to reduce cancer mortality after the removal of trihalomethanes and synthetic organics, risk estimates have been selected to reflect the range suggested by evidence from animal and short-term tests and from epidemiological studies.

20. These figures were based on (1) estimated U.S. resident population of 217,-599,000 as of April 1, 1978 (U.S. Bureau of the Census, *Current Population Reports*, series P-25, *Population Estimates and Projections*, no. 724, "Estimate of Population of the United States to April 1, 1978" [Government Printing Office, 1978]); (2) annual incidence rates of 3,000 per million population for all types of cancer and 929 for gastrointestinal and urinary tract cancer (U.S. Department of Health, Education, and Welfare, National Cancer Institute, *The Third National Cancer Survey: Advanced Three Year Report, 1969–71 Incidence*, DHEW[NCI] 74-637 [HEW, 1974]); and (3) annual mortality rates of 1,673 per million population for all cancer and 536 for gastrointestinal and urinary tract cancer (HEW, National Center for Health Statistics, *Vital Statistics of the United States, 1973*, vol. 2, pt. A [HEW, 1977]).

Unfortunately, the epidemiological studies that relate excess cancer mortality to drinking water do not distinguish the possible effects of trihalomethanes from those of synthetic organics that may have been in the water. Although water has been chlorinated since about 1910, many synthetic organics are of recent origin. During the chemical revolution of the past thirty years, the annual production of synthetic organic chemicals increased from approximately 5 billion pounds to 500 billion pounds per year. Given a probable twenty- to forty-year latency for most chemical carcinogens, it is likely that most of the effects of synthetic organics have not yet been expressed in total U.S. cancer rates. Those synthetics that have been present long enough to affect current cancer rates may have had a minor impact in comparison with the trihalomethanes.[21] Therefore, currently observed excess cancers demonstrated in epidemiological studies may primarily result from chlorination by-products and may not reflect the risk from exposure to current levels of synthetic organics.

Chlorinated and brominated organic compounds, including those that form after chlorination, and synthetic compounds are not naturally found in mammalian metabolism. Since these compounds' chemical properties make them or their metabolic intermediates prone to interact with genetic material, it is not surprising that a high percentage of them have been shown to be carcinogens or mutagens.[22]

Chlorination by-products to which the public is exposed form continuously over time, and it is impossible to identify exactly the compounds contained in them. The concentration and mix of trihalomethanes to which the public is exposed also depend on how the water is used and processed in the home (see table 1).

Knowledge about chlorination by-products is sparse. Only one of these compounds—chloroform (a trihalomethane)—has been adequately studied in animal tests and found to be carcinogenic. A short-term cancer test (lung adenoma assay) for several drinking water contaminants, including all four trihalomethanes, showed clear positive

---

21. R. H. Harris, T. Page, and N. A. Reiches, "Carcinogenic Hazards of Organic Chemicals in Drinking Water," in H. H. Hiatt, J. D. Watson, and J. A. Winsten, eds., *Origins of Human Cancer,* Cold Spring Harbor Conferences on Cell Proliferation, vol. 4, book A: *Incidence of Cancer in Humans* (Cold Spring Harbor, N.Y.: Cold Spring Harbor Laboratory, 1977), pp. 309–30.

22. Bruce N. Ames, "Identifying Environmental Chemicals Causing Mutations and Cancer," *Science* (May 11, 1979), pp. 587–93.

Table 1. Percentage Increase or Decrease of Three Trihalomethanes above or below Levels Present in Cincinnati Cold Tap Water

Compound	Cold tap	Boiled 5 seconds	Boiled 30 minutes	Hot tap
Chloroform	0	+96.5	−94.0	+108.0
Bromodichloromethane	0	+72.4	−97.2	+78.6
Dibromochloromethane	0	+121.9	−100.0	+141.9

Source: R. Melton and others, "The Analysis of Purgeable Organics in the Drinking Water of Five U.S. Cities" (U.S. Environmental Protection Agency, 1975).

results only for bromoform.[23] In this test, which is relatively insensitive to chemical carcinogens, chloroform—well established as a carcinogen in other tests—yielded negative results. This is consistent with the general observation that brominated analogs are usually more potent carcinogens than the chlorinated species. Short-term mutagenicity tests (Ames test) demonstrated that all trihalomethanes except chloroform were mutagenic and therefore probably carcinogenic.[24] In addition, Ames tests conducted on the nontrihalomethane component showed substantial mutagenic activity in comparison with the same water before chlorination.[25] Similar studies have demonstrated mutagenic activity of raw surface waters[26] and of organic nontrihalomethane concentrates of finished drinking water.[27] Although precise estimates have not been made, the mutagenic activity of the nontrihalomethane fraction would appear to be in the same range as the mutagenic activity of the trihalomethane fraction.

23. Jeffrey C. Theiss and others, "Test for Carcinogenicity of Organic Contaminants of United States Drinking Waters by Pulmonary Tumor Response in Strain A Mice," *Cancer Research,* vol. 37 (August 1977), pp. 2717–20.

24. Vincent F. Simmon, Kristine Kauhanen, and Robert G. Tardiff, "Mutagenic Activity of Chemicals Identified in Drinking Water," in D. Scott, B. A. Bridges, and F. H. Sobels, eds., *Progress in Genetic Toxicology* (New York: Biomedical Press, 1977).

25. Kim Hooper, Cheryl Gold, and Bruce N. Ames, "Development of Methods for Mutagenicity Testing of Wastewater and Drinking Water Samples by the Ames *Salmonella* Test," prepared for the State of California Water Resources Control Board (University of California–Berkeley, 1977).

26. William Pelon, Beth F. Whitman, and Thomas W. Beasley, "Reversion of Histidine-Dependent Mutant Strains of *Salmonella Typhimurium* by Mississippi River Water Samples," *Environmental Science and Technology,* vol. 11 (June 1977), pp. 619–23.

27. J. C. Loper and others, "In Vitro Mutagenic and Carcinogenic Testing of Residual Organics in Drinking Water" (University of Cincinnati Medical School, 1977).

In light of this information, chloroform may be only the tip of the iceberg with respect to the cancer hazard posed by chlorination. Chloroform appears to be only a moderately potent carcinogen, and if it is a mutagen, it may be only a weak one compared with the other trihalomethanes. It thus appears that the carcinogenic potential of the trihalomethanes is probably much greater than that of chloroform alone; indeed, chloroform may be less important than the other trihalomethanes even though it is usually present in higher concentrations. Furthermore, the nontrihalomethane chlorinated component is clearly mutagenic and probably carcinogenic. The trihalomethanes appear to constitute, by weight, only 10 to 20 percent of the total chlorinated organic compounds, most of which remain uncharacterized.[28] This evidence suggests that the cancer risk resulting from chlorination may be grossly underestimated if the risk estimate is based on chloroform alone.

Risk Estimates Based on Animal and Epidemiological Evidence

Hoel and Crump discuss some of the limitations of animal and epidemiological studies. Keeping these limitations in mind, we present here a few additional risk estimates for the few carcinogens in Miami and New Orleans drinking water (both highly contaminated) for which animal data and monitoring data were available. We used two generally accepted and conservative (yielding higher risk estimates) methods of risk estimation: a linear surface area method used by the National Academy of Sciences drinking water committee,[29] and a linear lifetime accumulated dose method recommended by the National Academy of Sciences pesticide committee.[30] The latter method is based on a study of six human carcinogens, and the former is based on theoretical and empirical considerations of chemical carcinogenesis and mammalian metabolism.

The total risk estimations for New Orleans (see table 2), using the surface area and lifetime dose methods, respectively, are approximately 23 and 102 cancers per million people each year; for Miami (see table 3) they are approximately 19 and 34 cancers per million people each year.

28. H. E. Sontheimer and others, "The 'Muheim Process'—Experience with a New Process Scheme for Treating Polluted Surface Water," *Journal of American Water Works Association* (forthcoming).

29. National Academy of Sciences, *Nonfluorinated Halomethanes in the Environment,* pp. 187–92.

30. National Research Council, Environmental Studies Board, *Pest Control,* pp. 64–86.

Table 2. Cancer Risk Estimation for New Orleans Drinking Water for Carcinogens Identified in Environmental Protection Agency Survey Using Surface Area Method and Lifetime Accumulated Dose Method

| | | Risk to most sensitive animal | | | | Risk estimates (cancer per million population annually) | |
| | | Dose (micrograms per kilogram daily) | Exposure (weeks) | Tumor incidence (percent) | Concentration in drinking water (parts per billion) | | |
Carcinogen	Species					Surface area method	Accumulated dose method
1,2-Dichloroethane	Rats	34	78	30	8	0.3	1.6
Hexachloroethane	Mice	421	78	32	4.3	0.0	0.1
Tetrachloroethylene	Mice	382	78	55	0.2	0.0	0.0
Dieldrin	Rats	0.005	104	36	0.07	13.2	83.8
Chloroform	Mice	51	96	22	200[a]	9.7	15.3
1,1,2-Trichloroethane	Mice	279	78	89	8.5	0.2	0.6
DDE	Mice	15	78	43	0.05	0.0	0.0
Bis (2-chloroethyl) ether	Mice	33	78	72	0.16	0.0	0.1
Total risk estimates	...	...	...	...	...	23.4	101.5

Sources: U.S. Environmental Protection Agency, Region 6, *Analytical Report: New Orleans Area Water Supply Study* (EPA, 1975); National Cancer Institute Bioassay Program Report; D. E. Stevenson and others, "The Toxic Effects of Dieldrin in Rats: A Reevaluation of Data Obtained in a Two-Year Feeding Study," *Toxicology and Applied Pharmacology*, vol. 36 (May 1976), pp. 247–54; F. J. C. Roe, "Preliminary Report of Long-Term Tests of Chloroform in Rats, Mice and Dogs" (unpublished paper, London, 1976); and J. R. M. Innes and others, "Bioassay of Pesticides and Industrial Chemicals for Tumorigenicity in Mice: A Preliminary Note," *Journal of the National Cancer Institute*, vol. 42 (June 1969), pp. 1101–14.

a. Based on Environmental Protection Agency analysis of samples from distribution system, 1978.

Table 3. Cancer Risk Estimation for Miami Drinking Water for Carcinogens Identified in Environmental Protection Agency Survey Using Surface Area Method and Lifetime Accumulated Dose Method

Carcinogen	Risk to most sensitive animal				Concentration in drinking water (parts per billion)	Risk estimates (cancer per million population annually)	
	Species	Dose (micrograms per kilogram daily)	Exposure (weeks)	Tumor incidence (percent)		Surface area method	Accumulated dose method
Vinyl chloride	Rats	5.4	104	15	5.6	0.6	2.6
Vinylidene chloride	Rats	1.2	82	18	0.1	0.1	0.6
Hexachlorophene	Mice	421	78	32	0.5	0.0	0.0
Tetrachloroethylene	Mice	382	78	55	0.1	0.0	0.0
Trichloroethylene	Mice	1,169	78	47	0.2	0.0	0.0
Dieldrin	Rats	0.005	104	36	0.002	0.4	2.4
Chloroform	Mice	51	96	22	366	17.8	28.4
Total risk estimates	...	...	...	...	...	18.9	34.0

Sources: Environmental Protection Agency, Office of Toxic Substances, Suspected Carcinogens in Drinking Water: Report to Congress (EPA, December 1975); C. Maltoni, "Vinyl Chloride Carcinogenicity: An Experimental Model for Carcinogenesis Studies," in H. H. Hiatt, J. D. Watson, and J. A. Winsten, eds., Origins of Human Cancer (Cold Spring Harbor, N.Y.: Cold Spring Harbor Laboratory, 1977), pp. 119–46; National Cancer Institute Bioassay Program Report; C. Maltoni and others, "Carcinogenicity Bioassays of Vinylidene Chloride: Research Plan and Early Results," Medicina Del Lavaro, vol. 68 (July–August 1977), pp. 241–62; Stevenson and others, "The Toxic Effects of Dieldrin in Rats"; and Roe, "Preliminary Report of Long-Term Tests."

Table 4. Selected Carcinogens and Mutagens Found in an Eleven-City Survey

Compound	New Orleans	Miami	Seattle	Ottumwa (Iowa)	Phila-delphia	Cincinnati	Tucson	New York	Lawrence	Grand Forks	Terrebonne Parish
*Benzene	X			X	X	X					
*Carbon tetrachloride	X	X		X	X	X		X	X	X	X
*Bis (2-chloroethyl) ether	X				X						
*Chloroform	X	X	X	X	X	X	X	X	X	X	X
*1,2-Dichloroethane	X	X			X	X					
*Dieldrin	X	X	X	X		X					
*DDT, DDE	X										
*Heptachlor	X										
*Hexachlorobenzene	X										
*Hexachlorocyclohexane						X					
*Lindane						X				X	
*Polychlorinated biphenyls						X					
*Tetrachloroethylene	X	X		X	X	X	X	X	X	X	
*Trichloroethylene	X	X		X	X	X	X		X		
*Vinyl chloride		X			X	X					
Bromodichloromethane	X	X	X	X	X	X		X	X	X	X
Chlorobenzene	X	X	X	X	X	X		X	X	X	X
Chloromethylether	X										
Dibromochloromethane	X	X	X		X	X	X	X	X	X	X
1,3-Dichlorobenzene	X	X			X	X			X		
Dichloroiodomethane	X	X			X	X		X	X	X	X
Methylene chloride	X	X	X	X	X	X		X	X	X	X
Vinylidene chloride	X	X			X	X			X	X	X

Source: Talbot Page, Robert Harris, and Judith Bruser, "Removal of Carcinogens from Drinking Water: A Cost-Benefit Analysis," Social Science Working Paper 230 (California Institute of Technology, September 1978).
* Carcinogens.

These risk estimates, however, are incomplete and possibly misleading. The concentration of each carcinogen listed in tables 2 and 3 is based on limited sampling data, and there were present in both waters several additional carcinogens (see table 4) for which either exposure data or carcinogenicity data were not available.

With the lifetime accumulated dose method, which produces the higher risk estimate, it can also be calculated that a trihalomethane level of 250 parts per billion parts of water—a level above which most utilities would probably require granular activated carbon to meet the proposed trihalomethane standard of 100 parts per billion—represents a risk of approximately twenty cancers per million people each year. This contrasts with the National Academy of Sciences drinking water committee's risk estimate of twelve cancers per million people each year and the Council on Wage and Price Stability's estimate of 1.3 cancers per million people each year. These estimates assume that all the trihalomethanes present are as potent as chloroform, an assumption likely to result in an underestimate of the risk since, as discussed above, the brominated trihalomethanes are probably more potent carcinogens than chloroform.

Epidemiological studies suggest substantially higher risks from drinking chlorinated water.[31] In a recent policy statement, the National Cancer Institute referred to a study by Hogan and others[32] that implied that reducing chloroform by 250 parts per billion would result in percentage reductions of combined large intestine and bladder cancer mortality equivalent to approximately twenty-two to fifty-five deaths per million people each year.[33] Another study using a slightly different data base

31. It should also be noted that the epidemiological studies have focused on risk of mortality, while the animal studies have focused more, though not entirely, on cancer incidence. However, the difference between mortality and cancer incidence is relatively small (roughly a factor of two) when compared with the range of risk estimates (one or two orders of magnitude). See Page and others, "Removal of Carcinogens from Drinking Water," app. C.

32. Michael Hogan and others, "Drinking Water Supplies and Various Site-specific Cancer Mortality Rates," *Journal of Environmental Pathology and Toxicology*, vol. 2 (January–February 1979), pp. 873–87.

33. Letter, A. C. Upton to D. M. Costle, April 10, 1978. As the letter noted, one ecologic study implied that reducing chloroform by 100 parts per billion would result in the following percentage reductions in cancer mortality: bladder, 1.3 percent to 7.5 percent for males and 5.3 percent to 10.0 percent for females; and large intestine, 4.0 percent to 8.5 percent for males and 3.0 percent to 7.5 percent for females. To calculate the reduction in cancer mortality that would result from a 250 parts per billion reduction of chloroform, these percentages were multiplied by 2.5 and then applied to the U.S. cancer mortality rates. The results are, for bladder

showed significant associations between chloroform and additional cancer sites, implying that the excess deaths might be somewhat greater.[34]

Two epidemiological studies involving eighty-eight Ohio and sixty-four Louisiana counties suggested that contaminated surface water was responsible for approximately 8 percent and 15 percent, respectively, of the total cancer mortality rate.[35] Given the total U.S. annual cancer mortality rate of about 1,673 deaths per million people, these studies suggest that contaminated surface water similar to surface water in Ohio and Louisiana may be responsible for between 135 and 250 cancer deaths per million people annually. Although the data on the quality of the water included in these studies are insufficient for determining the average exposure to the communities involved, it appears that the risk estimates suggested by these studies are not unreasonable for drinking water with 250 parts of trihalomethanes, as well as synthetic organic chemicals, per billion parts of water. Data on Cincinnati tap water from the Ohio River (gathered before the chlorination procedures were changed) indicate that trihalomethane levels ranged between about 70 and 280 parts per billion within one year, while a one-time reading taken in the fall from the treatment plant for New Orleans showed trihalomethane levels of approximately 140 parts per billion, and summer readings taken from the distribution system ranged from 170 to 250 parts per billion.[36]

A 1977 case control study of cancer rates in seven New York counties indicated that urban areas served by chlorinated water supplies have combined gastrointestinal and urinary tract cancer rates 2.7 times higher than

---

cancer, 61.7 percent reduction for males and 21.0 percent for females; and colon/rectum cancer, 222 percent for males and 231 percent for females (National Center for Health Statistics, *Vital Statistics of the United States, 1973*). The risk calculation for bladder cancer is virtually the same as that given by Hoel and Crump. Inclusion of cancer of the large intestine increases the total.

34. Kenneth P. Canter and others, "Associations of Cancer Mortality with Halomethane in Drinking Water," *Journal of the National Cancer Institute,* vol. 61 (October 1978), pp. 979–85.

35. Harris, Page, and Reiches, "Carcinogenic Hazards of Organic Chemicals in Drinking Water," pp. 320–21; and Talbot Page, Robert H. Harris, and Samuel S. Epstein, "Drinking Water and Cancer Mortality in Louisiana," *Science* (July 2, 1976), pp. 55–57.

36. Data on Cincinnati tap water were provided in a personal communication from A. Stevens, Environmental Protection Agency, Cincinnati, Ohio, July 11, 1978; data on New Orleans were taken from a fall 1975 reading of the Environmental Protection Agency and a personal communication from B. Lykins, Environmental Protection Agency, Cincinnati, July 12, 1978 (summer readings).

urban areas with nonchlorinated water supplies; in rural areas, the cancer rate is 1.8 times higher for chlorinated supplies.[37] (It is not known to what extent higher rates are associated with the level of chlorination by-products, other drinking water contaminants, or other unforeseen factors.) Using the nationwide combined gastrointestinal and urinary tract cancer rate of 536 deaths per million people as an estimate of the rate for areas served by chlorinated water supplies, the above findings suggest that each year 238 to 335 excess deaths per million people are associated with chlorinated drinking water.[38] The estimates derived in this section are summarized in tables 5 and 6.

Selection of Risk Estimates

Because of the pervasive uncertainty surrounding risk assessment for carcinogens in drinking water, it is useful to compare the two sources of estimates—epidemiological and animal bioassays. These two sources rely on completely different data sets: one human and the other rodent (usually). Moreover, they rely on two different methodologies for their calculations of risk. Hoel and Crump have noted the "excellent agreement" between the two sources of estimates.[39] Our own estimates span a wider range than those of Hoel and Crump, primarily because we add cancers of the large intestine to Hogan's estimate and make explicit calculations of risk done in other epidemiological studies. Even so, the estimates from epidemiological studies are only an order of magnitude or two apart from the estimates derived from the animal bioassays. One or two orders of magnitude are well within the range of precision that can reasonably be expected with either of the two approaches. Thus, despite the explicit estimates derived from epidemiological studies, the two sources are in basic agreement, which is surprising in light of the uncertainties of each.[40]

37. Michael Alavanja, Inge Goldstein, and Mervyn Susser, "Case Control Study of Gastrointestinal Cancer Mortality in Seven Selected New York Counties in Relation to Drinking Water Chlorination," prepared for the Environmental Protection Agency, Health Effects Research Laboratory (Columbia University, School of Public Health, September 1977), p. 29.

38. These numbers are not precise, since the cancer data are based on age-standard rates.

39. See the paper by Hoel and Crump in this volume.

40. Hoel and Crump note many of the sources of uncertainty. See also Page and others, "Removal of Carcinogens from Drinking Water."

Table 5. Summary of Risk Estimates from Animal Studies

	Cancer per million population annually	
Model	*Surface area method*	*Lifetime accumulated dose method*
New Orleans	23	102
Miami	19	34
80-city survey of chloroform[a] (250 parts per billion)	12	20

Source: Tables 2 and 3 in this paper.
a. See page 211 for assumptions.

Table 6. Summary of Risk Estimates from Epidemiological Studies

Model	Cancer per million population annually
Ohio (surface water)[a]	140
Louisiana (Mississippi River water)[b]	250
80-city survey of chloroform (250 parts per billion)[c]	22–55
New York counties (chlorinated water)[d]	240–340

a. Calculated from R. H. Harris, T. Page, and N. A. Reiches, "Carcinogenic Hazards of Organic Chemicals in Drinking Water," in Hiatt, Watson, and Winsten, eds., *Origins of Human Cancer*, pp. 309–30.
b. Calculated from Talbot Page, Robert H. Harris, and Samuel S. Epstein, "Drinking Water and Cancer Mortality in Louisiana," *Science* (July 2, 1976), pp. 55–57.
c. Calculated from Michael Hogan and others, "Drinking Water Supplies and Various Site-specific Cancer Mortality Rates," *Journal of Environmental Pathology and Toxicology*, vol. 2 (January–February 1979), pp. 873–87.
d. Calculated from Michael Alavanja, Inge Goldstein, and Mervyn Susser, "Case Control Study of Gastrointestinal Cancer Mortality in Seven Selected New York Counties in Relation to Drinking Water Chlorination," prepared for the U.S. Environmental Protection Agency, Health Effects Research Laboratory (Columbia University, School of Public Health, September 1977).

As shown in tables 5 and 6 there is about one order of magnitude difference between the risk estimate based on lifetime accumulated dose and the risk estimate based upon the epidemiological studies of the Mississippi River and chlorinated drinking water in New York State. The surface area method would have produced a risk estimate of approximately one cancer death per million (the Council on Wage and Price Stability's estimate). There appears to be no decisive scientific basis for choosing between the two extrapolation techniques recommended by the National Academy of Sciences so, to be on the conservative side, the higher estimate was chosen to reflect the likelihood that (1) brominated trihalomethanes are considerably more potent (ten to one hundred times) than chloroform, and (2) the trihalomethanes represent as little as 10 percent of the total chlorinated organics resulting from chlorination.

Therefore, the following risk estimates were selected for this study:

Level of risk	Annual excess cancer deaths per million population
Low	20
Medium	150
High	300

Since the average annual cancer mortality rate is about 1,673 per million population for all cancers and 536 for gastrointestinal and urinary tract cancer, these low, medium, and high risk factors imply that drinking water carcinogens are responsible for about 1 percent, 9 percent, and 18 percent, respectively, of total cancer mortality, or 4 percent, 28 percent, and 56 percent of gastrointestinal and urinary tract cancer mortality in those communities whose water quality resembles that of cities with an excess risk indicated by the epidemiological studies.[41]

The low risk estimate is based on the death rate of the laboratory animal (mouse) most sensitive to chloroform; the medium risk estimate is a midpoint between the low and high estimates; and the high risk estimate is based on the epidemiological studies of chlorinated water in New York and of Mississippi River water in Louisiana. In neither of these studies was it possible to separate the risk posed by trihalomethanes from the risk posed by synthetic organics. In the New York study, the apparent risk from chlorinated water may have been confounded by the association of chlorination with the presence of synthetic organics; in the Louisiana study, both trihalomethanes and synthetic organics were present in the analysis conducted in 1974.[42] The extent to which they were present in the 1930s and 1940s and thus expressed in the 1950–69 cancer mortality rates upon which the epidemiological studies were based can only be speculated. However, given the recent industrial origin of most synthetic organics and the twenty- to forty-year lag before the effects of newly introduced chemicals would be reflected in cancer mortality rates, it is quite possible that synthetic organics contribute little to the risk estimates derived from the New York, Louisiana, and Ohio studies. The calculated benefits of granular activated carbon treatment, which are based on these risk estimates, may reflect only the benefits of reducing chlorination by-products; the benefits of removing synthetic organics would be largely

41. These percentages are based on current cancer rates. If the total of gastrointestinal and urinary tract cancer rates double in the next forty years, these estimated percentages would halve.

42. Environmental Protection Agency, Region 6, *Analytical Report: New Orleans Area Water Supply Study* (EPA, 1975).

excluded. Therefore, to the extent that synthetic organics pose a health hazard, the benefits of granular activated carbon treatment calculated from these risk estimates are underestimated (in cases in which granular activated carbon is required to meet only the trihalomethane standard).

In addition to causing fatal cancer illnesses, drinking water carcinogens can also be expected to cause nonfatal cancer illnesses. For example, about 51 percent of bladder cancer victims survive, compared with the 1 percent of pancreatic cancer victims who survive. If all the excess deaths associated with drinking water were due to bladder cancer, the amount of nonfatal illness would be far greater than would be the case if the excess deaths were due solely to pancreatic cancer. The annual incidence of nonfatal gastro-intestinal and urinary tract cancer cases is about half the number of annual deaths caused by these cancers. If it can be assumed that excess cancers caused by drinking water carcinogens are gastrointestinal and urinary tract and that these cancers are increased to the same degree by drinking water carcinogens, then these carcinogens may be responsible for an annual number of nonfatal illnesses equal to about half the number of excess deaths. However, since it is unknown whether or not these assumptions are true, such an estimate of nonfatal illness caused by drinking water contaminants is uncertain. Although the cost of nonfatal illness is much lower than that of mortality, the difference in the range of estimated risk of death by cancer caused by waterborne carcinogens has a much larger impact on the estimated benefits of water treatment than does a reduction of the incidence of nonfatal disease. For this reason we will not attempt to quantify the cost of nonfatal illness, except to note that it is substantial. A more refined cost-benefit analysis should include as far as possible the benefit of reduced morbidity.

Costs of Removing Organic Contaminants from Drinking Water with Granular Activated Carbon

In this section we analyze the cost of removing organic compounds with granular activated carbon. Requirement of this process was the more comprehensive proposal that the Environmental Protection Agency first suggested but which it then decided not to implement. The trihalomethane standard that the agency finally promulgated is analyzed by Kimm and others in this volume. The granular activated carbon treatment analyzed here is a more expensive and comprehensive solution to the problem of

Table 7. Annual Costs per Resident of Granular Activated Carbon Adsorption
Costs in 1978 dollars

	System size (*population served*)[b]		
Increase in annual residential water bill[a]	*Small* (*75,000–100,000*)	*Medium* (*100,000–1,000,000*)	*Large* (*over 1,000,000*)
Standard cost			
9-minute contact time	16.20	10.50	7.10
18-minute contact time	23.00	15.00	11.40
High cost (25 percent extra site-specific capital expenditures)			
9-minute contact time	18.50	11.90	7.90
18-minute contact time	26.10	17.00	12.70
Annual revenue requirements for standard cost, 18-minute contact time	1,418,310.00	2,632,000.00	10,259,800.00

Source: Temple, Barker and Sloane, Inc., "Revised Economic Impact Analysis of Proposed Regulations on Organic Contaminants in Drinking Water," prepared for the U.S. Environmental Protection Agency, Office of Drinking Water (July 5, 1978), pp. II-21 and III-7.

a. For a family of three.

b. Cost estimates are based on plant production on the average day in the month of maximum production.

waterborne carcinogens than is the trihalomethane standard. If it can be shown that the treatment is justified by the benefits derived from it, the less comprehensive trihalomethane standard is likely to be even more clearly justified.

The economies of scale associated with granular activated carbon will lead to significant differences in water costs for different-sized communities. In the Environmental Protection Agency's economic impact analysis of the proposed regulations, communities of 75,000 or more were divided into three size categories: communities with populations of 75,000–100,000, 100,000–1,000,000, and over 1,000,000. The most representative population size in each category was 92,700, 263,200, and 1,193,000, respectively.[43]

Annual costs to the representative communities (see table 7) include annual operating and maintenance costs and initial capital expenditures amortized over the life of the adsorption system, based on how capital expenditures are likely to be financed. Standard costs were estimated on the basis of a sixty-day regeneration cycle and nine- and eighteen-minute

43. Temple, Barker and Sloane, "Revised Economic Impact Analysis of Proposed Regulations on Organic Contaminants in Drinking Water," p. II-21.

contact times, longer contact times being necessary for raw water of poorer quality. High cost estimates incorporate 25 percent more capital expenditures, which may be necessary for site-specific construction problems.

We have evaluated the benefits of granular activated carbon for the representative populations in each size category; presumably the results can be generalized to all communities within the same size category. To account for the variations in cost in a moderately conservative manner, the standard costs for the eighteen-minute contact time is used. For the small, medium, and large systems, these annual total costs are $1.4 million, $2.6 million, and $10.3 million, respectively, resulting in residential water bill increases (for a family of three) of $11 to $23 annually.

Evaluating Benefits and Costs

Because of the latency period involved in cancer, the distribution over time of the benefits of granular activated carbon treatment differs markedly from the distribution of costs. This creates the problem of fair cost distribution over time. This problem is especially important when human lives are involved and when effects span several generations, as is the case with granular activated carbon treatment. Accounting satisfactorily for distributional or equity effects across generations is not easy.[44]

One approach that appears to be fair to future generations is the steady state comparison test, which was used in both the National Academy of Sciences and the Council on Wage and Price Stability studies. The first seventy years or so after the installation of granular activated carbon can be considered a transition period during which cancer rates decline; during this time the benefits of granular activated carbon grow while the costs remain relatively constant (in real terms). After seventy years, the ratio of benefits to costs remains fairly steady for the foreseeable future. As a way of taking into account the future's perspective, which is longer term than the transition period, evaluation of granular activated carbon is based on the comparison of costs and benefits in the steady state.

44. See John Ferejohn and Talbot Page, "On the Foundations of Intertemporal Choice," *American Journal of Agricultural Economics*, vol. 60 (May 1978), pp. 269–75; and Erza Mishan and Talbot Page, "The Methodology of Cost Benefit Analysis with Particular Reference to the Ozone Problem," Environmental Protection Agency Program on Biological and Climatic Effects Research, 1978.

For comparison we also calculate present values of costs and benefits at 3 percent, 7 percent, and 10 percent discount rates. Some have recommended a lower discount rate to provide for intergenerational equity,[45] but we consider the steady state comparison more equitable in this case.

Quantitative Analysis

For the discounted benefits and costs, a time horizon of one hundred years was selected to fully capture the stream of benefits, which we have assumed will increase steadily during seventy years and then remain at the same level for an infinite length of time. (The difference between discounting over a hundred years and an infinite period is insignificant.) Costs are in 1978 dollars.

The quantitative analysis of benefits is limited to cancer deaths prevented. This approach ignores the several additional benefits of granular activated carbon and thus biases the results of the analysis against this procedure. The rationale for adopting this approach is pragmatic. If the cost of granular activated carbon appears justified when it is assumed that the only benefit is prevention of cancer deaths, then it is not necessary to assess the value of the additional benefits. The benefits of reduced anxiety and improvements in tap water's taste and odor would be particularly difficult to measure, and the magnitude of additional health benefits is uncertain. Such an assessment will be necessary, however, if the cost of granular activated carbon does not appear justified when only cancer deaths prevented are considered.

In evaluating the benefit of cancer deaths prevented, the saving of a human life is not assigned a dollar value. Instead, for a variety of cancer mortality and discount rates, the cost of granular activated carbon per life saved is indicated, thus allocating the total costs of granular activated carbon adsorption to saved lives. If this cost is less than a reasonable expenditure for saving a human life, then it can be said that the benefits exceed the costs, precluding the need to quantify other benefits.

Use of the risk estimates of 20 to 300 excess cancer deaths per million people annually implies that the community for which this analysis most directly applies is one which depends for its water supply on moderately

45. Robert M. Solow, "The Economics of Resources or the Resources of Economics," *American Economic Review*, vol. 64 (May 1974, *Papers and Proceedings, 1973*), pp. 1–14.

polluted surface water, with trihalomethane levels in the distribution system of approximately 250 parts per billion parts of water. Communities with lower trihalomethane levels could probably meet the Environmental Protection Agency's standard of one hundred micrograms per liter at considerably lower cost than granular activated carbon treatment by adjustments in the disinfection method. Although epidemiological studies cannot be used to estimate the risk from exposure to current levels of synthetic organics, limited risk estimates for New Orleans and Miami (see tables 3 and 4) suggest that these risks are in the same range as for the trihalomethanes and may be higher, considering the presence of numerous carcinogens and suspected carcinogens (mutagens and structural analogs of carcinogens) for which data are not available in a form appropriate for estimating risk. Furthermore, for communities that are required to install granular activated carbon to reduce the level only of synthetic organics, benefits will also accrue from concurrent reductions of trihalomethanes and other chlorination by-products.

Although it is assumed that granular activated carbon would reduce cancer risk from drinking water by 90 percent, there is some uncertainty about this estimate. It is impossible to determine how much the reduction in organic contaminants would reduce cancer risk. From studies conducted by the Environmental Protection Agency, it is clear that granular activated carbon is at least 60 percent effective in removing trihalomethanes and is highly effective—in some cases more than 90 percent—in removing industrial chemicals such as polycyclic aromatic hydrocarbons and polychlorinated pesticides (for example, dieldrin and kepone). Since the latter are likely to be more potent carcinogens and mutagens than the former, granular activated carbon would probably reduce the risk of cancer by at least 60 percent and possibly more than 90 percent.

Method of Calculation

The costs of granular activated carbon per life saved are calculated according to the following steps. First, the total number of excess cancer deaths is calculated by applying each risk factor to the total population of each representative community. For example, for the large community with a population of 1.193 million, the high cancer risk rate of 300 deaths per million annually would yield 358 (300 times 1.193) excess deaths annually. Second, the number of lives that would be saved annually after the excess cancer rate had ceased declining (after seventy years) is calculated as 90 percent of the number of excess deaths, since it is assumed that granular activated carbon adsorption would eliminate 90 percent of the excess deaths. For example, 358 excess deaths times 90 percent equals 322 lives saved.

To calculate the costs of granular activated carbon per life saved in the steady state, the number of lives that would be saved annually after seventy years is divided into the annual cost of granular activated carbon, irrespective of expenditures in earlier years, when fewer lives per year were saved. To calculate the cost per life saved under discounting, three additional steps are taken.

First, for seventy-one to one hundred years, the number of lives saved per year would be the same as under the steady state. For the first seventy years, it is assumed that the number of lives saved each year would be zero initially, then increase more and more rapidly, and then taper off to a steady state.[46] For example, for the large community, assuming that the cancer risk is high, the number of lives saved would be none the fifth year, 51 in the twenty-fifth year, 271 in the forty-fifth year, and 322 in the sixty-fifth year. Second, the cost of granular activated carbon for each representative community is discounted. Third, a cost per life saved is chosen so that when discounted back at the same rate, the total would be equal to the granular activated carbon's discounted costs.[47]

Results

The results of the quantitative analyses for the large, medium, and small communities are presented in table 8. These results are depicted graphically in figures 1, 2, and 3. The cost per life saved ranges from about $32,000 to $17.4 million. In sixteen out of thirty-six cases, the cost per life saved is less than $500,000 and is about $100,000 or less in eight cases. In twelve cases the cost per life saved exceeds $1 million.

Because of economies of scale, the cost per life saved for the small community is 1.5 to 2 times that for the large community, and the cost for the medium community is about 1.1 times the cost for the large community. For any assumed level of cancer mortality, applying the steady state comparison test or the various discount rates causes the cost per life

46. Page and others, "Removal of Carcinogens from Drinking Water," app. E.
47. This approach incorporates one definition, but not the only one, of intertemporal opportunity cost per life saved. See Mishan and Page, "The Methodology of Cost Benefit Analysis."

Table 8. Allocation of Granular Activated Carbon Costs to Reduced Cancer Mortality Alone

System size and population[a]	Excess cancer mortality rate (annual deaths per million)[b]	Cost per life saved (thousands of dollars)[c]			
		Steady state	3 percent	7 percent	10 percent
Large (more than 1,000,000)	20–300	32–489	93–1,434	269–4,147	545–8,789
Medium (100,000–1,000,000)	20–300	37–526	108–1,552	308–4,620	639–10,197
Small (75,000–100,000)	20–300	57–709	166–2,132	476–7,206	1,000–17,474

Source: Based on data in Temple, Barker and Sloane, "Revised Economic Impact Analysis of Proposed Regulations on Organic Contaminants in Drinking Water."

a. Calculations are based on the following representative systems in each size category: large, population 1,193,000, annual granular activated carbon costs of $10.3 million; medium, population 263,200, annual granular activated carbon costs of $2.6 million; small, population 92,700, annual granular activated carbon costs of $1.4 million.

b. Based on trihalomethane concentrations of 250 parts per billion parts of water. It is assumed that treatment by granular activated carbon adsorption will reduce the excess cancer mortality rate by 90 percent.

c. Discount rate applied over one hundred years.

saved to vary by a factor of 17 to 25. For any selected discount rate, or in the steady state of cancer mortality, the cost per life saved will vary by only a factor of 12 to 17. Thus the decision of how to treat the intergenerational equities has a greater impact than the choice of risk within the range of estimates used here.

Conclusion

Can the cost of granular activated carbon be justified when only the benefits of cancer death reduction are taken into account? The cost per life saved is an amount dependent on an objective judgment of the cancer risk associated with organic drinking water contaminants and on social judgments about how the interests of future generations should be weighed against those of the present generation. In addition to considering these issues, decisionmakers must consider how much should be spent to save a human life.

Figures 1, 2, and 3 show that the steady state approach, taking intertemporal equity into account, is the most favorable to the future. The highest curves in the figures show net benefits discounted at 10 percent under the assumption that prevention of cancer deaths is the only benefit of granular activated carbon. The curves can be interpreted as calculations omitting consideration of intertemporal equity. The curves labeled 3 and 7 percent represent intermediate steps between the steady state and discount approaches.

The figures indicate that if three unconservative assumptions are taken together, granular activated carbon treatment will not be justified. The unconservative assumptions are that (1) little or no weight be given to the epidemiological evidence, so that the risk of cancer is estimated low—fewer than twenty deaths per million; (2) little or no benefit be assigned to preventing mutagenic disease, birth defects, and improvements in tap water's taste and odor, so that the cost per life saved is allocated totally to cancer deaths prevented; and (3) no consideration be given to intertemporal equity, so that cancer deaths would be discounted over periods of forty years and more. The Council on Wage and Price Stability and the National Academy of Sciences use the first two assumptions but not the last one.[48]

48. Broder, "Analysis of Proposed EPA Drinking Water Regulations"; and National Academy of Sciences, *Nonfluorinated Halomethanes in the Environment*, pp. 228–51.

Figure 1. Allocation of Cost of Granular Activated Carbon to Reduction in Cancer Mortality Alone, Communities of over 1,000,000

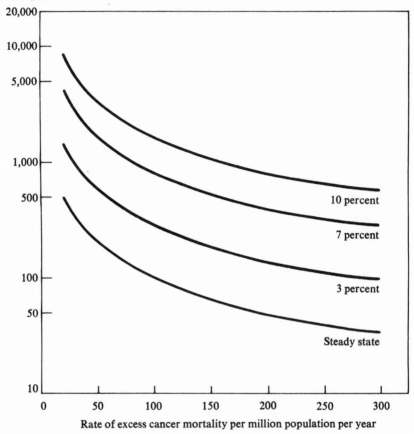

Cost per life saved (thousands of dollars)

Rate of excess cancer mortality per million population per year

Source: Curves generated for this paper based on data in Temple, Barker and Sloane, Inc., "Revised Economic Impact Analysis of Proposed Regulations on Organic Contaminants in Drinking Water," prepared for the Environmental Protection Agency, Office of Drinking Water, July 5, 1978.

An important issue in evaluating granular activated carbon is how conservative an attitude society should have toward the risk of cancer. We believe that a prudent attitude would place some weight on the epidemiological and other evidence of the mutagenicity and carcinogenicity of organics other than chloroform and the other trihalomethanes. Nevertheless, an important conclusion to emerge from the calculations of cost per life saved, under varying assumptions, is that justification of granular activated carbon need not be based on the epidemiological evidence at all,

Figure 2. Allocation of Cost of Granular Activated Carbon to Reduction in Cancer Mortality Alone, Communities of 100,000 to 1,000,000

Cost per life saved (thousands of dollars)

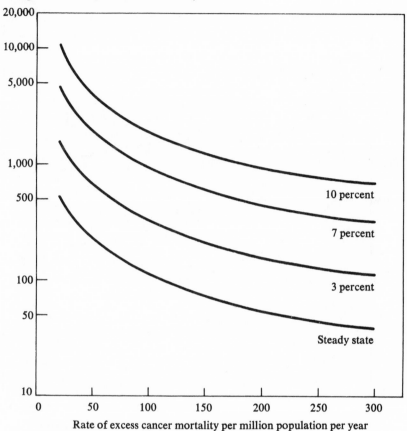

Rate of excess cancer mortality per million population per year

Source: Same as figure 1.

or on the inclusion of other benefits besides cancer deaths prevented. Applying the accumulated lifetime dose method instead of the surface area adjustment method and use of the steady state represent relatively conservative approaches toward cancer risk and yet justify, without the epidemiological evidence, the cost of granular activated carbon.[49]

49. In the steady state, assuming a minimum risk of twenty deaths per million, the cost per life saved is $709,000 or less, depending on community size (see figures 1–3). This cost per life saved falls within the range of estimates of willingness to pay per life saved of $200,000 to $1.5 million. Page and others, "Removal of Carcinogens from Drinking Water."

Figure 3. Allocation of Cost of Granular Activated Carbon to Reduction in Cancer Mortality Alone, Communities of 75,000 to 100,000

Cost per life saved (thousands of dollars)

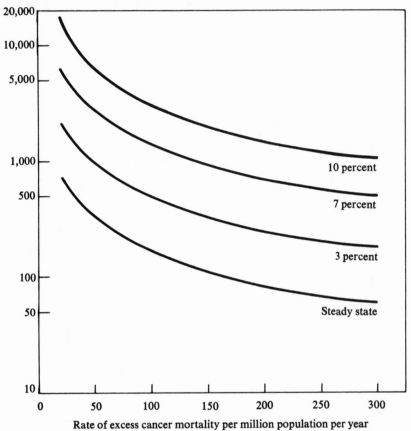

Rate of excess cancer mortality per million population per year

Source: Same as figure 1.

But benefits other than cancer prevention should be included in decisionmaking, at least to the extent that they can be quantified. Some sense of the value of the benefits of taste and odor control is indicated by the costs of bottled water and home filtration devices, which are used primarily to produce good-tasting drinking water and which would no longer be necessary if granular activated carbon treatment were implemented. Compared with the annual household cost of such treatment—$11 to $23— regular household use of bottled water costs about $65 to $115 per year, depending on geographic region.[50] Home filtration devices cost about $5 to $12 per year for filter replacement, after an initial cost of $20 to $40.[51] About forty communities seek good-tasting drinking water at lower household costs by using granular activated carbon in sand filter beds; the cost of this use of the carbon is about 15 to 20 percent of the cost of using it in contactors as a postfiltration adsorbent.[52]

Taken together, these additional benefits may have substantial value, and some portion of the total costs of granular activated carbon should be allocated to securing them. For this reason, the actual cost of saving a life will be less than the costs per life saved already discussed. If the value of the additional benefits can be assessed in relation to the value of the total benefits, the cost per life saved could be adjusted downward proportionally to determine the cost of saving a life by itself. For example, if the additional benefits were valued at one-third of the total benefits, then the cost of saving a life would be one-third less than the costs per life saved. This type of adjustment is a more appropriate basis for evaluating the cost of saving lives by granular activated carbon treatment.

One of the major problems in such an evaluation is the large range of uncertainty in estimating cancer risk. Until more information becomes available, it may at first seem sensible to delay decisions so that granular activated carbon filtration plants will not be built unnecessarily. If the risk of cancer from drinking water contaminants turns out to be negligible, society would have to live with its mistake for the life of the treatment plant (about forty years). However, against this irreversibility one must balance the irreversibilities of cancer, mutagenic disease, and birth defects, as well as their costs. The period of irreversibility for cancer is forty years or more, due to the latency factor; for mutagenic disease the period of irreversibility is in terms of generations. Thus if the true cancer risk turns out to be twenty deaths or more annually per million people, and if the building of granular activated carbon treatment plants is delayed, society

50. Based on consumption of five gallons every two weeks (a common minimum order for home delivery) and per gallon costs of 50 to 90 cents.

51. Based on recommended retail prices of three major brands.

52. For the three sizes of water treatment plants upon which this analysis is based, the annual costs of using granular activated carbon in filter beds for taste and odor control would be $2,342,800 for a large system; $574,000 for a medium system; and $219,500 for a small system. These costs include the construction of a filter shell and are based on a three-year carbon replacement cycle. Environmental Protection Agency, Municipal Environmental Research Laboratory, Cincinnati, Ohio, personal communication to the author, August 23, 1978.

will have to live with the unnecessarily caused diseases generated during this delay for a longer time than it would have to live with the irreversibility of carbon plant construction. More important, unnecessarily caused genotoxic disease is potentially more severe than unnecessarily built plants.

During the first few years after a decision to build granular activated carbon plants is made—in the planning and permit stage—the decision to build is reversible at low cost. Once the physical plant is constructed—perhaps five or more years after the decision is made—the original decision becomes in part irreversible because of sunk capital costs. Operating and maintenance costs, however, remain reversible. In contrast, every year of exposure to carcinogens and mutagens is largely irreversible in ultimate effect. Consideration of irreversibility usually suggests delay until more is known, lest highly valued options be irreversibly foreclosed. In the case of drinking water treatment, preservation of options suggests earlier introduction of preventive measures because the potentially more severe irreversibilities are on the side of cancer and mutation. The two potential uncertainties suggest the following strategy: an early commitment to plan and build granular activated carbon treatment plants so as to reduce the expected costs of irreversibility of cancer, coupled with intensive research on cancer and drinking water during the treatment plant planning stage to reduce the expected costs of irreversibility of treatment plant construction.

Social risk aversion implies a greater avoidance of the potentially more costly mistake than would be indicated by expected value calculations. The potential costs of granular activated carbon are fairly well defined by engineering calculations, but the potential costs of genotoxic disease are poorly bounded—cancer being the only one even partially quantified. Because the calculations of cost per life saved with granular activated carbon are based on expected values in this paper, consideration of risk aversion adds an additional factor in favor of preventive treatment.[53]

53. Expected value calculations are also used in Broder, "Analysis of Proposed EPA Drinking Water Regulations"; and National Academy of Sciences, *Nonfluorinated Halomethanes in the Environment*.

Waterborne Carcinogens:
A Regulator's View

VICTOR J. KIMM, ARNOLD M. KUZMACK,
and DAVID W. SCHNARE

COST-BENEFIT analysis is useful in the regulatory decision process because it helps identify many anticipated effects of regulations and establish program priorities and the order in which potential regulatory actions should be followed. However, there are serious problems in quantifying various factors in such analysis, especially those related to health effects. The widespread use of cost-benefit analysis may not lead to improved decisionmaking.

Risk of death, injury, or serious illness is an ever-present aspect of daily living. Indeed, we all take measurable risks for benefits that are small or even frivolous. Every time we drive to another city instead of flying, or every time we get impatient while trying to make a left turn and do not wait until all oncoming cars have passed, we are showing that we place a finite value on our own lives. And though we may take those risks voluntarily, they are involuntary for the friends and family members riding with us.

In the broad range of societal activities called "regulation," implicit valuation of human life and the resulting limitation on what we as a society are willing to pay to save lives are commonplace. No regulatory agency would, for example, seriously consider requiring the installation of a technically perfect air bag system costing $10,000 for each car, even if the law explicitly required the maximum feasible protection. No government regulatory agency is trying to achieve a "zero-risk society." The

The views expressed in this paper are those of the authors and do not necessarily represent the official position of the U.S. Environmental Protection Agency.

Delaney clause in the 1958 Food Additive Amendments, for example, is one of the few cases in which Congress itself balanced risk and benefit rather than delegating this judgment to a regulatory agency.[1] Congress concluded (whether correctly or not) that no food additive had sufficient benefits to justify any carcinogenic risk.

Such balancing is not new. When the Food and Drug Administration set allowable levels for mercury in fish, it had to make a whole series of assumptions involving such things as the level of fish consumption, the reliability of toxicity studies, the proportion of the mercury that is in the more toxic organic forms, and the magnitude of the safety factor. There would be a substantial difference in the final mercury level, for example, if it were based on the 90th percentile of fish consumption or on the 99.9th percentile. Thus, depending on these and other similar assumptions, the Food and Drug Administration could be more or less conservative, more or less stringent in the level eventually set. The point is that judgments about the costs and benefits of alternative mercury levels are buried in the choices that were made. So what is new is not that the balancing of risks and benefits is going on, but that it is becoming more explicit, particularly in the regulation of carcinogens. Since we assume that there is no safe level for a carcinogen, we can no longer pretend that our standards are safe levels—that is, levels at which no risk would occur.

As society grapples with the problems of regulation of carcinogens, regulatory agencies are being urged to quantify risks and benefits and to conduct cost-benefit analyses. President Carter's Executive Order 12044 encouraged the performance of such analyses, and President Reagan's executive order goes considerably further in this direction.[2] A variety of regulatory reform bills have been introduced in Congress that would require them with varying degrees of strictness. Some of these proposals seem to be based on the naive notion that the agencies do not balance risks and benefits and should, and that doing so would clearly show that many regulations are unjustified. A more sophisticated version of this argument maintains that the quality of decisionmaking would be vastly improved if agencies' implicit judgments about risks and benefits were made explicit and subjected to as much rigorous and quantitative analysis as possible. The regulatory agencies certainly have problems and should take advantage of whatever will enable them to make correct choices. But the

1. 72 Stat. 1785.
2. E. O. 12044, "Improving Government Regulation," 3 C.F.R. 152 (1978); E. O. 12291, *Federal Register,* vol. 46 (February 19, 1981), pp. 13193–98.

Environmental Protection Agency's experience with the drinking water regulations leads to serious doubts that formal risk-benefit or cost-benefit analyses will actually improve decisionmaking.

To understand why, it is important to understand how carcinogens are regulated. All the federal regulatory agencies have made the policy judgment to treat carcinogens as though they have nonthreshold effects—that is, as if any exposure to such a substance, no matter how small, causes a small but nonzero probability of a cancer that could result in death. This is a policy judgment that has been developed over a long period, not a statement of scientifically proven fact. The basis of the judgment can be summarized briefly.

First, the existence of a threshold cannot be experimentally proven. Suppose that at some dose level, an experiment fails to show any positive response. Empirically the possibility cannot be ruled out that an experiment with a much larger sample size would have shown an effect. (Even if the larger experiment were then performed, the same argument could be applied.) Although this holds true for all toxicants, carcinogens and certain other categories of toxicants are treated differently.

For conventional toxicants a threshold is assumed, and the experimental data are used to estimate it, usually by taking the lowest no-effect dose and applying a series of safety factors that have been developed in the folklore of toxicology to allow for the genetic variability of the population and other factors. A threshold is assumed because the kinds of toxic effects in question are those in which a substantial number of cells must be functionally impaired to produce an adverse effect on the whole organism. For example, most of us could have a few liver cells damaged with no ill effects, since proliferation of new cells would compensate for the loss. It is only when a large portion of the cells in a particular organ are affected that the body is unable to compensate and a toxic effect occurs. In chemical carcinogenesis, on the other hand, a complex and poorly understood process occurs in a single cell and transforms that cell into a tumor cell that will multiply uncontrollably and eventually kill the host. However the chemical carcinogen participates in that process, it is likely that a single molecule or only a few molecules are involved. For that molecule to reach the cell's vulnerable point, another complex series of metabolic transformation and transport (pathways) must occur. That process may not be linear in dose, of course, and may include a large number of minor, virtually immeasurable, pathways along with the major pathways. In only a few cases is anything known about the major pathways, and it is impossible to reliably link knowledge about metabolism to the carcinogenic process.

For these reasons, the federal agencies involved in regulating carcinogens have reached the policy judgment to treat all carcinogens as though there were no threshold to their action. This means that when there is evidence that a substance causes cancer at high doses, it should be assumed that there is some risk at low doses as well. This assumption is consistent with what is known about carcinogenesis, but cannot be tested scientifically. This does not mean, however, that the substance should be banned or otherwise regulated. The decision about whether to regulate depends on a balancing of risks against benefits.

Evidence of Risk

Three kinds of evidence typically indicate that a substance is a carcinogen. First, in a few cases, there is clear-cut human evidence. This can be expected only when there are well-defined highly exposed and unexposed groups in the population, as with those who smoke and those who are exposed to some occupational chemicals, or when the tumors involved are of such a rare type that any clustering is strong evidence, as with liver angiosarcoma caused by vinyl chloride. While such evidence should obviously be exploited when it exists, it is likely to be available only in these special circumstances.

Second, there may be ambiguous human evidence in a few cases. When the exposures are low, as is usually the case with environmental contaminants, the magnitude of the effects is also likely to be small and therefore difficult to detect in an epidemiological study. When a positive association is observed, it is difficult to be certain whether it is caused by the substance or substances under consideration or by some other unrelated factor that happens to be correlated with the substance or by possible confounding factors. In the case of organic contaminants in drinking water, most of the dozen epidemiological studies that have been done demonstrate an association between cancer rates and some aspect of drinking water. Yet such association does not prove that chemicals in drinking water cause cancer but rather adds weight to the hypothesis of an effect on cancer rates.

Finally, in most cases, we will be forced to rely on animal experiments. Unlike the second type of epidemiological study, most animal studies generally show that the effects observed are in fact caused by the chemicals being studied. But these studies have their own problems. The two most obvious are extrapolation from animals to humans and from high to low doses, the latter problem being shared with most occupational epidemiology studies. In any case, the federal regulatory agencies have judged that substances that cause cancer in animals present a risk of cancer to humans at low doses. This consensus has been expressed in the National Academy of Sciences' *Drinking Water and Health,* a report produced under a mandate of the Safe Drinking Water Act.[3]

This consensus reflects a social decision that has been made in the face of scientific uncertainty. In most cases concerning environmental exposures to carcinogens, science can neither prove nor disprove that a risk exists, although the judgment that a risk does exist at low doses is consistent with what is known about carcinogenesis. Furthermore, since epidemiology is usually not sensitive enough to detect possible effects of carcinogens, it will also be too insensitive to verify that a reduction of cancer risk has in fact occurred after regulatory action. Thus, not only do we not know for sure whether regulatory action will actually reduce the incidence of cancer (and, of course, nobody knows for sure that they will not), but we will also probably never know from direct empirical evidence. The only hope of reaching greater certainty in this area is through greater understanding of the fundamental mechanisms of carcinogenesis and the metabolism and transport of chemicals in the body.

Risk Extrapolation

Until a few years ago substances that caused cancer in animals were regulated without attempts to measure the impact of the regulations. The balancing of risks and benefits required under the pesticide law, for example, was largely a matter of determining whether substitutes existed for particular uses: if a substitute was available, it was generally assumed that the benefits of use were smaller than the risks.[4] Air and water pollution control requirements were based on use of the best available control technology.

3. National Academy of Sciences, Safe Drinking Water Committee of the National Research Council, *Drinking Water and Health* (Washington, D.C.: NAS, 1977).
4. Federal Insecticide, Fungicide, and Rodenticide Act of 1972 (86 Stat. 973).

Recently, however, interest has increased among regulatory agencies in the use of mathematical risk extrapolation models to derive quantitative estimates of the risks posed by exposure to carcinogens. This interest has evolved from several sources. Since the agencies' resources are limited and the regulatory process arduous, some way was needed to set priorities, to determine which of the thousands of potential regulatory targets should be high on the list. There was also concern that action might be taken in cases where the exposures were so small that the effects would be insignificant when evaluated. There was a feeling in some of the agencies that decisionmakers should have some estimate of the magnitude of the risks they were attempting to reduce, no matter how crude.

It is probably fair to say that the Environmental Protection Agency took the lead, among regulatory agencies, in applying risk extrapolation models to actual regulatory decisionmaking involving chemical carcinogens. Some of the models had been used for decades in the regulation of exposure to ionizing radiation, and the Food and Drug Administration had made limited use of them in regulating food contaminants. The process was tried out as part of the rulemaking on air emissions of vinyl chloride and has been institutionalized in the agency through establishment of the Carcinogen Assessment Group in 1976. Other agencies have adopted risk extrapolation models to varying degrees, and a recent decision of the Supreme Court, though ambiguous, appears to require some form of quantitative estimate of risk levels as a prerequisite for regulation under the Occupational Safety and Health Act of 1970.[5] The federal government's ambivalance toward these methods is indicated by the interdepartmental Regulatory Council's official government-wide policy statement, "The Regulation of Chemical Carcinogens," which says, in part, the following:

After it has been determined that a chemical substance is likely to be carcinogenic, the next step in regulatory decision-making is to assess the risk that people face of developing cancer from their exposure to the substance. . . .

The form, methodology, and elaborateness of the assessment may vary substantially. . . .

Except where a statute, as in the case with the Clean Water Act, explicitly indicated which substances are to be controlled and how, every regulatory proposal will be accompanied by some form of risk assessment which includes,

5. *Industrial Union Department, AFL-CIO* v. *American Petroleum Institute,* 448 U.S. 607, 100 S.Ct. 2844, 48 U.S.L.W. 5022 (1980). The statutory citation for the Occupational Safety and Health Act of 1970 is 84 Stat. 1590.

at a minimum, an analysis of the substance's carcinogenicity and a determination that people are likely to be exposed to the substance. . . .

Where the available data are scientifically adequate to support them, quantitative risk estimates can provide useful information for proposed regulatory decisions. . . . However, quantitative risk estimates are not yet sufficiently developed to be regarded as more than rough indicators of the level of human risks.[6]

Thus, the Regulatory Council has taken the position of encouraging the agencies to use risk extrapolations but is not willing to require their use. One of the concerns about the use of extrapolation models is based on the limitations of the models themselves. Those that are usually used to assess risk fall into two groups. The first, of which the Bryan-Mantel procedure is the best known,[7] is based on the assumption that the fraction of the population responding at a range of doses follows a log-normal function; the underlying assumption is that the susceptibility of individuals in the population is log-normally distributed. This leads to a mathematical formulation that never reaches zero as dose approaches zero but that falls off much faster than linearly. The second group of models, which includes the one-hit, multiple-hit, and linear no-threshold models, all have linear dose-response curves at low doses.[8] These models are based on a conception of carcinogenesis in which infinitesimal increments of doses randomly cause changes in target cells (for example, molecules that bind to DNA), some portion of which will transform the cell into a tumor cell.

Both sets of models are rich enough mathematically to fit the experimental data as well as anyone could ask (at least when the data are monotonic). Thus, one cannot distinguish between them empirically on the basis of fit. And for both of them, doses are typically extrapolated by factors of perhaps one thousand to one million. With such a range of extrapolation, the scientific certainty of the results is unclear at best. These extrapolations fall far short of being predictions based on a chain of logic whose steps are empirically verified. Since present knowledge does not rule out the possibility that a dose threshold may in fact exist, particular environmental

6. Regulatory Council, "Regulation of Chemical Carcinogens" (September 1979), pp. 8–10.

7. Nathan Mantel and W. Ray Bryan, "Safety Testing of Carcinogens," *Journal of the National Cancer Institute,* vol. 27 (August 1961), pp. 455–70.

8. P. Armitage and R. Doll, "Stochastic Models of Carcinogenesis," in *Proceedings of the 4th Berkeley Symposium on Mathematical Statistics and Probability,* vol. 4 (University of California Press, 1961), p. 19; and K. S. Crump and others, "Fundamental Carcinogenic Processes and Their Implications for Low Dose Risk Assessment," *Cancer Research,* vol. 36 (September 1976), pp. 2973–79.

carcinogens may actually pose zero risk. It is also not difficult to develop a model in which the response would be higher than that predicted by the one-hit model.

In spite of the models' serious shortcomings, there is a need, perceived by both the agencies and their critics, for some kind of answer to the question, "What are we buying with this regulation?" In response to this need, there has been a tendency to choose as a working model the linear no-threshold model and its variants. It has a preferred place both in the Environmental Protection Agency guidelines issued in 1976[9] and in the Interagency Regulatory Liaison Group guidelines issued in 1979.[10] The reasons usually given for this choice are that the model is conservative and is consistent with what is known about the biological mechanism of cancer. By the term *conservative* people seem to mean that the model gives higher risk estimates than other models. So few usable data exist for low doses that no one really knows whether the linear model is in fact conservative. The linear or one-hit model is consistent with the theory of carcinogenesis as involving random binding to a cell's DNA, but it is not consistent with the other parts of scientific knowledge. In many cases, the substance that interacts with the DNA is not the same as what people swallow or breathe, but rather a metabolite of the contaminant found in the environment. Metabolites can be more or less toxic than the original compound. In fact, the way the body deals with a particular carcinogen is likely to consist of a complex sequence of metabolites and competing pathways, one or more of which may be involved in carcinogenesis. These various processes may be more or less active at different doses, so the effects may not be linear with dose.

Probably the best thing that can be said about the linear one-hit model is that it is the simplest index of carcinogenic risk scientists have been able to develop. If compound A produces tumors in 50 percent of the experimental animals at a given dose and compound B produces the same response at 1/100 of that dose, and if both are present in the environment at the same levels, then we should probably be one hundred times as worried about compound B as about A. This logic is basically what the linear model generates. Unfortunately, things are not quite that simple.

9. U.S. Environmental Protection Agency, "Interim Procedures and Guidelines for Health Risk and Economic Impact Assessments of Suspected Carcinogens," *Federal Register,* vol. 41 (May 25, 1976), pp. 21402–03.

10. Interagency Regulatory Liaison Group, "Scientific Bases for Identification of Potential Carcinogens and Estimation of Risks," *Federal Register,* vol. 44 (July 6, 1979), pt. 3, pp. 39859–79.

Many questions or methodological choices have to be resolved before applying the linear model or one of its variants. These questions include the following:

1. How can animal doses in a laboratory experiment be converted to equivalent human doses? The most popular solutions are to scale the conversion either on body weight or on surface area.

2. How can the data from different experiments and different species-sex-dose groups in a single experiment be combined? For example, the most sensitive single point in the data could be used or some method of curve fitting to all the data could be adopted.

3. Given the possibility that the observed effect may not be caused by the substance in question, should data from human epidemiological studies be used, and if so, how?

4. How can the statistical uncertainty in the animal tests resulting from the limited sample sizes used be accounted for?

5. How can intermittent dosing schedules—for example, doses given five rather than seven days a week—be accounted for?

6. How can data from experiments in which the dosing does not continue for the animals' lifetime be incorporated?

7. How can data from experiments in which animals are killed before their natural deaths be incorporated?

8. How can differing mortality in various experimental groups be incorporated?

9. How should benign tumors or other lesions that, in the opinion of some experts, would have been likely to develop into malignant tumors in the future be dealt with?

10. How can data on the time of tumor occurrence be incorporated?

11. How should situations in which a substance appears to cause tumors at more than one site be dealt with?

12. How can the fact that humans are frequently exposed to substances in utero and experimental animals usually are not be accounted for?

This list is probably not exhaustive, and legitimate differences of opinion exist on all or most of the points. The impact of these questions is significant. For example, the first on the list, conversion from animal to human equivalent doses, changes the result by a factor of thirteen when extrapolating from data on mice. The range of outcomes that would result from reasonable solutions to each of these problems could easily be greater than a factor of one thousand. This is not just an abstract possibility, as two examples will show.

The National Academy of Sciences produced two reports within a year of each other that use the same experimental data and contain risk extrapolations for chloroform using the one-hit model. In one report the lifetime cancer risk was estimated at 2 times 10^{-7} for each microgram of chloroform consumed per day.[11] In the second report the risk was estimated at 22 times 10^{-7} for every microgram of chloroform consumed per day.[12] These estimates differ by a factor of eleven. A second example is the results of a comparison the Environmental Protection Agency made recently between the risk extrapolations made by the National Academy of Sciences for a number of different carcinogens and those made independently by the agency's Carcinogen Assessment Group for some of the same substances. Some comparisons were very close, but others differed by factors as large as one hundred in both directions.

The magnitude of these ranges is important: it is hard to imagine many cost-benefit analyses whose conclusions would not be changed if one side of the balance were multiplied or divided by one hundred or one thousand. The situation is even more precarious if a true risk of zero is considered possible, since the possibility cannot be excluded that a threshold may actually exist, or that the risk could be larger than calculated if the linear model is not conservative enough or if synergistic effects occur with other environmental contaminants.

This range of uncertainty is not as serious if one requires less from the models—that is, not an absolute estimate of the number of cancer cases anticipated but only a comparative index for setting priorities, based on expected carcinogenic potency, and for getting a very rough idea of a problem's seriousness. For these purposes, it probably does not matter much which way the questions listed above are resolved. What is important is that a single methodology be generally accepted, so that comparisons can be made among cases.

The Trihalomethane Regulation

It is clear from this discussion that estimating the health benefits of carcinogen regulations is fraught with uncertainty. Further difficulties in

11. National Academy of Sciences, Panel on Low Molecular Weight Halogenated Hydrocarbon of the Coordinating Committee for Scientific and Technical Assessments of Environmental Pollutants of the National Research Council, *Nonfluorinated Halomethanes in the Environment* (NAS, 1978), p. 197.
12. National Academy of Sciences, *Drinking Water and Health*, p. 716.

applying cost-benefit or risk-benefit analysis can be illustrated by the example of the regulation of organic contaminants in drinking water.

Recently promulgated was a regulation for trihalomethanes, which set a maximum contaminant level of 100 micrograms per liter, applicable to all public water systems serving ten thousand or more people.[13] Trihalomethanes are a group of compounds, of which chloroform is the most common, which form during water treatment as a by-product of disinfection with chlorine. Varying amounts of these compounds, therefore, are found in all public water systems that chlorinate their water and are most concentrated in systems whose raw water contains relatively large amounts of naturally occurring organic matter.

The Environmental Protection Agency performed a cost-benefit analysis for this regulation. The agency had to assume that (1) the trihalomethane levels found in a series of nonrandom surveys were representative of the entire nation; (2) specific treatment technologies would be chosen by systems to comply with alternative standards under various conditions and with the trihalomethane standard set at different levels; (3) the trihalomethanes other than chloroform had the same carcinogenic potency as chloroform; and (4) other disinfection by-products pose no health risks. The agency also had to pick a risk extrapolation method.

There are problems with these assumptions, but the limitations in the available data forced the agency to make them. Under these assumptions, the agency made a point estimate of the number of cancer cases avoided as a result of the promulgated regulation—322 cases per year. The costs of compliance had been estimated at $18.7 million per year. The agency was thus able to derive an average cost per case avoided of about $60,000 and a marginal cost per case avoided (relative to the maximum contaminant level) of about $200,000. It is unclear what significance should be ascribed to these figures. It is our impression that the trihalomethane regulation compares favorably in terms of cost per life saved to other regulations for which similar computations have been made, but it is not known if this has any meaning without determining whether the assumptions and methodologies are consistent.

What is perhaps more interesting is that the information captured by this calculation does not include the considerations the agency wrestled with in its attempt to balance costs and benefits. For example, there was

13. Environmental Protection Agency, "National Interim Primary Drinking Water Regulations: Control of Trihalomethanes in Drinking Water," *Federal Register,* vol. 44 (November 29, 1979), pt. 3, pp. 68624–707.

concern that the regulation of trihalomethanes not interfere with adequate disinfection of water, particularly in smaller systems where unsophisticated operators might try to reduce trihalomethane levels by reducing the amount of chlorination. The agency therefore proposed that the standard not be applied to systems serving populations below seventy-five thousand, a position modified in the final regulation to include phased implementation down to systems serving ten thousand people. Similarly, it was the fear of making too great a change in a process closely intertwined with disinfection that led the agency to set the standard as high as 100 micrograms per liter, although the agency believes that much lower levels ultimately will be attainable.

The agency also wrestled with another aspect of the trihalomethane problem. Little is known about the chemistry and toxicology of the by-products of disinfectants other than chlorine whose use would be stimulated by a trihalomethane regulation. Since any disinfectant is a biologically active substance that kills bacteria, this is an area of serious concern. The agency has attempted to deal with the immediate problem by writing provisions into the regulation that limit the addition of other disinfectants to water with high disinfectant demand. The agency has also initiated a series of research programs to gather basic data in this area. Ultimately, a limitation on disinfectant demand may be implemented that would force systems to clean up the water before adding disinfectants. The important point is that these are considerations that do not easily fit into the cost-benefit analysis, yet they are the ones that are most bothersome. It is almost as though cost-benefit analysis, at least in this case, helps deal with the easy part of the problem but does not help with the hard part.

Because cost-benefit analysis requires the inclusion of *all* costs and benefits, the Environmental Protection Agency's analysis is incomplete. The agency has not been able to quantify some of the most important aspects of the trihalomethane regulation. However, we believe that this experience is typical of attempts to use methods of cost-benefit analysis on actual problems in the field of health and environmental regulation.

In the second part of the proposed organics regulation—a treatment technique requirement for granular activated carbon or an equivalent in large vulnerable water systems to remove synthetic organic chemicals—the agency was totally unsuccessful in capturing a significant part of the problem in the cost-benefit analysis framework. Many commentors on the regulation, including the U.S. Council on Wage and Price Stability, urged the agency to perform such an analysis.[14] The council presented its own attempt, which the agency does not think is valid; but the agency has not been able to come up with a valid approach. The problem is that no one knows what levels of which chemicals would be removed with granular activated carbon. There are many thousands of organic chemicals in drinking water. Already identified are over 700, which represent only 15 percent by weight of all organic matter found in drinking water.[15] Only a few have been tested for carcinogenicity in the usual animal tests. The agency has conducted several surveys of water from different systems and has found that the levels of measurable chemicals vary widely from system to system and even from day to day. It would therefore be difficult to derive a risk estimate based on this fragmentary occurrence data, even for those measurable chemicals that have been tested for carcinogenicity. The agency has not been able to think of any way to estimate the risk to public health posed by compounds that cannot be measured or that have not been tested for carcinogenicity. Nor do methodologies exist for dealing with the potential effects of human exposure to mixtures of carcinogens, including possible synergistic effects. Yet the value of granular activated carbon is that it removes a wide variety of these compounds from water. The agency has suggested that it makes sense to spend a nominal amount, less than ten dollars per family each year, to take advantage of a known technology that will remove a variety of organic contaminants. Yet neither the agency nor its critics have been able to develop a method of analysis that would help determine whether or not granular activated carbon is worth its costs.

Thus, the agency has not found cost-benefit analysis to be a powerful tool, at least for developing a regulatory strategy to deal with the presence of organic carcinogens in drinking water. The agency is concerned that little thought has been given to the results of inserting cost-benefit analysis into the adversary process of rulemaking. It is predictable that both (or all) sides will be able to introduce analyses that support their points of view. Each will then bring forward analysts, of equivalent credentials, who will argue among themselves about the superiority of their particular

14. Ivy E. Broder, "Analysis of Proposed EPA Drinking Water Regulations" (U.S. Council on Wage and Price Stability, September 1978).

15. National Academy of Sciences, *Drinking Water and Health,* pp. 489–92; and Environmental Protection Agency, Office of Water Supply, "Statement of Basis and Purpose for an Amendment to the National Interim Primary Drinking Water Regulation on a Treatment Technique for Synthetic Organic Chemicals" (January 1978), p. 1.

analyses in a language all their own. Incomprehensible analysis may then drive out understandable argument. This might be worth enduring if the issues being debated were central to the decision at hand. However, if the drinking water regulation's problems are at all typical (and we believe they are), the cost-benefit analyses are likely to capture only a small part of the problem and deflect attention from the rest. This will not contribute to better decisionmaking.

If cost-benefit analysis becomes a legal requirement, these difficulties will be multiplied. There will be a period of uncertainty until a body of case law is developed that will show what the courts consider an adequate analysis. This delay will benefit the opponents of any change in regulations. A great deal of energy and attention would probably then be focused on how well the analysis satisfies whatever criteria have developed. Given the limitations of cost-benefit analysis, this allocation of the limited resources of time and personnel does not seem to be warranted.

An alternative to cost-benefit analysis is the use of technology-based standards. This approach is most clearly exemplified in the provision of the Federal Water Pollution Control Act Amendments of 1972[16] that requires effluent limitations on water polluters based on the "best available technology." The use of the best available technology seems particularly attractive in the case of carcinogens. Since it is assumed that there is no safe level, it seems reasonable to reduce exposures as much as possible. But the technological approach does not preclude the necessity of balancing costs and benefits. It is always possible to spend more money to reduce exposures. Even if no more advanced technology is known, more of the old technology can always be used. So there is a considerable range of judgment as to what constitutes best available technology, and the degree of stringency chosen depends implicitly on the perceived magnitude of the risk.

Another approach to regulation is to continue balancing risks and benefits intuitively. With this approach, risk extrapolation models would be used when possible. Over time, regulators would develop a feeling for the ranges of risk that will have been judged socially acceptable in previous decisions and would aim for that range of risk unless there were reasons to be more or less stringent in a particular case. When possible, regulators could even calculate the marginal cost of each cancer case avoided and develop a feeling for what ranges have been judged socially acceptable in

16. 86 Stat. 816.

previous decisions. But we would be wary of overformalizing the approach. Ideally, each case would lead to a creative resolution of conflicting goals.

Another problem is that of communicating regulatory activities to the public. Ultimately, the success of any social enterprise in a democratic society depends on the informed support of the people. Yet many discount the reports of carcinogens in their environment and do not believe, for example, that smoking causes cancer; and others go to ridiculous lengths to avoid minuscule risks, such as avoiding products containing polyvinyl chloride for fear of getting liver cancer. Because the adversary process tempts people to either exaggerate or minimize risks, almost nobody understands that although the risks may or may not exist, it is rational to treat them as real; that any reduction in cancer rates is likely to be small but still worth achieving; and that probably no one will ever know the true impact of preventive action. Sooner or later, regulatory agencies will have to face the consequences of their failure to communicate.

Appendix: Net Benefits of Several Trihalomethane Levels

The Environmental Protection Agency published a final regulation to control trihalomethane levels on November 29, 1979.[17] The regulation imposes a maximum contaminant level allowing no more than 100 micrograms of trihalomethanes per liter of finished drinking water. The requirement for granular activated carbon filtration systems to remove all organics was not promulgated. While the trihalomethane standard was being developed, other potential levels were suggested. There was a vigorous discussion of the cost estimates of control technology, and many issues related to risk estimation were raised. Within this highly charged atmosphere, the agency was challenged to analyze the economic efficiency of the proposed standards. As already discussed, there are several practical difficulties associated with refined cost-benefit analysis. The following case study presents the basic methodology used to determine the net benefits of alternative levels for the trihalomethane standard and discusses the dramatic effect produced by changes in basic assumptions.

Benefits associated with control of trihalomethanes essentially consist

17. Environmental Protection Agency, "National Interim Primary Drinking Water Regulations."

of a reduction in the number of cancer cases that could be attributed to the contaminant. The National Academy of Sciences presents the general formula for estimating cases avoided in *Drinking Water and Health*:[18] annual number of cases avoided equals RVT/E, where R equals risk per microgram per liter, V equals liters per day consumption, T equals total (national) reduction in exposure (in micrograms), and E equals life expectancy.

Knowing the number of cases avoided allows for estimation of the dollar value of the benefits. Assuming that each case avoided is a life saved and that it is possible to ascribe a value to human life, the annual benefits are merely the cases avoided times the value per life. However, these benefits vary depending on selection of risk estimates, reduction in exposure, and value of life.

Estimation of the risk posed by each microgram per liter of drinking water is a function of many variables. The Environmental Protection Agency's Office of Drinking Water reviewed the methodology used to develop two different risk estimates, one presented by the National Academy of Sciences and the other by the agency's Carcinogen Assessment Group.[19] The estimates are essentially the same, although arrived at using slightly different assumptions. A value of 2.08 times 10^{-6} cases per microgram per liter was used. The estimate reached by the Carcinogen Assessment Group was used in the analysis presented here to maintain consistency within the agency. The estimate is based on data from several animal studies and derived from a linear no-threshold risk model.

The consumption of drinking water per day varies according to climate and individual habits. Although recent data suggest that average daily consumption may be as low as 1.2 liters, the National Academy of Sciences' estimate of 1.95 liters per day was used in this analysis. Also taken from the academy, and generally accepted by analysts, is a life expectancy of seventy years.

The remaining independent component is the total reduction in exposure to trihalomethanes. The agency developed an estimate of this parameter. In a perfect world, one would first ascertain the exposure of the public to trihalomethanes and then assess how that exposure would change through use of various engineering alternatives. Unfortunately, it was not possible to define the exact preregulation exposure. The only data available

18. National Academy of Sciences, *Drinking Water and Health*, pp. 489–92.

19. National Academy of Sciences, *Drinking Water and Health;* and Environmental Protection Agency, "Interim Procedures and Guidelines for Health Risk and Economic Impact Assessments of Suspected Carcinogens."

Figure 1. Percentage of Population Served by Surface Water Systems according to Trihalomethane Level (Preregulation, 1977)[a]

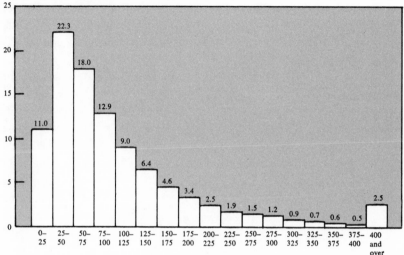

Percent of population served

Trihalomethanes, micrograms per liter

Source: Memorandum to Arnold M. Kuzmack from John Clark and T. J. Glauthier of Temple, Barker and Sloane, Inc., February 25, 1977.
a. Includes only systems that chlorinate.

to assist in this estimate was the National Organic Monitoring Survey, which analyzed the water from 113 water supplies representing various types of sources and treatment processes.[20] About nineteen different contaminants were measured, including some of the trihalomethanes. These data were used to represent the preregulation distribution of trihalomethanes in water supplies. Although taken from a nonrandom sample, the data are the only basis upon which to estimate trihalomethane exposure. The number of people served by surface and ground water systems of various sizes was calculated from a statistical survey of the operating and financial characteristics of community water systems. Multiplying the percentages of the population affected by the population using drinking water, weighted by source of supply, leads to an estimate of the total preregulation national exposure. Figures 1 and 2 show the distribution of people exposed to trihalomethanes by concentration of the contaminant. Table 1 shows this exposure level for various population sizes.

20. Environmental Protection Agency, Office of Water Supply, Technical Support Division, "The National Organic Monitoring Survey," unpublished data.

Figure 2. Percentage of Population Served by Ground Water Systems according to Trihalomethane Level (Preregulation, 1977)[a]

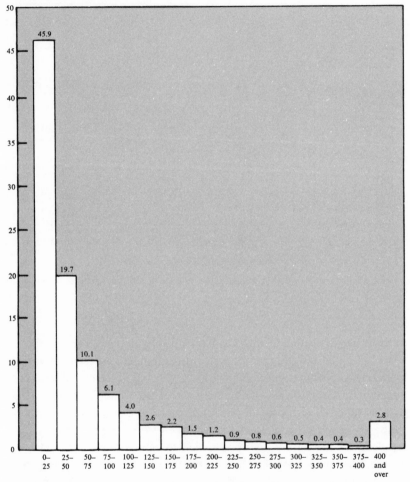

Percent of population served

Trihalomethanes, micrograms per liter

Source: Same as figure 1.
a. Includes only systems that chlorinate.

The following net benefit analysis is for all systems serving more than ten thousand people—about 80 percent of the national population regulated under the safe drinking water legislation.[21]

21. Environmental Protection Agency, *Economic Impact Analysis of the Promulgated Regulation for Drinking Water*, EPA-520/9-79-022 (EPA, 1979), p. I-1.

Table 1. National Exposure to Trihalomethanes[a]

Level (micro-grams per liter)	Population			
	Over 100,000	*Over 75,000*	*Over 50,000*	*Over 10,000*
Preregulation	6.1	7.1	8.6	11.4
150	4.1	4.7	5.7	7.4
100	3.1	3.6	4.3	5.8
50	2.0	2.4	2.7	4.0

Source: Calculated from U.S. Environmental Protection Agency, Office of Water Supply, Technical Support Division, "The National Organic Monitoring Survey," unpublished data.

a. The units of the table are in micrograms of trihalomethane levels multiplied by the number of people exposed, aggregated over the entire nation, or 10^6 gram persons.

To determine how the exposures presented in figures 1 and 2 would change after a regulation was implemented, a decision tree was constructed from information provided by water engineers asked to estimate the effectiveness of various water system treatments. The decision tree reflected assumptions about the combination of treatments that would be used, depending on the conditions within the different water supply plants. Further, the trihalomethane concentrations that will result from the treatments usually will be well below the maximum contaminant level standards. Only with the very expensive treatments (ozone and granular activated carbon) are final concentrations expected to be at the maximum contaminant level.

The national reduction in exposure to trihalomethanes is derived by subtracting the postregulation exposures from the preregulation exposures. These numbers, when combined with risk, consumption, and life expectancy, yield the number of cancer cases avoided each year by using various regulatory alternatives. To convert these cancer cases avoided to dollar benefits requires a simple multiplication with the value of life chosen by the analyst.

The national costs of the trihalomethane regulation are described in the economic impact analysis.[22] The particulars of the analysis are not unusual enough to warrant attention here. But it is important to recognize that even the cost analysis is subject to assumptions that can dramatically modify the national cost estimate. For example, the analysis included a contingency cost of up to 25 percent of capital to cover needs of the real world. If such contingencies are not really needed, as some environmental interest groups suggest, then costs would be significantly lower. On the other hand, certain water supply engineers, specifically

22. Ibid.

Table 2. Changes in Economic Efficiency with Various Risk Estimates[a]

Basis of risk estimate	Maximum national net benefit (millions of dollars)	Economically efficient standard (micrograms per liter)
Roe mouse	77	75
National Cancer Institute mouse	45	100
Roe rat	5	127

Source: Cost estimates were derived from cost data in Environmental Protection Agency, *Economic Impact Analysis of the Promulgated Regulation for Drinking Water*, EPA-520/9-79-022 (EPA, 1979).
a. A value of $200,000 per life was used in each calculation.

those now suing the Environmental Protection Agency over this regulation, believe that most systems would use the more expensive treatments, causing national costs to increase significantly.

To emphasize this point, consider the effects of a change in assumptions on risk. Table 2 represents the range of net benefits when the risk assumption is varied. The risks associated with three different animal tests were used to develop the net benefits shown.[23] The only parameter varied in the risk estimates is the set of animal data used. Models of risk estimation remain the same, and the value of life used is $200,000. Yet this relatively minor adjustment in risk results in greatly different net benefits. The maximum net benefits vary sufficiently to allow for selection of several different trihalomethane standards. This phenomenon can be reemphasized by the interested analyst through selection of different extrapolation models, which can provide risk estimates two orders of magnitude apart.

Variation in cost assumptions produces a similar picture, as table 3 indicates. The relatively modest changes in engineering assumptions described above result in not so modest changes in maximum contaminant levels, which are economically different. The point is made again in table 4, where net benefit is described for various values of life. Again, only a small range of values of life is shown. Some estimates have gone as high as $158 million per life, which was the value of life imputed from coke oven emission standards.[24] Some are as low as ten thousand dollars per

23. National Cancer Institute, *Report on the Carcinogenesis Bioassay of Chloroform* (Government Printing Office, 1976); F. J. C. Roe, "Preliminary Report of Long-Term Tests of Chloroform in Rats, Mice and Dogs" (unpublished paper, London, 1976).

24. Talbot Page, Robert Harris, and Judith Bruser, "Removal of Carcinogens from Drinking Water: A Cost-Benefit Analysis," Social Science Working Paper 230 (California Institute of Technology, September 1978), app. D.

Table 3. Changes in Economic Efficiency with Various Cost Assumptions[a]

Basis of cost estimate	Maximum national net benefit (millions of dollars)	Economically efficient standard (micrograms per liter)
Public interest group	50	83
Environmental Protection Agency	45	100
Industry group	25	125

Source: Same as table 2. The public interest group and industry group cost estimates were derived from high- and low-range cost estimates.
a. A value of $200,000 per life was used in each calculation.

Table 4. Changes in Economic Efficiency Assuming Various Values of Life[a]

Value of life (thousands of dollars)	Maximum national net benefit (millions of dollars)	Economically efficient standard (micrograms per liter)
500	150	50
300	75	75
200	45	100
100	15	125
20	(−5)	150

Source: Same as table 2.
a. A value of $200,000 per life was used in each calculation.

life, which is the amount society is willing to pay to preserve the life of an unknown individual through public nursing homes.[25] Within that range, nearly any national standard could be justified.

There is no obvious way to resolve these differences of opinion about technical assumptions, assumptions about risk, or, for that matter, the value of life. It is the tenuousness of these assumptions that reduces the utility of careful cost-benefit analysis, even for the relatively straight-forward trihalomethane regulation.

25. Ibid.

Part Five

Sulfur Dioxide:
A Scientist's View

BENJAMIN G. FERRIS, JR.

THERE ARE limited data that can be used to determine the relation between health and exposure—whether short- or long-term—to air pollutants. These relationships vary and need further documentation with better control of the confounding variables. In the studies on mortality described in this paper, especially those involving chronic exposure, much less effect of air pollution is noted when as many of the confounding factors as possible are included in the analysis; in fact, the effects attributable to air pollution virtually disappear.

Presented in this paper are short-term (twenty-four-hour) and long-term (annualized twenty-four-hour mean levels) exposure-effects relationships from selected studies. Because sulfur dioxide and suspended particulate matter (particles) have tended to come from a common source, their levels have moved together. At the various levels discussed there is a range of health effects from small, transitory decreases in pulmonary function to increased hospital admissions. The former finding may not have medical significance, although it can be shown to have statistical significance.

Based on the data it seems that a short-term (twenty-four-hour) exposure level for sulfur dioxide and particles could be set at about 380 micrograms per cubic meter, not to be exceeded more than once a year. For long-term exposures, sulfur dioxide particle concentrations could be set at 150 micrograms per cubic meter as a twenty-four-hour annual average without significant impact on public health. The current standards of the Environmental Protection Agency are, respectively, 365 (sulfur dioxide) and 260 (particles) micrograms per cubic meter for twenty-four hours and 80 (sulfur dioxide) and 75 (particles) micrograms per cubic meter annual mean.

The studies presented here do not permit the clear separation of the relative contribution of sulfur dioxide and particles. There is some evidence that the particulate matter is more important. There are no data that truly apply to sulfates, nor are there adequate data on mass respirable particulate matter. Twenty to 60 percent of this may consist of sulfates. There is a need for data on the health effects of exposure to mass respirable particulate matter and for better characterization of their chemical composition—equal mass does not necessarily mean equal effect.

Caveats and Questions

Before discussing the data, it seems appropriate to define certain caveats and comment on some principles that should be considered by economists and regulators using the data, even at face value.

Exposures to sulfur dioxide and particles are generally estimated from data collected at a central station. This central station, for various reasons, is likely to be on top of a building that may be three or four stories high. Occasionally, measurements are made at ground level or in areas where people congregate. At times, modeling is done to determine the spatial variation. Only occasionally are actual measurements made to assess the adequacy of the modeling to estimate exposure or to obtain data on actual exposure concentrations. So far, little use has been made of measurements of indoor pollution concentrations—a large part of the exposure pattern, since people spend a lot of their time indoors. Indoor levels may be lower or higher than outdoor levels, depending upon the pollutant being measured, time of year, air changes, and whether there are sources or sinks for that pollutant indoors. Also, the central monitoring site is likely to have been selected for control purposes and may be subjected to higher levels than those in the areas where people congregate. Thus, the outdoor concentrations measured may not properly represent concentrations the population is actually exposed to.

Another problem is that most of the data from Europe have been based on black smoke measurements. This method does sample the small respirable particulate matter that can penetrate deeply into the lung. These measurements do not measure weight directly but estimate it from the reflected light measurement of the sample. This reflectance has been calibrated against a standard black smoke. In the United States, suspended particulate matter is collected on a preweighed filter, usually by a high-volume system that can collect particles of considerable size that are probably not respirable, although they could be deposited in the nose. These two techniques have been compared in England.[1] A correction factor can be applied, but it is only a very coarse adjustment. There seems to be reasonable agreement between the two methods at levels above 500 micrograms per cubic meter. There is a trend in the United States to collect both the high-volume samples and mass respirable samples designed to measure mass respirable particulate matter. Both are direct gravimetric methods. The latter is probably more comparable to the European black smoke method but has the advantage that other colored smokes, or particles, can be measured. It is also the fraction that will contain most of the sulfates, which may range from 20 to 60 percent of the small particles.

A further step is needed, and that is to characterize the chemical composition of the particles, because equal mass does not necessarily mean that there will be an equal effect for all particles. The chemical composition of particulate matter varies. Some attempts have been made to identify chemical composition by measuring water-soluble sulfate or nitrate. In some cases, specific elements are identified by x-ray fluorescence, atomic absorption, or neutron activation. But to identify elements requires sophisticated equipment and is expensive. The sulfate and nitrate determinations give only partial answers; there is evidence that the activity or irritating quality of the sulfate is more dependent on the other part of the chemical compound. For example, sulfuric acid is more irritating than ammonium sulfate, which in turn is less irritating than ferric sulfate for equal amounts of sulfur or sulfate and similar size below one micrometer. Ferrous sulfate appears to be nonirritating.[2] These data were obtained from experiments with guinea pigs and are probably applicable to humans. Thus, it is important to identify the type of sulfate.

In most instances, data are expressed as twenty-four-hour values or as the annualized twenty-four-hour mean values. There is a need for a description of the frequency distribution of the data that go into the value. For some gases, it may be important to measure exposure in shorter

1. B. T. Commins and R. E. Waller, "Observations From a 10-Year Study of Pollution at a Site in the City of London," *Atmospheric Environment,* vol. 1 (1967), pp. 49–68.
2. Mary O. Amdur, "Some Comments on the Toxicology of Sulfur Dioxide and Particulates," paper presented at the Conference on Sulfur Oxides in Northeastern Ohio, John Carroll University, Cleveland, Ohio, November 18–19, 1976, pp. 28–38.

periods than twenty-four-hour averages. For example, one can have two mean values that are extremely close or identical and yet have different effects because one has very little variation around the mean value, whereas the other has a number of close together but high peaks interspersed with extremely low values. Intuitively, one would expect the series with the high peaks to have the greater effect. Thus, there is a need to express in some standard way the frequency distribution of the data and to relate this to effects on health.

Another question concerns thresholds and safety factors. These concepts are included in the Clean Air Act[3] and are a carry-over from classical toxicology, where experimental results obtained on animals are translated to effects on humans. It would be better to evaluate the data developed from the study of human populations, to develop dose or exposure-response relationships, and then to decide whether the threshold concept and safety factors are truly applicable. Most biological processes exhibit continuity rather than a threshold. This continuity can also reflect a gradation in the type of response to varying exposure concentrations. This is particularly true when a complex organism, such as man, is the responder.

When discussing exposure-response relationships, it should be clear what effect is being measured. This effect, severe or minor, will determine how big the safety factor should be. For example, if death is the effect, then a large safety factor would be appropriate; if the effect is minor irritation or an occasional cough, no safety factor may be required. Knowing the exposure-response relationship should make it possible to select an exposure level that represents an acceptable risk. As measuring methods improve, scientists will be able to detect smaller and smaller changes that may not be medically significant. Thus, any detectable change is not necessarily a significant health effect. For example, exposures to carbon monoxide show a continuum of increasing carboxyhemoglobin as the concentration is increased. Not until a concentration of 2.5 percent carboxyhemoglobin is reached is it considered to be a significant change. Unfortunately, there are no such convenient markers for sulfur dioxide or particulate matter.

Following is a discussion of the possible relationship between sulfur dioxide and health effects. This review will not be an exhaustive survey of the literature, but rather will highlight selected studies that could be used to develop further evidence of such a relationship, particularly at exposure concentrations near the present U.S. primary standard.

3. Clean Air Act of 1963, 77 Stat. 322.

Short-Term Effects

It is well documented that high levels of sulfur dioxide and particles are related to increased mortality.[4] High levels are in excess of a thousand micrograms per cubic meter for both sulfur dioxide and black smoke. At lower levels (see table 1), slight increases in mortality have been reported in various studies.[5] Schimmel has pointed out some of the problems associated with such time-series analyses.[6] He suggests that, at the present concentrations observed in the United States, sulfur dioxide has little effect and the effect of particulates is weak.

At levels of 500 micrograms or above of both black smoke and sulfur dioxide per cubic meter, an increase in hospital admissions has been reported, especially for patients with cardiovascular disease who are over fifty years old.[7]

At lower concentrations, Lawther and others have reported increased symptoms in patients with chronic bronchitis when black smoke and sulfur dioxide concentrations exceeded 250 and 500 micrograms per cubic meter, respectively.[8] They also noted that most of the controls in England were intended to reduce black smoke. After controls were implemented, sulfur dioxide occasionally reached concentrations as high as before, but with the low levels of black smoke no increase in symptoms was noted. Van der

4. M. Firket, "Sur les Causes des Accidents Survenus dans la Vallée de la Meuse, lors des Brouillards de Décembre, 1930," *Bulletin de l'Academie Royale de Médecine de Belgique,* vol. 11 (1931), pp. 683–739; and United Kingdom, Ministry of Health, "Mortality and Morbidity During the London Fog of December 1952," Report 95 on Public Health and Medical Subjects (London: Her Majesty's Stationery Office, 1954).

5. Patrick J. Lawther, "Compliance With the Clean Air Act: Medical Aspects," *Journal of the Institute of Fuel,* vol. 36 (1963), pp. 341–44; and A. E. Martin, "Mortality and Morbidity Statistics and Air Pollution," *Proceedings of the Royal Society of Medicine,* vol. 57 (October 1964), pp. 969–75.

6. Herbert Schimmel, "Evidence for Possible Acute Health Effects of Ambient Air Pollution from Time Series Analysis: Methodological Questions and Some New Results Based on New York City Daily Mortality, 1963–1975," *Bulletin of the New York Academy of Medicine,* vol. 54 (November 1978), pp. 1052–1108.

7. K. Biersteker, *Polluted Air Causes, Epidemiological Significance and Prevention of Atmospheric Pollution* (Assen, Netherlands: Van Gorcum, 1966), pp. 21–23, quoted in World Health Organization, *Environmental Health Criteria 8: Sulfur Oxides and Suspended Particulate Matter* (WHO, 1979), p. 69; and Martin, "Mortality and Morbidity Statistics and Air Pollution."

8. P. J. Lawther, R. E. Waller, and M. Henderson, "Air Pollution and Exacerbations of Bronchitis," *Thorax,* vol. 25 (September 1970), pp. 525–39.

Table 1. Short-Term Health Effects of 24-Hour Exposure to Air Polluted by Suspended Particles and Sulfur Dioxide

Study	Particles, 24-hour values (micrograms per cubic meter)	Sulfur dioxide		Effects
		Micrograms per cubic meter	Parts per million	
Biersteker	500	1,000	0.38	Slight increase in hospital admissions of persons over fifty with cardiovascular disease
Lawther	750[a]	710	0.25	Slight increase in mortality
Martin	500[a]	500	0.18	Above this level progressive increase in mortality and hospital admissions
Lawther, Waller, and Henderson	250[a]	500	0.18	Increased symptoms in patients with chronic bronchitis
Van der Lende and others	140[a]	300	0.11	Temporary decrease in pulmonary function
Cohen and others	150	200	0.07	Slight increase in asthmatic attacks, but these were more related to air temperature

Sources: K. Biersteker, *Polluted Air Causes, Epidemiological Significance and Prevention of Atmospheric Pollution* (Assen, Netherlands: Van Gorcum, 1966), pp. 21–23, quoted in World Health Organization, *Environmental Health Criteria 8: Sulfur Oxides and Suspended Particulate Matter* (WHO, 1979), p. 69; Patrick J. Lawther, "Compliance with the Clean Air Act: Medical Aspects," *Journal of the Institute of Fuel*, vol. 36 (1963), pp. 341–44; A. E. Martin, "Mortality and Morbidity Statistics and Air Pollution," *Proceedings of the Royal Society of Medicine*, vol. 57 (October 1964), pp. 969–75; P. J. Lawther, R. E. Waller, and M. Henderson, "Air Pollution and Exacerbations of Bronchitis," *Thorax*, vol. 25 (September 1970), pp. 525–39; R. Van der Lende and others, "A Temporary Decrease in the Ventilatory Function of an Urban Population During an Acute Increase in Air Pollution," *Bulletin de Physiopathologie Respiratoire*, vol. 11 (1975), pp. 31–43; and Adrian A. Cohen and others, "Asthma and Air Pollution from a Coal-Fuelled Power Plant," *American Journal of Public Health*, vol. 62 (September 1972), pp. 1181–88.

a. Measured as black smoke; to convert to total suspended particles, add 80 to 100 micrograms per cubic meter.

Lende and others reported a temporary decrease in pulmonary function.[9] A second study showed improved pulmonary function, in contrast to the expected decrease of pulmonary function with age. A review of the air monitoring data indicated higher levels of pollution when the earlier study

9. R. Van der Lende and others, "A Temporary Decrease in the Ventilatory Function of an Urban Population During an Acute Increase in Air Pollution," *Bulletin de Physiopathologie Respiratoire*, vol. 11 (1975), pp. 31–43.

was conducted. In a third study, the anticipated decrease with age in pulmonary function was present.[10] In what appears to be a valid observation, a temporary decrease in pulmonary function occurred with apparently no residual effect. This decrease could be considered an acceptable risk, since no permanent effect was produced.

Cohen and others followed a group of asthmatics that probably was fairly heterogeneous.[11] The researchers noted that the frequency of asthma attacks was more influenced by air temperature than by pollution. They showed that, after standardizing for the effect of temperature, there was a significant but weak effect of air pollution on the frequency of asthma attacks. The report did not give the number of attacks per day nor the subjects' pattern of attacks, did not comment on the changing composition of the group over time, and did not give clear criteria for the selection of participants. If these data are used, their instability must be taken into account. Probably not much medical significance should be given to these observations.

Thus, there are a few studies that could be used to assess the acute or short-term effects on health of sulfur dioxide exposure. Although all of the studies can be criticized, there is some sensible trend in the data, and the results appear to be consistent with medical knowledge. These data are listed in table 1, which also indicates probable acceptable risk. This was selected as a best estimate. Obviously, more data are needed to define this risk area with more assurance. It should be noted that there is a gradation of response type at different concentrations. The more severe responses occurred at the higher pollutant concentrations.

Long-Term Effects

In evaluating long-term effects, it would probably be more appropriate to relate the pollution levels that existed several years ago to current health effects rather than use current levels. Most of the studies discussed here are related to pollution levels measured at the same time the symptoms or other effects were noted. This may not be a serious problem, since Fletcher and others noted a progressive fall in phlegm production in a

10. R. E. Waller, "Discussion of Health Effects of Exposure to Low Levels of Regulated Air Pollutants," *Journal of the Air Pollution Control Association,* vol. 28 (September 1978), pp. 884–87.

11. Adrian A. Cohen and others, "Asthma and Air Pollution from a Coal-Fuelled Power Plant," *American Journal of Public Health,* vol. 62 (September 1972), pp. 1181–88.

group of working men over time.[12] This change paralleled a progressive fall in pollution concentrations. This may be a coincidental finding, since other factors were also changing, such as type of tobacco, the introduction of filter tips on cigarettes, the availability of or better chemotherapy, people's tendency to stay indoors more, and greater use of central heating.

Another study on adults melded the results of two studies—the general practitioners' study in the United Kingdom and the 1961 study in Berlin, New Hampshire.[13] In these two studies similar questionnaires were used and comparable tests of pulmonary function done. The exposure levels were obtained from Ferris and Anderson and from Holland and Reid.[14] The results were standardized according to age, lifetime cigarette smoking, and sex and indicate a monotonic increase in the prevalence of the complex bronchitic syndrome in both males and females, with an increase in males two to three times higher than that in females. The same could probably be said for black smoke or suspended particles.

Sawicki, in Poland, also found that his adult population living in a polluted area had more respiratory disease than adults living in a less polluted area.[15] He pointed out that because the people worked in different areas they could have been exposed to different pollutant concentrations at work.

Ferris and co-workers followed a cohort in Berlin, New Hampshire, and related responses to questionnaires and results of tests of pulmonary function to pollution concentrations.[16] Results were controlled for age, sex, and cigarette smoking habits. Unfortunately, sulfur dioxides were measured

12. Charles M. Fletcher and others, *The Natural History of Chronic Bronchitis and Emphysema* (Oxford University Press, 1976), pp. 60–63.

13. D. D. Reid and others, "An Anglo-American Comparison of the Prevalence of Bronchitis," *British Medical Journal*, vol. 2 (December 1964), pp. 1487–91.

14. Benjamin G. Ferris, Jr., and Donald O. Anderson, "The Prevalence of Chronic Respiratory Disease in a New Hampshire Town," *American Review of Respiratory Diseases*, vol. 86 (August 1962), pp. 165–77; and W. W. Holland and D. D. Reid, "Urban Factor in Chronic Bronchitis," *Lancet*, vol. 1 (1965), pp. 445–48.

15. Feliks Sawicki, "Chronic Nonspecific Respiratory Diseases in Cracow," *Epidemiological Review*, vol. 26 (1972), pp. 229–50.

16. Ferris and Anderson, "The Prevalence of Chronic Respiratory Disease in a New Hampshire Town"; Benjamin G. Ferris, Jr., and others, "Chronic Nonspecific Respiratory Disease in Berlin, New Hampshire, 1967 to 1973: A Follow-Up Study," *American Review of Respiratory Diseases*, vol. 107 (January 1973), pp. 110–22; and Benjamin G. Ferris, Jr., and others, "Chronic Nonspecific Respiratory Disease in Berlin, New Hampshire, 1967 to 1973: A Further Follow-Up Study," *American Review of Respiratory Diseases*, vol. 113 (April 1976), pp. 475–85.

by the sulfation rate, which is a crude method but was the original one used in 1961. After the study began, suspended particles fell progressively, and although the sulfation rate was low in 1967, it rose again so that in 1973 it was slightly higher than it was in 1961. Only during the first year of the study did there appear to be any effect on the population. A question can be raised whether these results from a pulp-mill community are relevant to other exposures. As noted above, the 1961 results were compared with data from the United Kingdom, where levels of pollution were higher and both the symptoms and pulmonary function were worse than in Berlin, New Hampshire.[17] Similarly, a comparison was made with a cleaner community in British Columbia.[18] The same observers, using the same techniques, found better levels of pulmonary function in the cleaner community. Thus, there seems to be consistency in the data. These observations indicate that the results from the Berlin, New Hampshire, studies might be more broadly applicable.

Some studies on children have also been done. In these the advantage was that the confounding factors of occupational exposure and, particularly, cigarette smoking were not present. Also, at the time the studies were done, most of the children lived close to the school where the studies were being conducted; thus their exposure to sulfur dioxide could be better estimated. Lunn and others studied children in Sheffield, England, and showed an increase in respiratory illness in the children living in the more polluted areas.[19] Levels at which these increases appeared are listed in table 2.

Douglas and Waller followed a cohort of children and noted an increase in lower respiratory tract illnesses in the children living in areas with greater pollution.[20] Their earlier estimate of the exposure concentration at which such illnesses occurred was based on coal use in the different areas. Later air monitoring essentially confirmed the qualitative categories and

17. Reid and others, "An Anglo-American Comparison of the Prevalence of Bronchitis."

18. Benjamin G. Ferris, Jr., and Donald O. Anderson, "Epidemiological Studies Related to Air Pollution: A Comparison of Berlin, New Hampshire, and Chilliwack, British Columbia," *Proceedings of the Royal Society of Medicine,* vol. 57 (October 1964), pp. 979–83.

19. J. E. Lunn, J. Knowelden, and A. J. Handyside, "Patterns of Respiratory Illness in Sheffield Infant Schoolchildren," *British Journal of Preventive and Social Medicine,* vol. 21 (January 1967), pp. 7–16.

20. J. W. B. Douglas and K. E. Waller, "Air Pollution and Respiratory Infection in Children," *British Journal of Preventive and Social Medicine,* vol. 20 (January 1966), pp. 1–8.

Table 2. Long-Term Health Effects of Exposure to Air Polluted by Suspended Particles and Sulfur Dioxide

Study	Particles, 24-hour annual means (micrograms per cubic meter)	Sulfur dioxide		Effects
		Micrograms per cubic meter	Parts per million	
Fletcher and others	280[a]	250	0.095	Increased phlegm production
Sawicki	170[a]	125	0.05	Increased respiratory disease
Lunn, Knowelden, and Handyside	200[a]	200	0.076	Increased respiratory illness in children
Douglas and Waller	140[a]	140	0.053	Increased lower respiratory tract illness in children
Hammer and others	85–110	175–250	0.067–0.095	Increased respiratory symptoms in children
Ferris and Anderson	180	55[b]	0.021	Increased respiratory symptoms, decreased pulmonary function in adults
Ferris and others (1973)	131	37[b]	0.014	None
Ferris and others (1976)	80	66[b]	0.025	None

Sources: Charles M. Fletcher and others, *The Natural History of Chronic Bronchitis and Emphysema* (Oxford University Press, 1976), pp. 60–63; Feliks Sawicki, "Chronic Nonspecific Respiratory Diseases in Cracow," *Epidemiological Review*, vol. 26 (1972), pp. 229–50; J. E. Lunn, J. Knowelden, and A. J. Handyside, "Patterns of Respiratory Illness in Sheffield Infant Schoolchildren," *British Journal of Preventive and Social Medicine*, vol. 21 (January 1967), pp. 7–16; J. W. B. Douglas and K. E. Waller, "Air Pollution and Respiratory Infection in Children," *British Journal of Preventive and Social Medicine*, vol. 20 (January 1966), pp. 1–8; D. I. Hammer and others, "Air Pollution and Childhood Lower Respiratory Disease, 1: Exposure to Sulfur Oxides and Particulate Matter in New York, 1972," in Asher J. Finkel and Ward C. Duel, eds., *Clinical Implications of Air Pollution Research*, proceedings of the American Medical Association Air Pollution Medical Research Conference, San Francisco, December 5–6, 1974 (Acton, Mass.: Publishing Sciences Group for the AMA, 1976), pp. 321–37; Benjamin G. Ferris, Jr., and Donald O. Anderson, "The Prevalence of Chronic Respiratory Disease in a New Hampshire Town," *American Review of Respiratory Diseases*, vol. 86 (August 1962), pp. 165–77; Benjamin G. Ferris, Jr., and others, "Chronic Nonspecific Respiratory Disease in Berlin, New Hampshire, 1961 to 1967: A Follow-Up Study," *American Review of Respiratory Diseases*, vol. 107 (January 1973), pp. 110–22; and Benjamin G. Ferris, Jr., and others, "Chronic Nonspecific Respiratory Disease in Berlin, New Hampshire, 1967 to 1973: A Further Follow-Up Study," *American Review of Respiratory Diseases*, vol. 113 (April 1976), pp. 475–85.

a. Measured as black smoke; to convert to total suspended particles, add 80 to 100 micrograms per cubic meter.

b. Converted from sulfation rate to sulfur dioxide equivalents, assuming that sulfation is due to sulfur dioxide.

gave quantitative figures for the areas. The researchers pointed out that their measured concentrations were probably lower than what had existed previously. Disease frequency increased at levels above the measured values given in table 2.

Hammer and others studied children in three different areas in New York City.[21] Their results are not clear-cut, but some increase in respiratory symptoms did seem to appear in the areas with greatest pollution. The researchers controlled for several variables—one of which was that two physicians were biasing the data by their choice of diagnosis. The best estimate of the range above which changes in symptoms occurred are presented in table 2. The studies on the long-term effects of exposure to sulfur dioxide are by no means perfect. Furthermore, studies can only show association, not causality. So the old question of whether these pollutant measurements are really indices rather than the causative factor has to be considered. Controlling emissions may still be appropriate, but Schimmel and Buechley have both shown that even with a marked reduction in sulfur dioxide, the same correlation exists between mortality and pollutants as before.[22] Buechley concluded that sulfur dioxide was still acting as a surrogate for some other factor(s) that had not been altered.

The mortality studies of Lave and Seskin have been criticized for not taking cigarette smoking into account adequately.[23] Also, other groups have used the same or similar data bases and, by using different techniques and sometimes different assumptions, have come up with different conclusions; that is, not as much of an effect was apparent.[24] Koshal and

21. D. I. Hammer and others, "Air Pollution and Childhood Lower Respiratory Disease, 1: Exposure to Sulfur Oxides and Particulate Matter in New York, 1972," in Asher J. Finkel and Ward C. Duel, eds., *Clinical Implications of Air Pollution Research,* proceedings of the American Medical Association Air Pollution Medical Research Conference, San Francisco, December 5–6, 1974 (Acton, Mass.: Publishing Sciences Group for the AMA, 1976), pp. 321–37.

22. Schimmel, "Evidence for Possible Acute Health Effects of Ambient Air Pollution from Time Series Analysis"; and R. W. Buechley, *SO₂ Levels, 1967–1972 and Perturbation in Mortality: A Further Study in the New York–New Jersey Metropolis,* National Institute of Environmental Health Sciences Report (Research Triangle Park, N.C.: Research Triangle Institute, 1975), p. 297.

23. Lester B. Lave and Eugene B. Seskin, *Air Pollution and Human Health* (Johns Hopkins University Press for Resources for the Future, 1977).

24. Thomas D. Crocker and others, *Methods Development for Assessing Air Pollution Control Benefits,* vol. 1: *Experiments in the Economics of Air Pollution Epidemiology* (Environmental Protection Agency, 1979); and L. A. Thibodeau and others, "Air Pollution and Human Health: A Review and Reanalysis," *Environmental Health Perspectives,* vol. 34 (February 1980), pp. 165–81.

Koshal did an analysis of levels of air pollution and mortality in forty cities between 1960 and 1967 similar to the analysis of Lave and Seskin.[25] Koshal and Koshal found an association between air pollution and health effects. They comment on the problems of collinearity and the complexity of the interactions, and whether these have been adequately controlled for. In those studies that account for more of the confounding variables, the effect of air pollution becomes less and less and for all practical purposes may disappear.[26] Another question that can be raised is whether the effects noted at higher pollution concentrations can be extrapolated down to the present relatively low concentrations.

Another problem with the large population mortality studies is that very small changes are being observed against a background of high variability, and the demonstration of significance is partly a numbers game —that is, the larger the sample (denominator), the greater the probability of demonstrating that a small difference in health is statistically significant. It also needs to be decided whether such health changes are medically or physiologically significant.

As scientists look at the types of symptoms and illnesses associated with lower sulfur dioxide concentrations, they need to discover whether they, too, have medical significance. Intuitively one would say yes. Although Van der Lende's study on adults indicated that the change in pulmonary function was reversible, it is not known whether repeated exposures would result in irreparable damage. In many of the other studies symptoms were minor. Adults with chronic respiratory disease seem to have had severe respiratory illness before the age of two.[27] This observation needs to be verified by prospective studies to determine the role childhood respiratory disease plays in adult respiratory disease. The rates at which these

25. Rajindar K. Koshal and Manjulika Koshal, "Air Pollution and the Respiratory Disease Mortality in the United States—A Quantitative Study," *Social Indicators Research,* vol. 1 (December 1974), pp. 263–78.

26. Crocker and others, *Methods Development for Assessing Air Pollution Control Benefits,* vol. 1.

27. Benjamin Burrows, Ronald J. Knudson, and Michael D. Lebowitz, "The Relationship of Childhood Respiratory Illness to Adult Obstructive Airway Disease," *American Review of Respiratory Diseases,* vol. 115 (May 1977), pp. 751–60; and J. R. T. Colley, J. W. B. Douglas, and D. D. Reid, "Respiratory Disease in Young Adults: Influence of Early Childhood Lower Respiratory Tract Illness, Social Class, Air Pollution and Smoking," *British Medical Journal,* vol. 3 (1973), pp. 195–98.

symptoms occur have not been developed, so it is extremely difficult to calculate their economic impact.

Sulfates

There are insufficient data to develop any exposure-response relationships for sulfates because the various study designs have not allowed the effect of this factor to be separated from sulfur dioxide and/or suspended particles. In fact, it is even difficult to separate sulfur dioxide from particulates, although there are indications that the particulate component is more important than the sulfur dioxide one.[28] When studies involving sulfates are done, the type of sulfate must also be taken into account.

A review of the effects of microparticulate-micronic sulfates has been presented in which these points are explored in more detail.[29] Some additional relevant studies have been done since. Sackner and co-workers exposed asthmatic and healthy subjects to sulfuric acid aerosols of submicronic size.[30] Even with mouth breathing and ten-minute exposures, no effect was noted with up to one thousand micrograms of sulfuric acid mist per cubic meter. Avol and co-workers exposed normal subjects and subjects with asthmatic histories and variable symptoms at the time of the study to various sulfate mixtures, including one hundred micrograms of ammonium sulfate, eighty-five micrograms of ammonium bisulfate, and seventy-five micrograms of sulfuric acid per cubic meter.[31] The different concentrations represented exposures to comparable amounts of sulfur or sulfate. Particles were submicronic in size; exposures lasted two hours; and

28. Fletcher and others, *The Natural History of Chronic Bronchitis and Emphysema;* Lawther, Waller, and Henderson, "Air Pollution and Exacerbations of Bronchitis"; and Schimmel, "Evidence for Possible Acute Health Effects of Ambient Air Pollution from Time Series Analysis."

29. Benjamin G. Ferris, Jr., *Microparticulate Sulfates: Effect on Human Health,* Air Quality Monograph 75-24 (Washington, D.C.: American Petroleum Institute, 1975).

30. Marvin A. Sackner and others, "Effects of Sulfuric Acid Aerosol on Cardiopulmonary Function of Dogs, Sheep and Humans," *American Review of Respiratory Diseases,* vol. 118 (September 1978), pp. 497–510.

31. Edward L. Avol and others, "Controlled Exposures of Human Volunteers to Sulfate Aerosols: Health Effects and Aerosol Characterization," *American Review of Respiratory Disease,* vol. 120 (August 1979), pp. 319–27.

the chamber temperature was 31° C, with relative humidity at 40 percent. No consistent effects were noted from these exposures, which simulated the worst conditions that had been recorded in Los Angeles.

The results of all these studies indicate that there are insufficient data to set a standard for sulfates. Ideally such a standard should be related to specific sulfates or to sulfuric acid. A factor not considered here is the action of acid rains and their ultimate effect on ecologic systems. Possibly this effect will be a controlling factor in regulating emissions of sulfur oxides.

Sulfur Dioxide: An Economist's View

LESTER B. LAVE

To SET intelligent policy for controlling air pollution, we must answer the following questions: (1) Which pollutants affect health? (2) What are the quantitative dose-response relationships between pollutants and resulting health effects? (3) Which emissions (that is, which chemicals at which locations) create air pollutants that damage health? (4) What are the costs of reducing those pollutants or of lowering individuals' exposure in other ways? These questions require input from the biomedical community, atmospheric chemists and physicists, engineers, and economists.

The pollutants regulated by the Environmental Protection Agency all cause severe health effects at high doses.[1] However, the questions above refer to low doses, beginning with the levels prevailing in many U.S. urban areas and continuing downward. As far as the first question goes, it is difficult to know which pollutants damage health at low doses; effects produced, if any, may have little to do with effects observed at high concentrations. The Clean Air Amendments of 1970 defined the primary air quality standard to be one that protects the population.[2] Thus the act

1. See David P. Rall, "Review of the Health Effects of Sulfur Oxides," *Environmental Health Perspectives,* vol. 8 (August 1974), pp. 97–121; and National Academy of Sciences, Commission on Natural Resources, *Perspectives on Technical Information for Environmental Protection,* Analytical Studies for the U.S. Environmental Protection Agency, vol. 1 (Washington, D.C.: NAS, 1977), and other volumes in the series. The National Academy of Sciences has also published studies on stationary sources of air pollution, automobile emissions, and specific pollutants such as nitrogen oxides, ozone and other photochemical oxidants, sulfur oxides, and carbon monoxide.

2. 84 Stat. 1676. According to legislative history, Congress wanted to protect even the most sensitive group.

assumes that a pollutant threshold level exists below which there are no health effects. This assumption has generated intense controversy.[3] The issue is not whether a threshold exists at extraordinarily low dose levels, but whether there is a threshold that can be attained by proposed abatement policies.

For carbon monoxide, there probably is a threshold level that can be achieved, particularly given natural levels of carboxyhemoglobin in the blood and other carbon monoxide sources.[4] But carbon monoxide is a special case because the mechanism by which it causes damage is known in detail. Not enough is known about the physiological mechanisms activated by other pollutants to identify the existence of a threshold. Thus, many pollutants must be assumed to have potential health effects at current and future air quality levels. However, additional information might help to establish that particular pollutants do have relevant thresholds—for example, sulfur dioxide—when there are no suspended particles.

Estimating health effects is complicated by vast differences in sensitivity among people. Health effects might be different, for example, in a healthy eighteen-year-old and a seventy-year-old with severe emphysema. Biological interactions further complicate the relationship between pollutants and health effects. Often the effect of two pollutants is greater than the sum of each individually.[5] Finally, many health effects have latency periods and become evident only after decades of exposure.[6]

Pollutants are not equally harmful, which leads to the second question. It is important to differentiate among them since it is impossible to abate them all in all media. According to the materials balance concept, the sulfur in coal, for example, must emerge in some chemical form and in

3. See the discussions in Bertram D. Dinman, " 'Non-Concept' of No-Thresholds: Chemicals in the Environment," *Science* (February 4, 1972), pp. 495–97; and Norton Nelson, "Discussion of Paper by Vaun A. Newill, R. Wyzga, and James R. McCarroll," *Bulletin of the New York Academy of Medicine,* vol. 54 (December 1978), pp. 1245–48.

4. See National Academy of Sciences, *Carbon Monoxide,* Report 02631-8 (NAS, 1977).

5. U.S. Department of Health, Education, and Welfare, Public Health Service, National Institutes of Health, National Institute of Environmental Health Sciences, *Human Health and the Environment: Some Research Needs,* Report of the Second Task Force for Research and Planning in Environmental Health Science (Government Printing Office, 1977), pp. 174–75, 342–43, and 435; and Rall, "Review of the Health Effects of Sulfur Oxides," p. 109.

6. For example, long latency periods are associated with cancers and with chronic respiratory diseases.

some medium when the coal is used.[7] It is possible to choose the chemical form and medium (including elemental sulfur), but it is not possible to eliminate the sulfur. Thus, knowledge is needed of the health effects of relevant chemical compounds at each dose level. This requires knowledge of the quantitative dose-response functions or their equivalents.

Once it is known which pollutants are harmful and the extent of harm, question three is, which emissions cause them? For some pollutants, no chemical change takes place after emission, and so one need only do the comparatively simple task of modeling the atmospheric physics of diffusion and deposition.[8] More often, chemical changes are important, and so the atmospheric chemistry must be investigated.[9] Reaction rates depend on the speed of mixing, temperature, amount of solar energy, catalysts, and so forth. The atmospheric physics and chemistry are terribly complex, and it is safe to assume that definite answers will not be available for some time. For example, sulfur compounds have been found to be transported much greater distances than had previously been believed possible.[10]

Assuming that it is known which pollutants in the emissions gases are harmful, question four is, what technologies are available for abatement, including redesigning the process, and how expensive is the resulting abatement? These are engineering questions whose answers depend on the particular technologies already in use. To answer them requires extensive and expensive work on particular technologies. Furthermore, there may be cheaper alternatives to abating a particular pollutant, including abating other pollutants that interact chemically or biologically with it. A host of possible alternatives must be explored.

Given answers to these four questions, the resulting health effects of various dollar expenditures on pollution abatement can be estimated. Assuming some dollar value of health, a formal cost-benefit analysis can

---

7. Allen V. Kneese, Robert U. Ayres, and Ralph C. d'Arge, *Economics and the Environment: A Materials Balance Approach* (Johns Hopkins Press for Resources for the Future, 1970).

8. See, for example, National Academy of Sciences, *Environmental Monitoring, Analytical Studies for the U.S. Environmental Protection Agency*, vol. 4 (NAS, 1977); and National Academy of Sciences, *Air Quality and Stationary Source Emission Control* (NAS, 1975).

9. For example, the review in Rall, "Review of the Health Effects of Sulfur Oxides," especially pp. 105–08.

10. See Organization for Economic Cooperation and Development, Environment Directorate, *The OECD Programme on Long Range Transport of Air Pollutants—Summary Report* (Paris: OECD, 1977).

be performed.[11] If no dollar value is assumed, a cost-effectiveness analysis can still be done.[12] These questions are spelled out in detail to illustrate how difficult it is to get the hard, scientific answers required for setting intelligent policy. Needless to say, if one or more of these questions are answered by vague statements or guesses, the resulting policy will be vague or subject to great uncertainties.

It is doubtful that policymakers ever have complete answers. At best, they have partial answers. For example, the typical dose-response curve from pharmacology has the shape of a cumulative normal distribution, illustrating that there are few very sensitive (or resistant) individuals in the population. To test the hypothesis that 0.1 percent of individuals are harmed by a given concentration of a pollutant would require thousands of subjects and extraordinary control for confounding effects. Yet at current levels of air quality, effects are subtle and the number of people displaying measurable effects is small. In addition, subtle effects will be known with confidence only after the theoretical prediction is compared with observed effects at a number of concentrations.

Making Estimates and Using Data

It is customary to make estimates by adopting the most conservative assumption at each stage. [13] However, such calculations are unrealistic and throw away much good information. It would be preferable to make three guesses at each stage: a best estimate, a conservative estimate, and an optimistic estimate. These three estimates could be carried through to produce the range of likely outcomes, along with a best guess about the outcome. However, outcomes based on the conservative and optimistic estimates are extremely unlikely. They can result only if the conservative (or optimistic) answer occurs at each stage; since that sort of consistency

11. For a review of the literature on the value of life, see Joanne Linnerooth, "The Value of Human Life: A Review of the Models," *Economic Inquiry*, vol. 17 (January 1979), pp. 52–74. For some qualifications on using the analysis, see Lester B. Lave, "Quantitative Analyses of Proposed Social Regulations" (working paper, Washington, D.C., 1979).

12. National Academy of Sciences, *Decision Making in the Environmental Protection Agency*, Analytical Studies for the U.S. Environmental Protection Agency, vol. 2 (NAS, 1977), p. 31; and Lave, "Quantitative Analyses of Proposed Social Regulations," p. 30.

13. National Academy of Sciences, *Decision Making in the Environmental Protection Agency*, pp. 32, 241–42.

is also unlikely, this procedure will tend to produce a wide range, the extremes of which are unlikely to occur.

More difficult and detailed questions emerge when interpreting experimental or epidemiological data and when extrapolating such data to current low level effects on humans. Epidemiological data are particularly difficult to interpret since many possible confounding factors might be present.[14] Imperfect data mean that the effects of air pollution can be underestimated or overestimated or the effects ascribed to the wrong pollutant. The problems are particularly vexing when the hypothesized effects occur over a long period of time. Experimental data are also difficult to interpret, but more because of the difficulty in extrapolating to humans.[15] A carefully planned and executed experiment has enough internal validity to enable one to know the effect of a particular pollutant at a particular level under certain conditions on a certain species of animal. However, it is not evident what the effect will be at different concentrations, under different conditions, and on other species. Experiments reveal detailed physiological responses and the underlying mechanisms that produce pollutants' effects. It is this knowledge of mechanisms that can be generalized to other species, settings, and concentrations.

Too little is known to pose sharp hypotheses for epidemiological experiments. There is a great deal of controversy about which chemical form of sulfur is likely to have the most effect, about the predicted resulting disease, and about whether observed statistical associations are causal or spurious.

The Effects of Sulfur Dioxide

According to Ferris and the literature generally, sulfur dioxide is not likely to pose significant health risks at currently observed concentrations without the presence of fine particles.[16] The gas is sufficiently water sol-

14. Lester B. Lave and Eugene P. Seskin, "Epidemiology, Causality, and Public Policy," *American Scientist,* vol. 67 (March–April 1979), pp. 178–86.

15. See Rall, "Review of the Health Effects of Sulfur Oxides," pp. 108–10; and Executive Office of the President, Office of Science and Technology Policy, "Identification, Characterization, and Control of Potential Human Carcinogens: A Framework for Federal Decision Making" (staff paper, 1979).

16. See the paper by Benjamin G. Ferris, Jr., in this volume; John R. Goldsmith and Lars T. Friberg, "Effects of Air Pollution on Human Health," in Arthur C. Stern, ed., *Air Pollution,* vol. 2: *The Effects of Air Pollution* (3d ed, Academic Press, 1977), pp. 493–94; Lester B. Lave and Eugene P. Seskin, *Air Pollution and*

uble to be absorbed by the mucous in the respiratory tract and the resulting weak acid buffered. Only under peculiar conditions is any appreciable
amount of sulfur dioxide likely to enter the lungs.[17]

However, Amdur and co-workers have hypothesized that sulfur dioxide
is likely to be absorbed into small particles, which can enter the lung and
deposit themselves on the lung's surface.[18] While experimental evidence
is somewhat equivocal, the hypothesis is plausible. Since it is much cheaper
to abate particles than sulfur oxides, the United Kingdom has concentrated on them and issued no regulations on emissions of sulfur oxides. As
Lawther points out, there has been a dramatic reduction in ambient
concentrations of suspended particles, little reduction in sulfur dioxide,
and a nearly complete absence of acute episodes such as the 1952 fog in
London that resulted in 4,000 excess deaths.[19]

If sulfur dioxide is believed to be the harmful agent, the best strategy
appears to be to reduce particle levels rather than sulfur oxide concentrations.

The Effects of Sulfates

An alternative hypothesis is that sulfates, particularly acid sulfates, are
the harmful agents.[20] These come in the form of aerosols or very fine
particles that can easily enter the lungs. Experimental evidence shows that
sulfuric acid mist is highly irritating to the respiratory tract; some sulfates
are more benign.[21] However, there are few accurate measurements of
sulfates in urban air.[22] Both the chemical composition and the size of the

---

Human Health (Johns Hopkins University Press for Resources for the Future,
1977); Symposium on Environmental Effects of Sulfur Oxides and Related Particulates, *Bulletin of the New York Academy of Medicine,* vol. 54 (December 1978);
and Rall, "Review of the Health Effects of Sulfur Oxides," p. 98.

17. Rall, "Review of the Health Effects of Sulfur Oxides."

18. See Rall, "Review of the Health Effects of Sulfur Oxides," p. 109; and Mary
O. Amdur, "Toxicologic Appraisal of Particulate Matter, Oxides of Sulfur, and
Sulfuric Acid," *Journal of the Air Pollution Control Association,* vol. 19 (Septem-
ber 1969), pp. 638–44.

19. Patrick J. Lawther, "Looking Backward and Forward," *Bulletin of the New
York Academy of Medicine,* vol. 54 (December 1978), pp. 1199–1208.

20. Mary O. Amdur, "Toxicological Guidelines for Research on Sulfur Oxides
and Particulates," in *Proceedings of the Fourth Symposium on Statistics and the
Environment* (American Statistical Association, 1977).

21. See ibid.; and Rall, "Review of the Health Effects of Sulfur Oxides."

22. See the paper by Ferris in this volume; and National Institutes of Health,
Human Health and the Environment, p. 30.

aerosols and particles must be known. Making these measurements is complicated by the chemical activity of the sulfates and their low concentrations.

Neither experimental nor epidemiological data have pinpointed sulfates as the culprits posing health risks. However, both kinds of data contain a good deal of suggestive evidence. Many scientists now believe that sulfates, not sulfur dioxide, pose a significant health risk.[23] For example, the investigation of daily deaths and daily sulfur dioxide levels in New York City over fifteen years found little or no relationship;[24] one possible explanation is that, although sulfur dioxide levels fell markedly, sulfate levels fell only slightly. My own work consistently shows total sulfur oxides (measured as sulfate) to be a more significant variable than sulfur dioxide.[25]

If sulfates are harmful, abating particles at their origin would have no effect. Instead, the focus must be on the atmospheric chemistry of converting sulfur dioxide to acid sulfates. Since only a tiny fraction of sulfur dioxide is transformed, simply abating it might not help much. Abatement of sulfur dioxide to the extent that sulfate concentrations would have to be reduced appears impossible. Instead, it must be determined whether effects are proportional to the sulfur dioxide concentration or whether the speed with which effects occur is governed by other pollutants, such as ozone, carbon monoxide, and the various oxides of nitrogen. If the latter is the case, then the focus of abatement policy must shift radically.

The Quantitative Relationship of Sulfur Dioxide to Health

Virtually all of the literature has focused on the underlying physiological mechanisms of air quality's effects on health, establishing a cause-

23. See Lave and Seskin, *Air Pollution and Human Health;* Symposium on Environmental Effects of Sulfur Oxides and Related Particulates, *Bulletin of the New York Academy of Medicine;* and Rall, "Review of the Health Effects of Sulfur Oxides."

24. Herbert Schimmel, "Evidence for Possible Acute Health Effects of Ambient Air Pollution from Time Series Analysis: Methodological Questions and Some New Results Based on New York City Daily Mortality, 1963–1976," *Bulletin of the New York Academy of Medicine,* vol. 54 (December 1978), pp. 1052–1108.

25. Lave and Seskin, *Air Pollution and Human Health;* Lave and Seskin, "Epidemiology, Causality, and Public Policy," p. 184; Michael Chappie and Lester Lave, "The Health Effects of Air Pollution Abatement II," report prepared for the Environmental Protection Agency (forthcoming), p. 70.

and-effect relationship, or seeking some threshold level. These studies will condition interpretations, but will not supply the needed evidence on the quantitative health effects of air quality.

The principal work attempting to estimate a quantitative relationship is my own. Some recent studies cast doubt on the sulfate estimates;[26] other studies confirm the basic results.[27] This is not the place to go into a detailed critique, but I think the doubting studies can be shown to have enough problems to vitiate their own conclusions.[28]

The Lave-Seskin work estimates a range of quantitative effects on mortality rates for both sulfate and suspended particulate reduction. I shall assume that these estimates indicate a cause-and-effect relationship and that the quantitative magnitudes are approximately correct. It is likely that the estimated effects of sulfates alone and of sulfates with particles cannot be differentiated.

Depending on the precise specification and data set, the combined effects of the two pollutants range on the mortality scale from an elasticity of about 0.04 percent to a "best" estimate of about 0.1 percent, with a high estimate not substantially larger than the best estimate. An elasticity of 0.1 percent means that a 50 percent reduction in ambient concentrations of the two pollutants is associated with a 95 percent reduction in the mortality rate. The corresponding estimates for sulfates alone are 0.006 percent and 0.07 percent.[29] Although there were one or two specifications in which the estimated elasticity of sulfates became negative, this seems due to multicollinearity.

26. F. W. Lipfert, "The Association of Human Mortality with Air Pollution: Statistical Analyses by Region, by Age and by Cause of Death" (Ph.D. dissertation, Union Graduate School, Yellow Springs, Ohio, 1978); and U.S. Environmental Protection Agency, Office of Health and Ecological Effects, *Methods Development for Assessing Air Pollution Control Benefits*, vol. 1: Thomas D. Crocker and others, *Experiments in the Economics of Air Pollution Epidemiology* (GPO, 1979).

27. L. Thibodeau, R. Reed, and Y. Bishop, "Air Pollution and Human Health: A Review and Reanalysis," *Environmental Health Perspectives*, vol. 34 (February 1980), pp. 165–83; Robert Mendelsohn and Guy Orcutt, "An Empirical Analysis of Air Pollution Dose-Response Curves," *Journal of Environmental Economics and Management*, vol. 6 (June 1979), pp. 85–106; and work at Brookhaven National Laboratory summarized in Leonard D. Hamilton, "Assessing the Health and Environmental Costs of Energy Production and Use: The Costs of Coal," Brookhaven National Laboratory, Biomedical and Environmental Assessment Division, 1979.

28. Chappie and Lave, "The Health Effects of Air Pollution Abatement II."

29. Lave and Seskin, *Air Pollution and Human Health;* the 0.04 value comes from regression 5.8-9, the 0.1 value from table 10.1, the 0.006 value from regression 5.8-7, and the 0.07 value from regressions 7.2-6 through 7.2-9.

These four estimates provide the basis of a cost-benefit analysis. The next step is to translate these estimates first into numbers of premature deaths and then into dollars. Approximately 1.9 million Americans die each year. Thus, assuming the Lave and Seskin statistical associations indicate a causal relationship and that the quantitative estimates are correct, a 1 percent abatement of particulate matter and sulfate levels would lead to from 760 (lower bound) to 1,900 (best guess) fewer deaths per year; a 1 percent abatement of sulfates alone would lead to from 114 (lower bound) to 1,330 (best estimate) fewer deaths per year. There is a factor of twelve between the highest and lowest estimates; this range is probably narrower than the true range of uncertainty. The narrowed range stems from the fact that these estimates come from a single piece of research; other investigators might extend both lower bound and best guess estimates by perhaps a factor of ten each.

A Cost-Benefit Analysis of Sulfur Abatement

To place a monetary value on the estimated decrease in premature deaths requires estimating the social benefit of delaying death. A range of numbers is currently used by economists, ranging from the Cooper and Rice estimate of the present discounted value of future earnings (about $63,000 for the average American) to some willingness-to-pay estimates of about $1.5 million.[30] I will take these two estimates to be lower and upper bound estimates and $300,000 to be my best guess estimate. The resulting dollar benefits are shown in table 1. The broad range is striking, particularly since the estimates of the effects of sulfates might be raised or lowered by a factor of ten.

The costs of abating sulfur dioxide, and presumably sulfates, are quite sensitive to the initial level of control. A minor reduction of sulfur pollu-

30. Based on data in Barbara S. Cooper and Dorothy P. Rice, "The Economic Cost of Illness Revisited," *Social Security Bulletin*, vol. 39 (February 1976), p. 30, updated to 1979 dollars; and Robert Stewart Smith, *The Occupational Safety and Health Act* (Washington, D.C.: American Enterprise Institute for Public Policy Research, 1976), p. 91. (The actual Smith value is $2.6 million but it is thought that this value is too high and a more accurate value is the $1.5 million cited.) Richard Thaler and Sherwin Rosen, "The Value of Saving a Life: Evidence from the Labor Market," in Nestor E. Terleckyj, ed., *Household Production and Consumption* (National Bureau of Economic Research, 1976), pp. 265–98; Linnerooth, "The Value of Human Life"; and W. Kip Viscusi, "Employment Hazards: An Investigation of Market Performance" (Ph.D. dissertation, Harvard University, 1976).

Table 1. Estimated Annual Social Benefits of 1 Percent Reduction in Atmospheric Sulfates

Millions of dollars unless otherwise specified

	Estimated benefit			
	Lives saved from sulfate reduction		Lives saved from sulfate and particulate matter reduction	
Value of life (dollars)	114 (low estimate)	1,330 (high estimate)	760 (low estimate)	1,900 (high estimate)
63,000	7.2	83.8	47.9	119.7
300,000	34.2	399.0	288.0	570.0
1,500,000	171.0	1,995.0	1,140.0	2,850.0

Source: See text for discussion.

tion can be achieved inexpensively by washing coal. Sulfur can be removed from oil at somewhat higher cost, and finally, sulfur can be scrubbed from the stack gases. Thus, there is an upward-sloping schedule relating the amount of sulfur dioxide emissions abated to the cost of abatement. Substantial abatement requires flue gas desulfurization of coal combustion, a new technology undergoing rapid change. Neither costs nor reliability can be estimated with confidence. However, generally quoted estimates of costs range from $600 to $1,000 per ton of sulfur dioxide removed, with a relatively constant cost per ton over a wide range.[31]

In 1976 the Environmental Protection Agency estimated that a total of 29.5 million metric tons of sulfur oxides were emitted into the atmosphere in the United States.[32] To remove 1 percent (0.295 million tons) would cost between about $177 million and $295 million per year. I assume that a 1 percent abatement of sulfur dioxide would reduce ambient sulfate levels by 1 percent. While modeling point sources with careful examination of air chemistry and dispersion would produce better local estimates, this "rollback" model gives a reasonable idea of what might happen to the nation as a whole.

31. Lewis J. Perl, "Alternative Estimates of the Benefits of Sulfur Dioxide Emissions Control," paper prepared for the National Commission on Air Quality, Benefit Estimation Methodology Panel (New York: National Economic Research Associates, Inc., 1979).

32. Environmental Protection Agency, *National Emissions Report, 1976,* EPA Report 450/4-79-019 (GPO, 1979), available from National Technical Information Service, Springfield, Va.

These marginal cost estimates can be compared with the marginal benefit estimates shown in table 1. For a value of premature death estimated from the present discounted value of future earnings ($63,000), none of the estimates of the effect of sulfur oxides on health would justify abatement. In contrast, if the cost of premature death is estimated by willingness-to-pay measures, particularly those from the top of the range of estimates ($1.5 million), virtually all estimated effects would justify stringent abatement.

My best estimate of the social cost of premature death presents the most interesting case. If the effect of a 1 percent decrease in atmospheric sulfates is estimated to cause fewer than 590 premature deaths per year (or 983 for the high cost abatement estimate), only minor abatement is warranted; if the effect is greater, stringent abatement is warranted.

If it were estimated that fewer than 590 premature deaths would result from a 1 percent decrease, abatement would be justified only in the low range when coal scrubbing or oil desulfurizing could remove the sulfur inexpensively. Before more complete sulfur removal would be justified, technological change would have to lower removal costs or the estimated benefit of abating pollution would have to be increased by considering effects other than premature death (such as morbidity, visibility, odor, and damage to plants and animals). If an estimate of more than 590 premature deaths were to result, abatement would be warranted over the full range where the cost of abatement was no higher than $600 per ton of sulfur dioxide removed. Indeed, abatement should stop only when expensive technologies needed for greater reductions show a marginal cost equal to the marginal health benefits of abatement.

My best guesses are that the average social cost of a premature death is $300,000 and that the effect of a 1 percent decrease in atmospheric sulfates would be 900 premature deaths per year. Thus, even without considering technological change (which would lower abatement costs) or the non-health benefits to be gained from abating sulfur oxides, I conclude that sulfur dioxide abatement should be at the level where its cost would be $915 per ton removed (which could buy perhaps 90 percent reduction of sulfur oxide emission for electric utilities).

Good estimates have not been made of the social benefit of any effects other than health of sulfur dioxide abatement. Some estimates put other benefits in a range of from $140 to $836 per ton of sulfur dioxide removed.[33] These estimates would raise the marginal benefit estimate to between $1,050 and $1,750 per ton and justify still more stringent abatement.

Table 1 helps define the goals of rational conservationists. They might attempt to cope with uncertainty by choosing an estimated effect from the high end of the range. They might also tend to choose a social cost of premature death from the high end of the range and to value the nonhealth effects highly. These people would focus on the lower right-hand corner of table 1—perhaps even choosing $2.85 billion as the appropriate estimate of benefits derived from sulfate reduction. A cost-benefit analysis based on such a high estimate of benefit would support a stringent abatement level and lead to impatience with decisions to abate sulfur dioxide by less than what could be done with the best available technology.

At the opposite extreme might be a risk-taking entrepreneur who would assume the best until proven wrong. Such a person would conclude that sulfur dioxide is not a real problem and that hysterical worriers are stopping progress.

This analysis cannot hope to get both extremes to agree because of differing views about whether the sulfate-mortality rate association is causal and if it is, what the quantitative estimates of effect are. Individuals will disagree about the social cost of a premature death, the nonhealth benefits of abatement, and the costs of abatement.

33. Based on figures in John E. Yocum and Roy O. McCaldin, "Effects of Air Pollution on Materials and the Economy," in Arthur C. Stern, ed., *Air Pollution,* vol. 1: *Air Pollution and Its Effects* (2d ed., Academic Press, 1968), p. 651, updated to 1979 dollars.

Sulfur Dioxide:
A Regulator's View

JOHN T. MIDDLETON

THERE WAS a sufficient data base in 1969 to establish descriptive criteria on the health effects attributable to sulfur oxides, taking into consideration the influence of undifferentiated particulate matter. Today's data base reasonably supports the national primary ambient air quality standards of 365 micrograms of sulfur oxides per cubic meter for twenty-four hours and 80 micrograms per cubic meter—measured as sulfur dioxide—for an annual average. A lot more information is needed to assess the health effects of sulfur dioxide alone and of specific sulfates and to establish air quality standards for them. The numerical values for the primary ambient air quality standards for sulfur oxides were based on effects reported in the criteria document that considered effects on sensitive populations in compromised environments and identified the lowest symptomatic or physiological effect level. A shift in abatement and control policy that would relax limitations on sulfur oxide emission and increase particulate matter emission restrictions is untenable, since sulfur oxide levels would increase with consequent increases in sulfate levels and attendant changes in acid precipitation and visibility degradation. Improved control systems should be considered for sulfur oxides—including processes using tall stacks. In addition, more emphasis should be placed on both abatement and control of atmospheric photochemical reactions and emission limits for nitrogen oxides to reduce the transformation of sulfur oxides, reduce the extent and severity of acid precipitation, improve visibility, and prevent significant deterioration of air quality.

279

Clean Air Legislation

Clean air is essential to human health. The issue of abatement and control of air pollution requires national legislation setting forth air quality goals and ways to achieve them along with provisions for coping with international pollution problems.

The first national pollution legislation was enacted in 1955 and was primarily concerned with problem recognition and description.[1] The first Clean Air Act, enacted in 1963, among other things, assisted state pollution control programs, provided federal control for pollution created by motor vehicles, and authorized the publication of air quality criteria as guides for municipal, state, and interstate air pollution control authorities.[2] The resulting *Air Quality Criteria for Sulfur Oxides* was published in March 1967.[3] The Air Quality Act of 1967 included expanded assistance to states and federal controls for motor vehicle emissions and motor vehicle fuels; characterized features to be considered in developing criteria reflecting identifiable effects on health and welfare; prescribed a protocol for states adopting air quality standards that used published air quality criteria; formulated a scheduled control plan to meet adopted standards in designated areas; and provided for a comprehensive federal report on the need for and effect of national emission standards for stationary sources.[4] That act did not stipulate a margin of safety in standards derived from criteria but did reserve the right for state and local air pollution control authorities to adopt standards and a plan for their implementation that would achieve a higher level of air quality than required by federal law. Following legislative directive, the sulfur oxides criteria issued in 1967 were reevaluated in accordance with a prescribed consultation procedure and reissued in 1969 simultaneously with *Air Quality Criteria for Particulate Matter.*[5]

1. "An Act to Provide Research and Technical Assistance Relating to Air Pollution Control," 69 Stat. 322.

2. 77 Stat. 392.

3. *Air Quality Criteria for Sulfur Oxides,* prepared by the National Center for Air Pollution Control for the U.S. Department of Health, Education, and Welfare, Public Health Service, Bureau of Disease Prevention and Environmental Control, Public Health Service Publication 1619 (Government Printing Office, 1967).

4. 81 Stat. 485.

5. Department of Health, Education, and Welfare, Public Health Service, National Air Pollution Control Administration, *Air Quality Criteria for Sulfur Oxides,*

The Clean Air Amendments of 1970 provided an air quality management scheme that increased responsibilities of both state and federal control authorities.[6] The amendments gave the federal government authority not only to issue air quality criteria but also to prescribe primary and secondary ambient air quality standards and establish national emission standards for stationary sources and hazardous pollutants. The primary air quality standards were chosen to protect the public's health with an adequate margin of safety, and the secondary standards were chosen to protect the public's welfare from any known or anticipated adverse effects. The use of ambient and emission standards and other requirements were detailed to ensure effective and timely state plans for abatement and control. The 1977 Clean Air Amendments built on and expanded requirements to (1) attain and maintain national air quality standards for sulfur oxides, particulate matter, four additional ubiquitous pollutants, and several other pollutants from specific emission sources; (2) enforce more stringent limitations on motor vehicle emissions; (3) implement consideration for ozone protection programs; and (4) prevent significant deterioration of air quality, especially from sulfur oxides and particulate matter.[7]

The twenty-two-year legislative history of air pollution control shows (1) continuing support for research on causes and effects and prevention and control of air pollution; (2) reliance on air quality criteria as a basis for ambient air quality standards to protect public health and welfare; (3) the setting of emission standards for mobile and stationary sources and for specific hazardous pollutants; and (4) a growing sense of urgency to attain and maintain air quality levels based on criteria and to protect and enhance national air quality.

Air Quality Standards

Have the standards for sulfur oxides and particulate matter been adequately derived and have implementation plans for their control resulted in improved public health and welfare?

NAPCA Publication AP-50 (GPO, 1969); and Department of Health, Education, and Welfare, Public Health Service, National Air Pollution Control Administration, *Air Quality Criteria for Particulate Matter,* NAPCA Publication AP-49 (GPO, 1969).

6. 84 Stat. 1676.
7. 1977 Clean Air Act Amendments, 91 Stat. 685.

Air quality criteria reflect what science has been able to measure of the obvious and insidious effects of air pollution on man and his environment. Criteria describe what occurs when ambient air concentrations of a pollutant have reached or exceeded a particular level for a specific time period. The criteria considered such factors as: (1) chemical and physical characteristics of pollutants; (2) techniques for measuring these characteristics and exposure, duration, and site conditions; (3) characteristics of receptors; and (4) the response to exposure including such variables as human health and effects on agriculture, materials, visibility, and climate.

The criteria issued for sulfur oxides recognize effects for various concentrations and exposure times for one family of pollutants commonly found in the atmosphere that includes sulfur dioxide, sulfur trioxide, their acids, and the salts of their acids. It is important to understand that the effects observed in ambient air conditions usually are not solely attributable to sulfur oxides in the atmosphere, since other pollutants probably have been present—most usually undifferentiated particulate matter—making distinction between effects of each class difficult. The effects reported are those that can be reasonably predicted when sulfur oxides are in ambient air and detected and measured by surrogate sulfur dioxide.

The range of health effects associated with sulfur oxides is discussed in a sulfur oxides criteria document, a National Academy of Sciences review, and in the paper by Benjamin G. Ferris, Jr., in this volume.[8] Aside from toxicological experimentation and certain industrial source exposures, few, if any, effects were believed to be directly associated with ambient sulfur dioxide levels, but were associated with sulfur dioxide and transformation products coexistent with other air pollutants, notably suspended particulate matter. These observations along with atmospheric parameters and other matters were considered in establishing the national primary and secondary ambient air quality standards for sulfur oxides.

The standards for sulfur oxides published in 1971 were based on a reevaluation of the criteria issued in 1969, which in turn were based on recently published information and a reappraisal of the first criteria published in 1967.[9] Consideration was again given to the prospect of

8. National Air Pollution Control Administration, *Air Quality Criteria for Sulfur Oxides* (1969); and National Academy of Sciences, National Research Council, Assembly of Life Sciences, Board on Toxicology and Environmental Health Hazards, Committee on Sulfur Oxides, *Sulfur Oxides* (Washington, D.C.: NAS, 1978).

9. "National Primary and Secondary Ambient Air Quality Standards," *Federal Register*, vol. 36 (April 30, 1971), pp. 8186–201.

establishing ambient air quality standards for specific components of the airborne sulfur oxides complex. Toxicological and epidemiological evidence of adverse health effects implicated concurrent exposure to sulfurous pollutants measured as sulfur dioxide and undifferentiated particulate matter. However, the considerable gravimetric variations in particulate levels and the modest variations in sulfur dioxide measurements precluded a combined particulate–sulfur dioxide standard that could be meaningfully related to observed clinical and epidemiological dose-response data. Likewise, while there was evidence of toxicants generated either through transformation of sulfur dioxide into other gas phase compounds or into particulate aerosols such as sulfuric acid and acid salts, there were no health effects data related to specific transient or terminal transformation products. While the atmospheric photooxidation system for sulfur dioxide was known when the standards were formulated, little was known of the heterogeneous sulfur dioxide oxidation reactions, especially those gas-to-particle conversions occurring in the hydrocarbon photooxidation system and resulting in organic aerosols and their potentially adverse health effects. Given the spare evidence on the specific health effects, no single standard for both sulfur oxides and particulate matter seemed tenable.

A particulate sulfate ambient air quality standard was also considered but rejected because there was no dose-response information or chemical and physical description of the purported toxicant to support such a standard.

An ambient air quality standard specifically for sulfur dioxide was rejected, for there were no useful data associating adverse health effects with measured ambient levels of the toxicant.[10]

The selection of a more meaningful surrogate or the designation of a specific compound for the monitoring of sulfur oxides and surveillance of the health effects now attributed to sulfur oxides and undifferentiated particulate matter awaits scientific evidence of the chemical and physical identity of the inciting pollutant and methods for detection, measurement, and data reporting. Sulfur dioxide measurements and gravimetric measurements should be continued for current air pollution control purposes and should be maintained for a specified time after any new related sulfur health standard is set to ensure a relationship of historical data with contemporary change.

10. The national primary air quality standards for sulfur oxides are measured in terms of sulfur dioxide by a reference method described in "National Primary and Secondary Ambient Air Quality Standards," 40 C.F.R., pt. 50, app. A (1979).

The data base available for establishing air quality standards for sulfur oxides and particulate matter does show a dose-response curve of decreasing adverse health effects matching decreasing pollutant levels. However, the dose-response evidence is not complete enough to show possible threshold effects, thus affecting the choice of an adequate margin of safety.

The allowance for an adequate margin of safety was based on the validity of the data and the applicable response time as well as on the minimal response effect or least significant impact on the population at risk under compromised environmental conditions. Handling the margin of safety in this way met some of the obstacles of the threshold concept and avoided the difficulties of setting a standard at an assured no-effect level. On the other hand, a larger margin of safety might have been provided by selecting biochemical or chemical-physical changes as markers for expected onset of observed clinical symptoms. This approach, however, would have had to await clearly established and confirmed dose-response information related to the onset of symptoms quite apart from professional judgment of the significance of the impact on health.

Using the scientific evidence presented in the sulfur oxides criteria documents and the guidelines for allowance of an adequate margin of safety, the current primary sulfur oxides and primary particulate matter standards were established.[11] Sulfur oxides standards are 365 micrograms per cubic meter for twenty-four hours and an annual average of 80 micrograms per cubic meter, measured as sulfur dioxide. Particulate matter standards are 260 micrograms per cubic meter for twenty-four hours and an annual average of 75 micrograms per cubic meter. The National Academy of Sciences report believes these standards reasonable in the absence of additional data, but Ferris claims there is no significant impact on health at 360 micrograms per cubic meter for twenty-four hours and 150 micrograms per cubic meter as an annual average for both sulfur oxides and particulate matter. He states that no clear separation of the relative contribution of each can be made yet suggests that particulates are somewhat more harmful than sulfur dioxide. He also reports that there are no data relevant to the assessment of the possible health impact of sulfates and mass respirable particles.

Costs associated with achieving and maintaining ambient air quality

11. "National Primary and Secondary Ambient Air Quality Standards," p. 8186; and *Air Quality Criteria for Sulfur Oxides* for both 1967 and 1969.

standards are excluded from consideration in the selection of sulfur oxides or particulate matter standards by legislative intent.[12]

Effects of Air Pollution

The paper on sulfates by Lester Lave gives an interesting account of the impact of sulfates on human health and the environment and a hypothesis that merits scrutiny. Transforming the hypothesis to theory and ultimately to regulation and practice calls for an adequate and well-documented information base. Well-planned and properly conducted epidemiological research on health effects of sulfur oxides and associated pollutants offers a challenging opportunity for biomedical and community health research. It is distressing to think that without appropriate and adequate financial support the next round of mandated reviews of air quality criteria and the consideration of possible air quality criteria for sulfur dioxide and toxic sulfates will probably be just another review and reevaluation of a well-worn information base.

Lave correctly cites the dramatic reduction in particulates without concomitant reduction in sulfur dioxide and the cessation of acute air pollution episodes in England. The control of fuel quality improved local air quality. But advocating and expanding the use of tall stacks, although helping to reduce sulfur oxides near emission sources, added to the sulfur oxides in the air far from emission sources and distributed sulfates over a wide area. This phenomenon is described and documented in a Swedish report on the European transboundary impact of sulfur in air and precipitation.[13] Clearly, tall stacks are not a means of emission limitation, and the processes using them should reduce their pollutant emissions before discharging them into the atmosphere.

12. See *Air Quality Criteria,* staff report prepared for the use of the Subcommittee on Air and Water Pollution of the Senate Committee on Public Works, 90 Cong. 2 sess. (GPO, 1968); *Clean Air Amendments of 1970,* conference report to accompany H.R. 17255, 91 Cong. 2 sess. (GPO, 1970); and *Executive Branch Review of Environmental Regulations,* Hearings before the Subcommittee on Environmental Pollution of the Senate Committee on Environment and Public Works, 96 Cong. 1 sess. (GPO, 1979).

13. *Air Pollution Across National Boundaries: The Impact on the Environment of Sulfur in Air and Precipitation,* Case Study for the United Nations Conference on the Human Environment, Stockholm, June 5–16, 1972 (Government of Sweden, Royal Ministries of Foreign Affairs and of Agriculture, 1971), pp. 19–24.

Similar adverse effects of the transport and transformation of sulfur oxides and their contribution to acid precipitation and decreased atmospheric visibility occur in North America.[14] Areas affected by acid precipitation have increased in the northeastern and southeastern states, and the pH of precipitation in those areas has also increased. Visibility degradation has also increased in many areas of the country. Sulfur and nitrogen oxides are believed to contribute to the acidity of precipitation; atmospheric sulfates are known to be associated with visibility degradation, but the lack of needed quantitative data precludes determination of their specific contribution.

Emphasis and priority for controls of sulfur oxides and particulate matter may be modified as new information on atmospheric chemical reactions becomes available. Lave is perceptive in his view that if in fact the adverse health effects are attributable to the joint and combined effects of sulfur dioxide and particulate matter, stringent abatement of particulate matter with little or no control of sulfur oxides would be a good strategy. On the other hand, if the health effects result from sulfurous particles produced as transformation products from gaseous sulfur dioxide, a different control strategy would be required. A report by David S. Brookshire estimates significant economic and health benefits that would result if particulates were reduced. These benefits would come from more time on the job and increased productivity—approximately a $36 times 10^9 per year benefit for a 60 percent reduction in particulate matter.[15] Between 1970 and 1974, particulate emissions were reduced by 29 percent, and sulfur oxide emissions were reduced by 8 percent.[16] Emission reductions for particulate matter between 1970 and 1976 were reportedly reduced by 41 percent and sulfur oxides by 8 percent, resulting in a substantial additional decrease of particulate matter but none of sulfur oxides.[17]

Despite the downturn in particulate matter and sulfur oxides, there was

14. Environmental Research and Technology, Inc., *International Aspects of the Long Range Transport of Air Pollutants,* prepared for the U.S. Department of State, ERT Doc. P-5252 (Washington, D.C.: Environmental Research and Technology, Inc., 1978).

15. U.S. Environmental Protection Agency, Office of Health and Ecological Effects, *Methods Development for Assessing Air Pollution Control Benefits,* vol. 5: David S. Brookshire and others, *Executive Summary* (GPO, 1979).

16. *Environmental Quality: The Sixth Annual Report of the Council on Environmental Quality, 1975* (GPO, 1976), p. 305.

17. *Executive Branch Review of Environmental Regulations,* Hearings, p. 237.

a concomitant increase in the occurrence and distribution of acid precipitation and visibility degradation associated with sulfates. Thus it appears that abatement and control systems to reduce sulfur emission sources further are needed. Reduction of nitrogen oxides and other chemical components supporting the formation of nitrates also appears necessary to lessen the acid precipitation problem.

Lave postulates a possible change in focus of abatement policy depending on route and rate of sulfur dioxide transformation in the atmosphere. Although understanding of the quantitative aspects of the problem is incomplete, it is clear that sulfates are formed in at least two ways: in a liquid droplet process and by the photochemical process involving hydrocarbons, nitrogen dioxide, and photochemical oxidants, including ozone. Rates of conversion for both process routes seem similar, ranging from 0.5 percent to 8 percent per hour in daylight. Source strength, density, and emission plume height affect sulfur dioxide concentrations and therefore the amount transformed to sulfate. In addition, since there are two conversion mechanisms, larger quantities of sulfates may be expected if emissions are subjected to atmospheres in which the photochemical process is active. Control strategy options allow consideration of not only reductions of sulfur dioxide emissions, but also simultaneous reductions of nitric oxide and additional controls for limiting the photochemical process.

Programs for the prevention of significant deterioration introduced in the 1977 Clean Air Amendments also appear to call for intensified and upgraded abatement and control systems to reduce emission sources of sulfur and nitrogen oxides and of particulate matter. These control efforts may be needed for particular land area classification "to protect the public health and welfare from any actual or potential adverse effect which . . . may reasonably be anticipated to occur from air pollution or from exposures to pollutants in other media, which pollutants originate as emissions to the ambient air, notwithstanding attainment and maintenance of all national ambient air quality standards."[18] The findings and procedures to be used in these particular areas may not only influence levels of control technology but may also affect the application of emission source control systems and strategies in other areas of the nation.

It appears that the national ambient air quality standards for sulfur

18. 91 Stat. 731.

oxides and particulate matter have been adequately derived and that implementation plans for their control have effectively reduced levels of each pollutant class. Economic and health benefits have been accrued from particulate matter control, and cost-benefit projections for sulfur oxide control have been reported. The complexities of sulfur dioxide transformation and long distance transport of sulfur oxides and their effects on health and the environment call for critical study, analysis, and consideration of abatement and control strategies.

Part Six

Comments

DAVID S. POTTER

I DO NOT represent businessmen around the world but only represent myself. There is as great a spectrum of viewpoints within the business community as there is within the economics profession. My views happen to fall in the middle of the business spectrum. In my opinion, 50 percent of businessmen are more liberal than I am and the other 50 percent are more conservative.

Whenever one attempts to view someone else's field, he or she perceives what appears to be a monolithic set of ideas. However, two or three points from the previous discussions suggest that it might be worthwhile for me to describe why the business community is not monolithic.

With respect to regulation, contributors discussed two different areas where the business community is regulated, and in this regard business treats each of these areas very differently. The first set of regulations deals with the regulation of the factory, from either an environmental or an occupational safety and health point of view. Whether it is inside the factory walls or outside, these regulations deal with the work place. The problems generated by these regulations are different from the problems that arise from regulating the product.

In the first case, plant regulation costs can be estimated fairly accurately. Furthermore, these costs are usually much lower than those of product-related regulation and do not involve the tremendous risks associated with the latter. When you deal with regulation of the environment in the factory or the effluents from the factory, you may still hear protests from the regulated firms, but at least the regulation costs are measurable. Furthermore, the consequences of related regulation can be examined, such as the cost of one strategy over another or which aspects of a business are likely to be most affected. When dealing with regulation of the work

291

place, it may be possible to make logical choices because at least the costs of your alternatives are discernible.

Events become less predictable when dealing with regulation of the product. Typically, product regulation involves areas without a perceived value to the customer. If there were a perceived value, the manufacturer would probably have brought the product to the marketplace in the form giving that value. Thus, product regulation requires additions to or restrictions on the product, which the customer may not want to pay for.

Product alterations create for the businessman a greater degree of uncertainty and risk. Will the altered product sell? The difference is potentially disastrous, not only for the producer or industry, but in some cases for the country.

Nonetheless, as a result of regulation industry has been forced to modify products to the point where some are no longer salable and are now off the market. Other products have experienced a 10 percent decrease in sales. These are huge effects, much larger than the known effects of capital improvements back at the plant. This, of course, is why businessmen react so negatively when their products or the acceptability of their products in the marketplace is interfered with.

In the economic area, most business people have experienced regulation and understand it reasonably well. Businessmen always expect more coordination in government than that which has actually been achieved, but I have learned that it is futile to expect such coordination. It is always frustrating to walk out of a meeting talking about inflation and the depressed state of the economy and then be told by one of the regulatory agencies that the inflationary impact of a proposed regulation doesn't make a bit of difference—Congress has demanded that the product be fixed, whatever the cost.

Businesses that are being affected by regulation span a large range in their annual gross volume, capital investment, and so forth. There is a rule of thumb that says, with about every order of magnitude of change in gross volume, businesses change in their character, in their management structure, and in the way they do business generally. The company with sales of $10 billion to $50 billion a year is very different from the company with sales of $10 million to $50 million a year. The managers think differently, the pressures are different, and the aspects of regulation that affect them are different. It is a mistake not to take into account the relative size of the industry being regulated.

Another factor that must be taken into account in regulating industry has to do with the stage of the industry in its regulatory experience. How educated is the industry? Some industries have been forced to undergo a detailed and lengthy educational process, and they understand much about the regulatory process. Others are just entering this process, and their level of understanding is not as high.

The education starts out this way. When a regulatory agency knocks on an industry's door the first time, the natural reaction is, "You can't do that [regulate] to me; it is un-American; it is illegal. I have rights!" The courts, however, will disabuse the factory manager of that notion. After a while the industry discovers that the regulators are there to stay.

In phase two the factory manager says, "Yes sir, I guess they can do that to me and, furthermore, all of my lawyers and outside consultants have said they can, and now I believe them."

Then comes phase three, which many of us in industry are rapidly approaching. This is a recognition that, yes, "they" can do it, but it is improper to give up on the whole subject and just quit. It is in the best interests of everyone to take the view that in certain cases where an industry is hurt, or will be hurt, by a regulation, the regulatory agency is obliged to explain the hurt. In a sense one says, "I now understand why you regulate me and what the basic rules are. I have also learned what legal recourse I have. If I don't have legal recourse, I at least know that legislative recourse is available." With this kind of mature attitude, responsible business people will come back to responsible regulators and try to work out what is in the best interests of the country.

But this process takes time. I suspect that only a few industries have reached such a degree of maturity. In my own case of the automobile industry, it is interesting to note the difference in this industry's response to the environmental regulation of our stationary sources as opposed to our mobile sources. In the mobile source area we said, "You can't do this to us." By the time regulators got to the stationary sources the industry knew better and has, I think, achieved a better understanding with the Environmental Protection Agency on the matter of regulation. Much more has been achieved in the stationary source area than in the mobile source area.

The approach taken here has been a philosophical one, which is worthwhile. But businessmen cannot really step back and look at the overall situation, particularly since their first interaction with the regulatory process is with the Occupational Safety and Health Administration fellow at the door saying, "I'm not going to shut you down."

The businessman must take the small view. He is basically results-oriented. If he is dealing with a subcontractor, he is apt to sit down and try to work out a deal between the two of them. He is willing to recognize that it snowed last week or that some other "act of God" might have interfered with a delivery. He is willing to recognize changes in circumstances. But dealing with regulations and the regulatory process is a relatively recent experience for the businessman, and he is only now coming to appreciate that regulations are necessary.

Obeying the law does not, in and of itself, achieve a result. When a businessman fails to obey the law—that is, comply with a regulation—but achieves the result intended by the regulation, he is miffed to be found not in compliance. The regulators, of course, insist that everyone comply with the law in each and every case.

It is important to remember the evolutionary nature of regulation. When a regulation is first conceived, there is usually some kind of real social need. For example, air and water pollution, solid wastes, and toxic substances were problems requiring regulation. When government acted on these problems, some business people objected. Yet such actions clearly provided benefits that exceeded the costs. But soon all of the easy gains will have been achieved. All of the easy benefits will have been accrued, and the regulators will move on to the benefits that are much more difficult to obtain. Finally, costs will begin to exceed the benefits.

When one finally reaches a state of regulatory maturity, new costs arise that are formidable. This year, for example, my company—General Motors—delayed by one week starting production of a diesel engine to be used in larger cars. General Motors lost seven thousand units of production because it was not granted a certificate by the Environmental Protection Agency to produce that diesel engine. It happens that the agency made a mistake, which I must admit does not often occur. Not only did General Motors lose seven thousand units of production, but the U.S. gross national product was off seven thousand units. General Motors is the only company producing that size engine domestically and is absolutely capacity constrained. The company has no way of making back the seven thousand lost units, and that is an effect on the country's gross national product that is never counted.

At the same time the Environmental Protection Agency made its mistake, General Motors made a mistake in another area; as a result, the company did not sell any diesel cars in California for approximately six months of the 1980 model year.

It doesn't matter whether General Motors or the Environmental Protection Agency is to blame. The fact is that there is an adverse national effect, not only from the lost production, but also because of the possibility that foreign companies will win the lost sales.

This is a cost of regulation that industry urges regulators to take into account. The difficulty comes not from the fact that industry is regulated, but from the mechanism of regulation. Industry must make decisions about whether or not to shut down production. It would have been much easier for General Motors to have negotiated with the Environmental Protection Agency a fine of $5 or $2 per unit for whatever pollutant was being regulated.

The business community urges policymakers to examine the total cost of regulation and recognize the increasing costs of product and plant control. When a manufacturer is forced to discontinue a product because of some new finding concerning health, for example, he must write off certain costs, such as the cost of the capital investment that is no longer useful or the cost of the product's conversion to some new purpose. These are the obvious surface costs; other associated costs are even larger.

Every industry that has been regulated has been through these uncertainties and may even have lost a product because of a situation such as I have described. The cost at this point is substantial enough, but the real cost to the nation is that the industrialist remembers uncertainty and is inclined not to take risks again. As a result, the producer may become less inclined to modify his product, even though such modification might produce a cheaper or better product. He is afraid to modify because of the risk that the product will be discontinued. Thus, industry is no longer as innovative or creative as it once was, partly because the costs of making a mistake have become far too high.

It must be recognized that various industries are at different stages of understanding of the regulatory process in this country. The uncertainty associated with regulation is very disconcerting to businessmen and in some instances may reduce national output. It is important to be careful and bring industry along slowly through the regulatory process.

Comments

MARVIN SCHNEIDERMAN

THE SCIENTIST'S perspective is neither unitary nor clear. Scientists have different desires and needs and consider different levels of evidence as adequate for "proof." I am a statistician so I think I may understand economists better than I sometimes understand the virologists, immunologists, molecular biologists, and a host of other people with whom I share the National Cancer Institute campus.

Clifford Grobstein, discussing the National Academy of Sciences report on saccharin, which found the animal evidence of carcinogenicity adequate and the human evidence inadequate, remarked that there are three kinds of science: basic, applied, and science for public policy. He implied that the knowledge needed for each of these is different, both in kind and in quantity. Most people believe that there is little difference in the quality of knowledge needed. It all needs to be good. Indeed, the quality of science may have to be better for public policy use, largely because actions taken in the public arena are hard to change, modify, or withdraw, and it would be best to be on firm ground the first time around. Basic science, since it only rarely leads directly to public action, benefits from the self-correcting and homeostatic mechanisms inherent in the small, self-critical community of practitioners who are concerned with the specific basic science. Applied science is also self-correcting, since if an airplane won't fly or a vaccine won't work, the people who need to know will find out quickly.

Bertram D. Dinman has commented on three other kinds of science: good science, bad science, and that in between. Where the pragmatic tests exist or the self-criticism acts quickly and incisively, the good science eventually drives out the bad. Science for public policy is different; the question is not how good or bad it is, but whether the public recognizes that far more goes into regulatory decisions than just science. How ad-

297

equate is the science for the purpose it must serve? At the start of the process, work in science follows from what scientists can measure. Good engineering makes good tools, which, in turn, make measurement possible.

Certainly regulation does not require science that is completely above criticism. Such science probably does not exist. Benjamin Ferris commented on this, noting that epidemiology is always subject to challenge. The epidemiologist is faced with the problem of trying to think of and account for all the factors and their interactions that might possibly influence the results of an unplanned experiment. This is an impossible task. Epidemiological studies are usually attempts to make sense of nature's experiments, but Mother Nature has not read Ronald A. Fisher's *Design of Experiments.*[1] Epidemiologists have their pet ideas of what must be done for a study to be good and, of course, not all epidemiologists agree.

Joseph Pechman has asked if in any of the specific regulatory actions discussed here additional data would have made the regulatory process easier, better, or less controversial. He has also asked if the estimates on which action would be taken could be made better, for example, in the case of passive restraints in automobiles. Estimates given here of deaths potentially averted with passive restraints now range from 6,000 to 9,000 a year. Earlier estimates had covered a much wider range. It seems to me that the difference between 6,000 and 9,000 will be of no consequence whatever in formulating regulations about passive restraints. In the saccharin case, the range of estimates given was wider, yet it seems extremely unlikely that any additional animal experimental data, of the kind already available, would modify the regulatory actions taken. The National Academy of Sciences found the human data inadequate. I suspect that with a weak carcinogen (as saccharin seems to be) any human data likely to be developed will be inadequate or equivocal and will not convince people not already convinced by the animal data.

The problem of saccharin and other possible carcinogens poses another issue that transcends science. The question of waiting for or looking for data on humans, which will arise only if humans are or have been exposed to potential carcinogens for the long period necessary to see effects (if any) in humans, is an ethical, economic, and political issue. In the case of saccharin, what are the costs of a false positive (from the animal experimental results) as opposed to the costs of a false negative? What are the costs of

1. Sir Ronald A. Fisher, *Design of Experiments,* rev. 7th ed. (New York: Hafner, 1960).

allowing a material to remain on the market thirty years or more while we seek to confirm possible carcinogenic effects in humans?

Such questions make it clear that regulatory actions depend only partly on scientific information. Usually by the time regulatory action is contemplated or is under way, substantial scientific information has already been collected, and further decisions and actions become data-insensitive. That is, additional data will be marginal and have little effect on the decisions eventually made. Scientists usually are aware of this. Most of them seem to be content to have the world operate this way. Scientists may seem to be cowardly when they say, "I can do only so much. I can only supply you, the regulator, with what data I have collected or can collect. The decision about what to do with the data is yours." But this kind of self-limitation makes sense. If this sharp division of labor always existed, I think most regulators would function easily. What sometimes happens, though, is that scientists collect some data, regulators take some action, and other scientists (whose sponsors may object to the actions) find fault with some of the data or their interpretation. This could and perhaps does lead to administrative paralysis. What is the regulator to do in the face of contradictory advice, information, or interpretation? I sense some annoyance among regulators who take on difficult actions and who then find themselves scolded as poor scientists for their interpretations of data that led to that action.

I think science and scientific data are absolutely essential to regulatory decisionmaking. Scientific data are most useful early in the regulatory process. Although regulatory action may sometimes be proposed to bring forth data that has not been made public, it seems to me that most of the time the marginal effect of additional data once the process is under way is rather small. Regulators need to be open and sensitive to new data, but the promise of new data should not lead them to avoid taking needed action.

Conference Participants

with their affiliations at the time of the conference

Glenn C. Blomquist *Illinois State University*
Peggy Connerton *Occupational Safety and Health Administration*
W. J. Coppoc *Texaco Inc.*
Morton Corn *University of Pittsburgh*
Robert W. Crandall *Brookings Institution*
Kenny S. Crump *Louisiana Technical University*
Martha Derthick *Brookings Institution*
Bertram D. Dinman *Aluminum Company of America*
Richard Dowd *Environmental Protection Agency*
George C. Eads *Council of Economic Advisers*
Benjamin G. Ferris, Jr. *Harvard University*
John Froines *National Institute for Occupational Safety and Health*
Bernard D. Goldstein *New York University Medical Center*
Michael Gough *Office of Technology Assessment*
Clifford Grobstein *University of California at San Diego*
Robert Harris *Environmental Defense Fund*
David Harrison *Council of Economic Advisers*
Thomas Hopkins *Council on Wage and Price Stability*
Neil Howe *Smith Richardson Foundation*
Donald F. Huelke *University of Michigan*
Victor J. Kimm *Environmental Protection Agency*
Alan V. Kneese *Resources for the Future*
Marvin J. Kosters *American Enterprise Institute*
Howard L. Kusnetz *Shell Oil Company*

Arnold M. Kuzmack *Environmental Protection Agency*

Lester B. Lave *Brookings Institution*

Alvin Lazen *National Academy of Sciences*

Ronald Lewis *Council on Wage and Price Stability*

Paul W. MacAvoy *Yale University*

James A. Merchant *National Institute for Occupational Safety and Health*

Richard A. Merrill *University of Virginia*

John T. Middleton *Consultant*

John F. Morrall III *Council on Wage and Price Stability*

Larry Moss *Sierra Club*

Carl E. Nash *National Highway Traffic Safety Administration*

Vaun A. Newell *Exxon Corporation*

Albert Nichols *Harvard University*

Roger G. Noll *California Institute of Technology*

James O'Day *Highway Safety Research Institute*

Gilbert S. Omenn *Office of Science and Technology Policy*

Talbot Page *Environmental Protection Agency*

Joseph A. Pechman *Brookings Institution*

Henry Peskin *Resources for the Future*

Paul Portney *Council on Environmental Quality*

David S. Potter *General Motors Corporation*

William Poundstone *Consolidation Coal Company*

Alan Pulsipher *Ford Foundation*

J. Thomas Ratchford *American Association for the Advancement of Science*

Robert D. Reischauer *Congressional Budget Office*

Joseph Rodericks *Food and Drug Administration*

Laurence Rosenberg *National Science Foundation*

Stephen Salop *Federal Trade Commission*

David W. Schnare *Environmental Protection Agency*

Marvin Schneiderman *National Cancer Institute*

Lawrence White *New York University*

Oliver E. Williamson *University of Pennsylvania*

Richard Wilson *Harvard University*

Index

Abramson, Fred P., 136
Acid precipitation, 286, 287
Air bags, 21–24, 26, 28–33, 61–63
Air pollution regulation. *See* Sulfates;
  Sulfur dioxide regulation
Air Quality Act of *1967*, 280
Alavanja, Michael, 187, 213n
Aldman, Bertil, 32n
Amdur, Mary O., 255n, 272
American Conference of Governmental
  Industrial Hygienists, 95, 110–11
Ames, Bruce N., 124n, 205n, 206n
Andelman, Julian B., 186n
Anderson, Äke, 32n
Anderson, Donald O., 260, 261n
Andreassend, D. C., 34n
Animal Drug Amendments of *1968*, 166
Animal studies: cotton dust risks, 88;
  drinking water risks, 176–83, 191–92,
  200, 205–07, 213–15; human risk ex-
  trapolation, 124–25, 177–80, 191–92,
  213–15, 271; saccharin risks, 119–20,
  122–25, 157–59; short-term, 123–24,
  205–06
Antweiler, Hubert, 85n, 86, 87
Arlidge, J. T., 82n
Armitage, P., 235n
Arrow, Kenneth J., 141n, 147n
Asberg, A., 25
Automatic belts. *See* Passive belts
Automatic crash protection standard.
  See Passive restraint standard
Automobile crashes: air bag activation
  level and, 28, 29; fatalities, 28, 45–46,
  62; financial incentive approach to,
  39–40; lap-shoulder belt effectiveness,
  24–26; lives-saved estimates, 27–28,
  62; passive restraint effectiveness, 22–
  24; restraint effectiveness evaluation,
  30–33; second collision injuries, 55–

56; severity, 28–29, 34, 62; survivability in, 26–27; value of safety and, 38–
  39, 41–42, 46, 65–66
Avol, Edward L., 265
Ayres, Robert U., 269n

Backstrom, C. G., 25
Bailey, Martin J., 49
Barbero, A., 73
Barton, Margaret F., 151n
Batawi, Mostafa A. El, 75n, 76n
Bates, David V., 73n, 79n
Beasley, Thomas W., 206n
Benefit-cost analysis: cotton dust stan-
  dard, 104–08; drinking water regula-
  tions, 197–99, 218–23, 230–32, 238–
  42; passive restraint standard, 40–42,
  47–51; regulatory actions and, 3–5,
  14–15, 229–32; saccharin ban, 133–
  34; sulfur abatement, 275–78; value
  of life, 48–49, 275–78; value of safety,
  38–39, 41–42, 46, 49, 65–66
Berenblum, Isaac, 124
Berry, G., 76n, 80
Biersteker, K., 257n
Bingham, Eula, 201n
Bishop, Y., 274n
Blomquist, Glenn C., 38, 42–44, 49, 50,
  54n
Boak, R. W., 24, 25
Bouhuys, Arend, 76n, 78n, 79–81, 85n,
  89n, 90n, 111
Boutwell, Rosewall K., 124n
Braun, Daniel C., 88
Breyer, Stephen, 146n
Bridges, B. A., 206n
Broder, Ivy E., 198n, 223n, 228n, 241n
Brookshire, David S., 286
Bruser, Judith, 200n, 248n, 249n
Bryant, Joseph, 43, 44n

303